The Emotional Computer

Lloyd Manford Herfindahl, *Sleeping City*, oil, 54 × 96 ins, reproduced by courtesy of the artist.

The Emotional Computer

José Antonio Jáuregui

Translated from the Spanish by
Eduardo Jáuregui
and
Pablo Jáuregui

BLACKWELL
Oxford UK & Cambridge USA

Originally published in Spanish as *El Ordenador Cerebral* by
Labor, Barcelona, 1990
English edition first published 1995

Blackwell Publishers Ltd
108 Cowley Road
Oxford OX4 1JF

Blackwell Publishers Inc.
238 Main Street
Cambridge, Massachusetts 02142
USA

British Library Cataloguing in Publication Data
A CIP catalogue record for this book is available from the British Library.
Library of Congress Cataloging-in-Publication Data
Jáuregui, José Antonio
[Ordenador cerebral. English]
The emotional computer / José Antonio Jáuregui
     p.   cm.
Includes bibliographical references and index.
ISBN 0–631–19843–1 (alk. paper). — ISBN 0–631–19844–X (pbk. : alk. paper)
1. Emotions—Physiological aspects. 2. Mind-brain identity theory.
3. Human behaviour. 4. Neuropsychology. I. Title.
QP401.J3813   1995
152.4—dc20   94–44904
                                                          CIP

Copy-edited and typeset in 11 on 13 Sabon
by Grahame & Grahame Editorial, Brighton
Printed and bound in Great Britain by Hartnolls Limited, Bodmin, Cornwall
This book is printed on acid-free paper

To my children:

Eduardo, Pablo, Javier, Elena and Maite

Contents

Foreword

In *The Emotional Computer*, Jáuregui uncovers, beginning with the very title, what in a less explicit manner also constituted the central theme of his earlier books, *The Rules of the Game: the Tribes* and *The Rules of the Game: the Sexes*. The author believes that co-existence and rivalry, attraction and repulsion, integration and exclusion, both on a collective as well as on an individual scale, follow the same natural guidelines. In his view, the key to understanding behaviour, and even conduct, lies in the workings of physiological mechanisms, which in turn depend on the brain's intricate system of networks.

Commenting on the characteristics which Jáuregui attributes to tribes, in 1977 José Botella Llusia wrote in the Spanish newspaper *ABC* that 'the movement orginated by Alexis Carrel, and which is currently being developed by the Oxford school with Jáuregui and the Harvard school with Wilson, considers that sociology is a branch of biology and obeys the same laws as the latter'. In his preface to the Selecciones Austral edition of *The Rules of the Game: the Tribes*, José Luis Pinillos referred to this view as 'a coherent and rigorous theory'. According to Jáuregui, the political, economic and cultural life should not only be interpreted as a 'class struggle', but also as a 'tribal or territorial game'. History is thus viewed as the result of a permanent, more or less peaceful interaction between communities, or owners of particular lands, habits and cultural identities.

The same idea permeates the whole book of *The Rules of the Game: the Sexes*. On both the philosophical and the anthropological level, the approach that was taken towards territories and tribes is repeated. Identical emotional systems, which are numerous and varied, but all controlled by the 'neural computer', explain and condition the behaviour and the relations between men and women. In this case as well, everything is subordinated to the supreme dictatorship of the brain, which orders the human being to act in one way or another by means of complex schemes of a biological nature. Jáuregui's 'programmed man' – as opposed to Heraclitus' 'constant flow', to the uniqueness of each person produced by the constant genetic and sociocultural transformations always in effect – explains sociological phenomena in biological terms, but subordinates all natural phenomena to the neural vertex of a pyramidal structure. And, when what characterizes the human brain is its creative capacity and lack of moderation, Jáuregui nevertheless reduces it to a command centre.

A disciple of Madariaga and Evans-Pritchard, he attributes certain functions of planning and regulation to what Locke referred to as the 'commonwealth of learning', which transform it into a very strict regime – into an undemocratic commonwealth? – where everything is interpreted on the basis of the relationship between the emotional system and the neural computer. His book develops an analysis of the brain as 'a computer which informs and orders the subject about what he must do in order to preserve his body and his society, by activating emotional mechanisms'. Pleasant and unpleasant feelings are, according to the author, 'mathematically foreseen responses based on programs registered via DNA or via culture'.

Jáuregui criticizes Descartes, Spinoza and St Augustine for having dismissed feelings as 'confused states of the mind', when in his view they constitute a precise, relentless system of information which aids human beings to maintain both their bodies and their society. Pleasure, he argues, does not actually exist; it is merely the absence of pain and appetite, or the cancellation of an unpleasant sensation.

If reading, in order to be fruitful, must establish an intense and even heated dialogue with the author, there can be no doubt that this book fully accomplishes this goal.

However divergent one's own opinions may be from Jáuregui's, the latter provoke thought, meditation and controversy. The result of this, the reader will discover, is a net gain in one's personal appreciation of essential issues and in the most intimate and subtle reflection on the things that really matter, on what are, in my view, the unyielding forces of the spirit.

Federico Mayor
Director General
Unesco

Preface to the English Edition

Since I wrote this book in Spanish in Los Angeles during the 1980s (published in 1990 as *El Ordenador Cerebral* by Labor, a prestigious scientific publishing house in Barcelona), interest in exploring the fascinating, undiscovered world of the brain has continued to grow. 'The Decade of Brain' has been launched in the United States and also in Japan, and recently the European Union has inaugurated 'The European Decade of Brain Research'. Numerous books on the subject have appeared, and are continuing to appear. The developing sophistication of computers, moreover, and the remarkable fact that these machines are capable of defeating a human being in a game of chess, has opened up new horizons, and has confronted us with new problems: can one say that a computer thinks? Is the brain a computer? In the words of Roger Penrose:

> Why is it that beings like ourselves should sometimes be troubled – especially when probed about this matter – by questions about 'self'? (I could almost say: 'Why are you reading this chapter?' or 'Why did I feel a strong desire to write a book on this topic in the first place?'). It is hard to imagine that an entirely unconscious automaton should waste its time with such matters . . . Of course there would be no problem about deliberately programming a computer to seem to behave in this ridiculous way (e.g. it would be programmed to go around muttering 'Oh dear, what is the meaning of life? Why am I here? What on earth is this "self" that I feel?'). But why should natural selection bother to favour such a race of individuals, when surely the relentless free market of the jungle should have rooted out such useless nonsense long ago! (*The Emperor's New Mind*, p. 528)

My book is situated in this context of questions and enigmas, and particularly tries to answer the question posed by Penrose: 'What on earth is this "self" that I feel?'

At the same time, a new controversial debate has broken out over the word 'sociobiology', which was coined by Edward O. Wilson. As with all new, unexplored fields, there is still much ground to cover. The relationship between biology and sociology, the brain and society, nature and culture, or what is innate and what is acquired, is, in any case, a fundamental issue about which we are still highly ignorant. My book is also situated in this context, and attempts to tackle the problem.

A few months ago, Richard Dawkins, Alex Kacelnik and I discussed the organization of an International Symposium entitled 'The Brain and Society', which will soon take place at the Ramón Areces Foundation in Madrid, with the collaboration of the European Decade of Brain Research (a scientific committee appointed by the European Commission). During the course of this interdisciplinary symposium, these issues will be approached from different academic perspectives. Richard Dawkins made a sharp observation during our conversation: 'We shall all be laymen in this symposium, except for a very restricted area.' This sensible remark has given me much to think about. We must all start off from the following premise with Socratic modesty and truth: we are laymen in almost everything, except with regard to the restricted areas of our individual disciplines. Hence, each one of us must patiently and rigorously investigate within his field, and then join everyone else in a fruitful dialogue where all will attempt to solve the same puzzle from different angles.

My initial academic training was philosophical. At the Gregorian University, where I was taught by great authorities – Father Copleston *inter alios* – we read Plato in Greek and Seneca in Latin. Every single class, as well as all exams, were in Latin: 'Sicut Darwinius dixit . . . '. I then became tempted by social anthropology, which I took as an optional course, and decided to pursue this field at the University of Oxford (Balliol College). There I had the good fortune and the privilege of being tutored by Sir Edward Evan Evans-Pritchard. I eventually became his teaching assistant, and in this way earned my first salary at the University of Oxford. My main responsibility was accompanying Sir Edward to the pub and to various restaurants. Besides introducing me to the world of social anthropology, and supervising my thesis, during those informal chats and meals (sometimes in the company of figures such as Claude Lévi-Strauss or Sir Isaiah Berlin), I contracted an academic debt of infinite proportions with this eminent anthropologist and true friend. My training, my limitations, my dogmas, and my prejudices hence originate from these two disciplines: philosophy and social anthropology. I have never stopped reading Plato and Aristotle in Greek, as well as Seneca in Latin, on an almost daily basis (my working tools are the magnificent bi-lingual editions of the Loeb Classical Library). I continuously read and reread Kant, Darwin, Hobbes, Descartes, Hume and Locke, as well as my contemporaries, in order to keep track of new ideas.

Several years have passed since this book originally came out in Spain, and numerous books and articles have since been published on these topics. Nevertheless, I believe that it still has the same interest now as it had when it originally saw the light of day, and I sincerely hope that the publication of this English edition will give me the opportunity to engage in dialogue and in friendly controversy with new colleagues from different disciplines, as well as to offer my own points of view, solutions and questions.

The book has been given a different title for this edition (the original Spanish edition was called *El Ordenador Cerebral*, The Neural Computer). My son, Eduardo, suggested that I change it to *The Emotional Computer* (I quote his arguments from memory):

> I think you should give it this title because it reflects the fundamental aspect of your theory, a view which contrasts substantially with those of others who have made the analogy between the brain and an automatic computer. According to your book, the brain is a machine which, in accordance with certain programs installed via the genes or via culture, informs us every day about when we should eat, play tennis or have sex through the activation of feelings, entities which have been for the most part left out of the reckoning by cognitive psychology. As you are dealing with humans who feel pleasure and pain rather than with chess-playing automatons, *The Emotional Computer* seems a more appropriate title.

If there is one word which I could say is sacred to me, it would be Oxford. I had always dreamed of studying and living there, and this cherished dream came true. I made the same mistake as the Queen of Sheba. They had told her so many wonderful things about King Solomon that she feared the reality would not live up to his fame. In the end, however, Solomon turned out to be greater than she had imagined. The same thing occurred to me at Oxford. If I was asked to define Europe or the academic life in one word, I would simply mention the name of this historic centre of study. At Oxford I also had the privilege of sharing a friendship with Salvador de Madariaga, a man whom Albert Camus referred to as 'one of the few Europeans worthy of being called a philosopher'. How can anyone who has lived in such an aesthetically and academically rich environment, in a college like Balliol, with mentors like the ones I was fortunate enough to study with, fail to be inspired?

Furthermore, Oxford is the city in which three of my children were born. Eduardo, the first-born, who graduated from the London School of Economics and has received a Master of Studies in Social Anthropology from Oxford (Exeter College), and Pablo, my second son, who has just received an Oxford BA (also at Exeter College), have translated this book. I could not have found two better candidates for the job, and I am eternally grateful to them for the dedication and the efficiency with which they have completed it.

The translators of this book queried with me the fact that I always used the male sex in my examples. I agreed that I really should have given examples in a more balanced way, but I leave my 'male' examples in the text as testament to my original literary inadequacy. However, I gently wish to point out that, except where specifically indicated, the theories presented here are applicable to both sexes.

From the moment I arrived at Oxford, Blackwell also became a very special name to me. Both the bookshop and the publishing house are undoubtedly two great ambassadors of the land that has given the world Shakespeare, Newton, football, the incomparable aesthetic beauty of its villages and gardens, the sharpness of its wit, and the brilliant combination of bacon and eggs (without which I would be a less happy man). I am proud to be a part of the Blackwell family, and to have established this new link with the city of Oxford. I would like to thank Alison Mudditt, Senior Commissioning Editor at Blackwell Publishers, for all her advice and efforts. I am also indebted to Professor Ian Michael and to Glyn Redworth, who supported the publication of this book in England.

I would like to express my gratitude to the Fundación Ramón Areces, which has supported this work with a very generous economic grant.

I am indebted to Federico Mayor Zaragoza, the General Director of Unesco, for writing a preface to this study. I also thank Javier, my third Oxonian child, for helping me in numerous ways with the preparation of the manuscript of this English edition, as well as my daughters, Elena and Maite. Finally, I must mention my wife, Dorita Narvaez, the mother of my five children, and a companion who has always lived up to her Christian name: Theo-dora, 'present-from-God'.

José Antonio Jáuregui
Universidad Complutense, Madrid

Part I

The Neural Computer and the Emotional System

1

The Emotional System

The Emotional System as an Informative System

As you begin to read this paragraph, you are not aware of what is going on inside your digestive system. Your brain, however, is fully informed about its present state. Perhaps at this very moment the nerves in your digestive system have informed your brain about the presence of a given gas exerting pressure on the wall of your large intestine. The brain has then automatically consulted its digestive program and discovered that if a gas of these characteristics is found in such a place, it must be expelled immediately. The brain has also learned from this program that it must inform the subject about such a state of affairs. You, the reader, suddenly feel an urge to expel a gas. The brain has sent you the following message: 'There is a gas which must be expelled via your lower organic pipe.' You have received this information. The brain has given you precise news about something you ignored completely. By what means or through what channels has the brain sent you such a message? The brain's postal or telegraphic service is the emotional system. You have suddenly felt something: an urge to expel a gas via a particular organic pipe (it could also have been via your upper organic pipe). The brain, upon being informed by the nervous system about the presence of this gas, found the following directive within its digestive program: 'Inform the subject about the presence of this gas and of the need to expel it by activating x degrees of the urge to expel it' (the degree or the emotional intensity of the urge is proportional to the degree of harm that this gas could bring to your digestive system). The brain sent you this message as you began to read the opening page of this book (let us suppose this for the sake of argument). You had no idea that such a gas was located in an unsuitable place; you did not know that gases must be expelled, nor from where this must be done, nor when, nor for what structural reasons it is necessary to expel certain gases in order to ensure the harmony of your digestive system. You have now been informed of the need to carry out this mechanical task with the help of your brain and your digestive system. One of the most ingenious, swift, precise and complex informative systems is the brain's emotional system.

The emotional system is a genetically implanted system of information by means of which the brain informs the subject (you, the reader, or myself, the author) about what he must do and about when, how and with what degree of urgency the task must be performed. The relationship is comparable to that which exists between the automatic controls of an aircraft and its pilot. The automatic controls of an aircraft are components of a complex machine equipped with certain programs. If this automatic system detects a loss of hydraulic fluid, and if there is an automatic program by means of which, if such a loss occurs, a phonic alarm is set off and a red light begins to flash, this automatic system thus makes the pilot – who at that precise moment may have been chatting about other matters with a charming stewardess – become aware of such a loss. The difference lies in the informative means or channels that the neural computer employs: the triggering of particular feelings (a toothache or the urge to eat), which are mathematically precise in their degree of intensity (minor urges to expel solids, liquids or gases on one end, or extremely intense urges to do so on the other). René Descartes,[1] amongst others, completely misfired when he attempted to uncover both the nature and the function of feelings in his celebrated work, *Meditations on First Philosophy*. He excommunicated them from the scientific church for being *confusi status mentis*, confused states of mind, or 'confused ideas'. It is this which seems to me a truly confused idea. In this book, my aim is to discover and explore the nature and function of feelings as components of a dependable, swift and mathematically precise informative system: the emotional system.

Given the enormous influence that Descartes has exerted on the intellectual community, his unfortunate observations have hindered the exploration of the emotional system, which has remained an undiscovered continent of the scientific world. Descartes, for what in his view were weighty reasons, decreed that not only should feelings be considered second-class citizens beneath ideas in the commonwealth of learning, but that they should be expelled for being *persona non grata* – in other words, for being undesirable foreigners who are to be stripped of their citizenship and of their residential rights. The argument employed by Descartes for this purpose consists in highlighting the deceptiveness of feelings: they may encourage the subject to drink when in his feverish state a particular drink will harm him, and they may even allow him to ingest a poisonous substance which will inevitably bring about his death, not warning him in time of its fatally hazardous effects. Descartes was right with regard to these specific examples. Feelings can deceive us. Like all human systems, the emotional system is not one hundred per cent perfect or precise, and it may not warn the individual in time of a toxic substance invading his digestive republic undetected by the brain's border patrol. Descartes made the mistake here of rejecting the emotional system as an informative system by allowing his vision to be clouded by its minimal and exceptional defects, and not pausing to discover and admire the marvellous wonders of one of the most ingenious and sophisticated informative systems imaginable. It would be neither a wise nor a prudent action to cut off my head in order to rid myself of a headache. It is true that eliminating the head will eliminate the headache, but the head generates more than mere headaches, and the emotional system is not principally a source of error that leads the subject to ingest harmful substances.

The brain is an extremely complex computer that is programmed to inform the individual, with both the precision of a Swiss watch and the speed of a lightning bolt, about what he must do to preserve his body and his society. It does so through the postal service of feelings. The neural computer will inform the subject about the presence of any foreign substance which may penetrate the frontiers of his body, for example a hair in his eye, and will let him know how to deal with such an intruder. The neural computer will inform the subject, if he is male, about when he ought to sow his seed, and about how, and with what degree of mathematically precise urgency he must perform this social task. The removal of a hair from one's eye is necessary for the proper functioning of one's organic cameras. The sowing of the male seed in the place foreseen by nature is necessary for the preservation of society. In this study I would like to demonstrate to René Descartes, and to any other interested readers, that one of the most remarkable genetic wonders is the communications link between the neural computer and the subject, a sophisticated, swift, complex, mathematically precise and integrated structure: the emotional system.

By activating a rainbow of feelings (a toothache, the pleasure of laughter, the joy of winning, the happiness of finding a lost child, the shame of having performed an act of incest, and so many others), the neural computer informs the individual of the state of his teeth, his eyes, his son or his territorial society, and gives him detailed instructions regarding what he ought to do with his genital antenna, his mouth, or his in-laws. Throughout the course of our lives, from the moment we come out of the maternal dwelling we have rented out for nine months (the current rental rate in the United States is ten thousand dollars, as deduced from recent litigation involving so-called surrogate mothers), the neural computer will send us millions and millions of messages, letting us know when and how we ought to expel a gas, make love, eat, laugh, cry, live, and even execute ourselves, always and on every occasion by means of the same channel: the emotions. The emotional system is an informative system.

The Emotional System as a Coercive System

When the neural computer triggers an unpleasant feeling, it informs the subject of something he did not know previously (e.g. 'there is a hair in your eye'), but at the same time it gives precise orders: 'Take that hair out of your eye immediately.' The emotional system is not only an informative system, but also an authoritarian system of government, an omnipotent coercive system. Each time the neural computer informs the subject of something he was unaware of, it simultaneously commands him to do something. Anyone who gives orders must be in a position of power (must have the power to give those orders). Anyone who governs, who rules and commands, needs to possess some set of coercive tools, of rewards and punishments, by means of which he may persuade his subjects to comply with the orders given. Feelings are 'the carrot and the stick', the rewards and punishments, the coercive tools with which nature has endowed the neural computer, so that it may persuade and pressure the subject to obey its commands.

The nerves in the index finger of the left hand may inform the neural computer that the surface of this finger has made contact with a scorching body at 120 degrees. The neural computer will then consult the temperature program prescribed for this somatic area, will detect an infraction of 90 degrees, and will discover that it must in this case trigger off a precise feeling (an unpleasant burning sensation) of 90 degrees (intense pain). When it releases this feeling, the neural computer informs the subject of something he was unaware of, having been previously occupied with other affairs: 'The surface of the index finger of your left hand is in contact with an extremely high temperature.' The neural computer simultaneously commands the subject as follows: 'Remove your finger from there immediately, or I shall continue to torture you with severe pain.' The neural computer treats the subject in the same way that the lion-tamer treats his animals at the circus: 'Jump through the hoop or I shall flog you with my whip.' The neural computer's whip is the emotional system. The subject can disobey the brain's orders (within certain genetically foreseen limits), but he cannot avoid its whip. He may keep his finger on the stove, but he cannot avoid suffering the torture foreseen by the neural computer's program.

The Emotional System as an Objective, Automatic and Mathematically Precise System

The emotional system is a genetically installed, automatic, independent, rigid and mathematically precise system that both informs and pressures. The subject – you, the reader, or myself, the author – is governed by the neural computer's emotional pressures. The difference between a computer and a brain appears to lie in the fact that the former can never feel anything. A computer can never feel sad, nor happy, nor bored, nor angry. This is a puzzle I have been trying to come to grips with for many years (I am tempted to write 'centuries', since in our species certain problems have been approached from different angles by various thinkers over hundreds of years. It is all part of a multi-secular process to which one hopes to add a fruitful contribution).

Feelings are on one level subjective and inaccessible, but they are also objective and mathematically precise. They can, therefore, become objects of study or scientific analysis. This is hardly an easy task, since feelings and ideas, what we call 'you' and 'I' (the subject), and the brain, are intimately connected and intertwined. We can and should, nevertheless, distinguish between two different worlds: the neural computer and the 'I', or subject. The neural computer, like any other machine, does not and cannot feel anything; only the subject feels. But this is only one side of the coin. If we flip this coin over we find another side, the most paradoxical aspect of this mysterious world: the neural computer, by means of programs that function with complete independence from the subject, controls all his feelings. The subject can never attain such control. The neural computer,[2] following the instructions contained in its programs, automatically decides what the subject must feel, when, and to what degree. Were the subject in control of his emotions, he would make himself permanently happy. He would do away with all the sensations and emotions that make his life burdensome (headaches, depressions, anxiety, sadness), and would provide himself with all the feelings that were agreeable to him. Nature (or whoever has designed the genetic constitution of human beings and their society) has decided that the subject must perform certain tasks in order to ensure the proper functioning and maintenance of his body and his society. Nature has created an ingenious system of biological wages and payments for this worker – what one could refer to as emotional salaries. The neural computer offers the subject the following contract: 'Carry out this task and I shall reward you with an emotional salary. Eat now and I shall pay you a certain amount of pleasure.' The subject cannot obtain this emotional reward unless he carries out the task commanded by the neural computer: 'As long as you refrain from eating, I shall not reward you with the pleasure of eating.' The neural computer never pays the subject in advance.

We can also find, in this ingenious contractual system between the neural computer and the subject, a genetic law that regulates the intensity of feelings: 'The more important the task, either for the body or for society, the higher the emotional salary that will

be paid, or the more intense the pleasure offered and provided.'
The neural computer pays the subject (if he is male) a meagre
emotional salary for sending images of a young woman's attractive
legs to the visual department of the brain. The neural computer
will pay this same subject a higher sum for exploring the lady's
legs with his hands, and will increase this salary if the manual
exploration is extended to other more intimate areas of her body.
But the subject will only 'hit the jackpot' when he performs the
task that nature has decreed, i.e. when he delivers the goods in
the prescribed place of the required female. (1) If the job is not
finished properly, the neural computer does not pay the sum of
pleasure stipulated in the contract. (2) For each particular task
there is a particular emotional salary. I shall attempt to demonstrate in this study that these two laws are innately installed in the
brain.

The neural computer, automatically guided by these two genetic
laws, directs and governs the subject. Only the subject feels, but
he feels what the neural computer decides for him throughout the
course of his life. The subject is compelled to feel (a particular
pleasure or a particular pain) with a precise intensity and for an
imposed duration, according to rigid, inalterable genetic laws, in
the same way he is forced to reside in a somatic dwelling which
is given to him: a body of a certain height, design, skin and eye
colour, with certain organic functions, and which will irreversibly
deteriorate and die. The subject finds himself under the despotic
government of the neural computer, which has an exclusive control
over feelings. Only the lion, but not the lion-tamer, feels the pain of
the latter's whip. Only the subject, but not the neural computer, feels
the pain of the latter's emotional floggings. The subject has no way
of seizing control over the neural computer's genetically designed
weapon.

The Emotional System as a Punitive System

In my initial exploration of the emotional system, I believed that I
had discovered that the neural computer negotiated with the subject
by offering him rewards, payments or salaries (pleasant feelings), or
by threatening him with punishments or tortures (unpleasant feel-

ings). However, I have ultimately reached the following conclusion: there are in actual fact no emotional rewards, but only punishments. Only pain, but not pleasure, exists. We can see how there are three phases in the course of the negotiating process between the neural computer and the subject: (1) before the action; (2) during the action; (3) after the action. Let us consider the following example: (1) before a meal; (2) during a meal; (3) after a meal. At first I believed that before a meal the neural computer, upon being informed of the state of the stomach, offered the subject a contract in the following terms: 'If you eat now, I shall pay you with the pleasant sensation of eating.' However, I have now reached a very different conclusion. The brain, once it has been informed of the need to send food to the stomach, and once the digestive program has been consulted, automatically triggers an unpleasant feeling: hunger.

The neural computer begins to negotiate by disturbing the subject. During the first phase, it does so as follows: 'If you begin to eat, I will gradually cancel this uncomfortable sensation as long as you continue providing the stomach with food.' Let us suppose that the subject decides to accept this contract: he begins to eat. We then enter the second phase. The subject experiences the illusion of receiving a pleasurable sensation for each bite he takes of, for instance, his roast beef. In fact, however, what happens is that the neural computer diminishes the uncomfortable sensation of hunger in direct proportion to the amount of food that the subject ingests: x degrees of hunger are eliminated for every bite that is taken. We finally reach the third phase: after the meal. The subject would not know when to stop eating, or what is the precise quantity that his stomach needs at a given moment. The neural computer will tell him when he has had enough by cancelling the last degree of hunger. 'What a great meal! I feel great now,' the subject might then say. What has really happened, however, is that the neural computer has fully cancelled the unpleasant sensations of hunger that it compelled the subject to experience.

Plato tells us in his *Dialogues* how Socrates, minutes before drinking the fatal hemlock which he was sentenced to drink, had his shackles removed from his ankles and exclaimed:

What a strange thing, my friends, that seems to be which men call pleasure! How wonderfully it is related to that which seems to be its opposite, pain, in that they will not both come to a man at the same time, and yet if he pursues the one and captures it, he is generally obliged to take the other also, as if the two were joined together in one head. And I think if Aesop had thought of them, he would have made a fable telling how they were at war and god wished to reconcile them, and when he could not do that, he fastened their heads together, and for that reason, when one of them comes to anyone, the other follows after. Just so it seems that in my case, after pain was in my leg on account of the fetter, pleasure appears to have come following after.[3]

I have often read and reread these dialogues of Plato. Only after having written *The Emotional Computer*, however, did the paragraph I have just quoted make me realize that here Socrates was on the verge of discovering the following genetic law: what appears to be pleasure, what the individual takes to be pleasure, is in fact nothing but the elimination of pain, of an uncomfortable sensation. It is not actually the case, as Socrates and common sense assume, that there are two types of feeling: pleasure and pain. Only pain, only uncomfortable feelings, exist. The subject, therefore, has to buy pleasure (the pleasure he mistakenly believes to exist) with the currency of pain. One who has not been shackled – one who has not previously acquired the currency of pain – cannot feel, or buy, the pleasure that eliminates pain. If a person wants to obtain pleasure, he must first undergo the pain of being in some way shackled. This is one of the genetic laws that I believe I have discovered and which I shall explore from different angles throughout the course of this study. The brain, an automatic, mechanical computer, negotiates with the subject in these terms: 'If you remove these shackles now – whatever the urges or the corresponding task that has to be performed may be – I shall cease to disturb you with these unpleasant feelings.'

The Subject's Limited Freedom

Is the human being, then, a mere emotional robot? If nature manipulates the brain with genetic mechanisms, and the brain in turn manipulates the subject with the emotional whip, is man a puppet that loves, hates, feels urges to read or to cease reading, a puppet controlled by the strings of nature, the ultimate puppeteer? In other words, are human beings nothing more than chess pieces moved by nature through the emotional mechanisms installed in their brains? The Spanish philosopher Miguel de Unamuno said that if chess pieces were granted the ability to reason, they would attribute their movements to themselves, mistakenly believing themselves to be free.[4]

Unamuno's comparison is inappropriate and exaggerated. Any process of negotiation, of lobbying, and even of threats, includes and presupposes a limited margin of choice and freedom in the subject, who may obey orders or reject them entirely. The neural computer informs, persuades, pressures and threatens the individual with the emotional whip, but the latter has the last word. The neural computer can inform the subject about what he can eat, and can begin to pressure him by releasing the sensation of hunger. The individual does not possess the freedom to cancel the sensation of hunger, but he may disobey this order and abstain from eating. The brain, following its automatic program, will augment the intensity of the hunger as time passes and the subject continues to disobey the order to ingest food. The conflict between the neural computer and the subject becomes increasingly tense and intense. The neural computer, as one, two, three, four and perhaps more days go by while the subject tenaciously ignores the former's commands, will escalate the emotional pressure until it is as unbearable as the tortures of the Holy Inquisition: acute pains, feelings of depression, dizzy spells, and so on. The subject, however, can withstand all these tortures, disobey the brain's orders, and die of starvation.

St Thomas Aquinas affirmed that *nemo sine delectatione vivere potest*,[5] that no one can live without pleasure, without experiencing pleasant feelings, whichever they may be. If this renowned medieval thinker was right (and this is one of the conclusions of the present study), *delectatio*, or pleasant feelings, are a condition *sine qua non*, a vital, indispensable energy, a kind of spiritual oxygen: oxygen is to the body what pleasant feelings are to the subject. A subject who disobeys the orders and the brutal blackmails of the neural computer until he dies of starvation is in actual fact exchanging exquisite emotions for psychological tortures. He buys gourmet pleasures for the steep price of intensely painful sensations. This brings us to one of the most important aspects of the brain's emotional world:

the phenomenon of conflicting emotions, of opposed torturers. The human brain is a computer that functions not only with feelings, but also with different programs which often stand in opposition to one another, and hence which simultaneously trigger antagonistic, irreconcilable emotions.

2

The Neural Computer

Hardware and Software of the Neural Computer

One of the reasons that led me to use the 'computer' metaphor is that *servatis servandis* (within the limits and reservations which will be noted in this study), the brain functions with both hardware and software. The brain's hardware includes the genetically designed physical components, a complex and unknown structure of neurons and specialized areas that function according to some type of operating system. This hardware can assimilate and operate with particular software, with certain programs and certain types of data, but not with others. Not all software is compatible with the hardware of a particular computer. Similarly, the hardware of a monkey's neural computer is incompatible with the software of laughter, cooking, religion, or ethics, which are compatible with a human being's hardware. We can define the brain's software as 'programs and data files compatible with the brain's hardware, which can be installed by the genetic plan or by sensory channels, and which allow the brain to inform and pressure the individual to carry out particular acts'.

Particular software packages have been genetically installed in the brain of a dog or of a human being. These are innate programs and data. The neural computer of a dog contains a genetic program by means of which it can, with its olfactory antennae, detect the species to which a particular specimen of urine belongs, as well as its sex, age and individual identity (its mate, its owner, a neighbour who kicks him regularly, and so on). The neural computer of a human being contains no such program. In a dog's neural computer this software is genetically installed, although it is also true that the program which contains the voice, the smell, the image, or the behaviour of its owner is software acquired by the neural computer of a particular dog. As we shall see, crying and laughter, amongst others, make up part of the genetic, innate software of a human being's neural computer, although a genetically installed timer included in the operating system will determine the initial functioning of certain programs, such as those mentioned. I would argue that there are two types of software, or program, in the neural computer: bionatural and biocultural programs.

Bionatural and Biocultural Software

We must distinguish between what is natural and what is bionatural. A banana is a natural product that exists independently of the human brain, but it becomes something bionatural when it becomes a product of the brain. The neural computer can create a data file of this fruit and store it within its memory banks: the image of a banana, its tactile qualities, its smell, and other ideas and feelings derived from it.

We must similarly distinguish between what is cultural and what is biocultural. The Oxford English Dictionary and the English language are cultural products of a particular society, which exist outside the human brain (in the form of, say, books or films in English). However, the English language is also a biocultural product in the sense that it can be an acquired, stored entity within the software of a particular individual. An Englishman, born and raised in England, carries in his neural computer a biological, biocultural dictionary which includes the grammatical rules that dictate the use of its words and sentences.

Any cultural system is a partly innate program, partly a cultural program, and partly a biocultural program. (1) It is innate in the sense that the hardware of the human being's neural computer has foreseen the acquisition of this software. For instance, every human being's neural computer has a place reserved for the acquisition of religious programs. (2) It is cultural in the sense that any human society will generate, amongst other cultural products, a religious system. The beehive produces honey and wax. A specific religion, a particular language, and other cultural products are the honey and the wax of human society. (3) It is biocultural in the sense that, once the neural computer has acquired a religious program, and depending on the quality and the quantity of this acquisition, the neural computer will inform and pressure the individual in order to force his observance of the rules of this system: what he ought to do, when, how, where and to what extent.

The Sensory, Mental and Emotional Branches of the Brain's Software

A program of the neural computer could be defined as a correspondence amongst three systems: the sensory, the mental, and the emotional systems genetically or experientially installed in the neural computer. The neural computer of a dog is equipped to grasp and file the sounds of human laughter or of a human language such as English, but these sounds cannot be translated by it into a mental system (ideas which correspond to these sounds), nor into an emotional system (feelings which correspond to these sounds). The neural computer of a human being is innately equipped to translate, amongst others, the phonic system of laughter: to translate it into a mental system (for instance, if a bearded male adult speaks in a high pitched voice, which is associated with the female sex according to a genetic code, the violation of this rule will be perceived); and also to translate it into an emotional system (pleasure in the subject who laughs at the male with the high pitched voice, and hurt feelings in the victim of this laughter, who is penalized by ridicule).

The Neural Computer's Automatic Translations

If the neural computer possesses a particular program, such as the English language or the crying system, it will be capable of automatically translating a sensory message into a mental or emotional message, and vice versa. We should take note of the fact that two characteristic products of the brain, ideas and feelings, belong to the category which Aristotle called Μέτα τα φυσικα,[1] 'beyond physical things'. Physical things are those that can be seen, touched, smelled, tasted, heard, or in some way perceived by the senses (oxygen has no smell, no colour, no taste and no 'feel', but its chemical composition can be analysed). Metaphysical things, those that lie 'beyond the physical', are those that cannot be perceived nor analysed by the sensory antennae of the human brain. God, angels and devils would belong to this category. More importantly, however, we must be aware of the fact that the two most important products generated by the human being's brain – ideas and feelings – are metaphysical.

Neither ideas nor feelings can be seen, heard, smelled, tasted or touched. They cannot be perceived by any of the sensory antennae of the brain. When Chekhov wrote that 'the soul of another is a dark jungle', he made a scientifically insightful point. The human being, with the help of the brain's sensory antennae, can analyse a tomato, a cloud or the body of other human beings. However, he has no way of analysing their 'souls'. In other words, he can neither see their thoughts nor touch their feelings. A human being's sensory antennae can perceive the physical world, but not the metaphysical one. An American gentleman whom I used to know very well was one day told by his secretary that his wife was secretly plotting a conspiracy with his enemies in order to oust him from the three hundred million dollar corporation of which he was both founder and president. This man would evidently have given anything to penetrate the metaphysical world of his wife in some way, and hence to uncover whether or not this was really true. Given his human incapacity to do so, at one point he told her about the rumours he had heard of a conspiracy in which she was supposedly scheming against him along with his enemies. She passionately denied the accusation, assuring him in a loving tone of voice that such neurotic misgivings must have been due to exhaustion and stress. He made the mistake of believing her words and her phoney affection. A few days later, his wife sued him and successfully expelled him from the corporation he had founded and directed for over forty years. Such an example highlights the human being's inability to look into the 'soul', into the private world of ideas and feelings of another human being. Ideas and feelings make up the daily correspondence that the subject receives from the neural computer. It is a secret and inscrutable postal service between the two. If a man is lying in bed with a woman, the former may hear the sounds which the latter emits, and may explore her body with his organic 'cameras' and with various different tactile antennae. He cannot, however, explore either her thoughts or her true feelings. She may tell him how much she adores him while thinking to herself how much she abhors this repulsive, decrepit old man to whom she pays attention only because of the economic advantage he represents for her. (Let us for now ignore the issue of clairvoyance, of those who claim to have 'psychic' powers and say they have access to the thoughts and feelings of other people.)

Nature, nevertheless, has conceived and installed an automatic translation system by means of which the neural computer translates ideas and feelings into the sensory world (images, sounds, tactile signs), and similarly translates images, sounds, tastes, smells, tactile signs, and other sensory signs, into ideas and feelings. Amongst its other roles, the brain is the quickest, most professional, concise and precise simultaneous translator imaginable, coding and decoding both bionatural and biocultural messages. A biological translation by the neural computer is bionatural when the correspondence between the sensory code and the mental or emotional code has been genetically installed. In the case of crying and laughing, for instance, the brain's translations are bionatural. The translation is biocultural when the correspondence between the sensory code and the mental or emotional code has been acquired.

The neural computer's sensory translations

The neural computer first presents the subject, who is both its master and its servant, with a sensory translation. It is interesting to note that the Italian people, as my mentor Sir Edward Evans-Pritchard revealed to me, are fond of saying *traduttore, traditore* ('translator, traitor'). Just as the subject can only penetrate the world of ideas and feelings of another human being by means of the neural computer's sensory translations, he can only penetrate the world of material objects by means of these same sensory translations. We could say, inspired by the words of Chekhov quoted above, that the body is also a dark jungle. Our own body, the body of others, and any other physical body (a tomato or a stone) is an impenetrable mystery. Kant and other philosophers attempted to decipher what St Thomas Aquinas, inspired by Aristotle, called *adequatio rei et intellectus*, the correspondence between our ideas and reality (the external world of sensible objects).[2] This is not the place to tackle such a complex and fascinating philosophical problem. However, it may be worth pausing briefly to consider the issue, in order to gain a better understanding of the first translation which the neural computer presents to the subject.

A tree is one thing, but a photograph of a tree is quite another. A photograph is a visual translation of reality, which is partly the result of something external that is 'out there', partly the result of the characteristics of a particular camera (its lens, its technical quality, and so on), and partly the result of other intermediary factors (the light, the angle, the distance, the relative motion and speed). We may mistakenly believe that the translations from tree to photograph are more accurate and reliable than those from the photograph to one's ideas of (and feelings provoked by) the photograph. In other words, we may think that we have better access to the world of material objects than to the world of ideas and feelings. This, however, is a vain illusion, although it may be commonly accepted as a self-evident, commonsensical truth. Our organic cameras (and all other sensory antennae) allow the brain to present the subject with an initial translation. However, like all translations, it is never entirely objective (all translators do indeed turn out to be 'traitors'). In one of his brilliant essays, the Spanish statesman, thinker and poet Salvador de Madariaga asks himself: 'If our eyes had X-ray vision, would the information about reality they presented to us be more objective, more accurate, more complete, more penetrating?' He then answers himself: 'Yes and no. A beautiful young woman would look like a walking skeleton to us. We would receive some information which our eyes hide from us – information about her bones – but we would never know what her face, her legs, her hands, her breasts, or the colour of her eyes are like. If our eyes had X-ray vision, we would describe a tree as a vertical liquid stream that springs from the ground and which, if approached, causes one to receive an awful bump on the head.'[3] The brain, with its genetically designed sensory antennae, is marvellously equipped to translate a tomato, a tree, or a cloud into images, smells, tactile sensations, tastes or sounds. The true reality of the tomato or of any other body, however, is a mystery.

The sun, seen from the earth, 'looks like a very small body',[4] smaller than a tree or a house. Descartes used this example to illustrate how the information we receive through the senses is extremely unreliable. When we look at clouds from the ground, they appear to have certain shapes, sizes and designs; but when we go through these clouds in an aircraft, these shapes, colours and designs look completely different. When the aircraft rises up above these same clouds, their appearance is transformed once again. The wooden desk on which I am writing appears to be smooth and solid. However, were I to look at it through a microscope, my view of it would be utterly metamorphosed. What appeared solid would now look hollow. What seemed solid would be transformed into an endless series of hills and valleys. Modern physics has done nothing but add weight to these Kantian points. This solid table, like any other solid object, is in reality made up of atoms. These are in turn made up of neutrons, protons and electrons, and these of even smaller particles as mysterious and inaccessible to our sensory organs as an angel.[5] The actual reality of a tree, of this table, or of any external body is a mystery about which the neural computer, by means of its sensory antennae, provides partially manufactured information: the sensory translations of the external world.

With regard to these sensory translations we must take note of the following points:

(1) *The external world*: a tomato, the sun, a tree. This is a world that exists independently of the individual and which is organized according to its own laws. In this case the external world sends the sensory message, in other words, the object which is to be translated. The sender is the external world.

(2) *The brain's antennae*: the organic cameras and their photographic laboratories (the eyes), the organic microphones and their recording studios (the ears), the tactile antennae and their respective laboratories (the penis, in the case of males, the hands, and other antennae), the olfactory antennae and laboratories, and other antennae and laboratories that can perceive and analyse electrical charges, degrees of dampness, degrees of temperature, and other physical and chemical properties of external bodies.

We must take notice of the wide variety of cerebral antennae throughout the animal kingdom and, consequently, of the wide variety of sensory perceptions which different brains receive of the same external world. The organic cameras of a human being, of a mosquito or of an eagle present very different visual reports to the brains of each of these animals. Furthermore, the quality of a subject's sensory information depends on the state of his sensorial antennae (perfect vision, as opposed to complete blindness, short-sightedness, cataracts, and so on).

(3) *The organic cables, or nerves*: the eyes are an organic system of translation or transformation. They translate, or transform, a tree or some other external body into a photograph. The eyes are the cameras and the photographic laboratories where pictures are taken and developed in colour. These labs then send the photographs, or developed films, to the neural computer's memory banks, by means of another ingenious system of transport: the nerves, or organic cables. If the nerves have deteriorated, the brain will receive distorted images and unclear sounds.

(4) *The brain*: the brain receives millions of images, sounds, smells, tastes, tactile sensations, and so on. This complex computer is genetically programmed to receive and process these numerous products, and in this way fulfils several biological purposes:

(a) It compels the individual to see, smell or otherwise perceive all the sensations that are received by the sensory antennae. The neural computer, like any other machine, neither sees, nor hears, nor tastes nor smells. Only the subject sees, hears, tastes and smells. The automatic controls of an aircraft do not see the red flashing lights or hear the sounds of an alarm. Only the pilot sees and hears these things. The automatic controls are the sole activators of these visual and phonic mechanisms, and the pilot is their sole witness. Similarly, the brain is an automatic machine which compels the individual to see whatever nature determines him to see: the subject successfully obtains a photograph of a tomato (with the help of the organic cameras, the photographic laboratories found in the eyes, the transport provided by the nerves, and the final processes in the brain). Only the subject sees, but he sees what the eyes, the nerves and the brain have manufactured for him to see in accordance with precise, inflexible genetic laws he has played no part in designing. A friend can lend us his camera, but he cannot lend us his eyes, his ears, his penis or his brain so that we may perceive the external world through them. The subject is granted a very limited margin of freedom to choose what, how and when he wants to see, hear or perceive in the external world with one of his sensory antennae.

(b) The subject can open or close his organic cameras, zoom in on certain objects, or, like a film director, choose a particular angle. However, as we shall see, even in this particular domain, the brain pressures the individual to see, hear, smell, touch or taste certain external objects and not others, prescribing the appropriate moment to do so, as well as the duration of such actions, and other precise details, according to various genetic and acquired programs. The neural computer of a vulture will pressure its 'pilot', a particular vulture, to see, smell and savour the carrion of a dead animal (a certain amount of pleasure is offered for smelling it and a greater amount is offered for ingesting it). The neural computer of a human being, on the other hand, will threaten the subject with highly unpleasant sensations if he approaches a decaying corpse, will augment these threats if he smells it, and will provoke extreme degrees of repugnance if he tries to eat it.

(c) The neural computer stores photographs, films, tastes, sounds, tunes, voices, tactile sensations and other perceptual experiences in different files. Each neural computer has numerous files with images, sounds and other stored sensory products of varying quality. The subject has not a clue about how these storage rooms or files are organized and plays no part in their operation. He does not decide which images or sounds are to be filed, or where, how, and for how long they are to be conserved. The neural computer is an extremely professional, efficient and swift archivist which simultaneously classifies and stores millions of images, sounds and all sorts of sensory products with which it is continually bombarded, in accordance with mathematically precise laws. The latter, as we shall see, are partly bionatural and partly biocultural. This archivist decides, independently of the subject, which images or sounds are to be eliminated, and which are to be filed, which are to be classified in particularly privileged places and which in some abandoned corner, and for how long each piece of information will be kept in a file (an entire lifetime, a few years, months, days or seconds).

(d) The neural computer is programmed to work for the subject as an archivist which will search and attempt to find whatever image, number, phrase or poem the subject asks it for as quickly as possible. In this case, the subject is the sender, and the neural computer is the worker receiving the orders. However, it is also true that the subject is to some extent at the mercy of the archivist's efficiency (all employers depend at least in part on the quality of their employees). A student would be able to answer every question on a memory test correctly if his performance was wholly dependent on him rather than on his neural computer.

(e) The neural computer is programmed to reproduce certain images, scenes or stored films. A person who owns a video camera can record moving pictures. If he also owns video equipment and an appropriate monitor, he can see these pictures as often as he wishes to do so. The neural computer is equipped with mechanisms that can perform similar tasks. It can record moving pictures, store them and reproduce them (the same applies to other sensory products, such as the taste of fish and chips, which it can store and reproduce for the subject). The subject can decide when and how often he wants to view a particular scene from his data files. His neural computer will obey this order according to the genetic plan. Sometimes, however, the subject becomes irritated when his neural computer is unable to reproduce a particular line from a poem, or a particular sequence from a musical composition. In this domain, the neural computer, as we shall see, will pressure the subject to view certain scenes, and to refrain from viewing others. The emotional pressure can be so powerfully persistent that the subject might be compelled to repeatedly view a scene he would much rather forget. The subject, although he may desire to do so, cannot destroy any scenes in his memory banks as if they were files on his home computer. Nature has given the brain exclusive access to these files. A criminal may hence be forced to witness, time and again, the scene in which he murdered his victim.

It sometimes happens that a particular melody we thought we had 'forgotten' is played over and over again by our neural computers. We may wish to destroy the 'record' and the 'record player', but this is something we simply cannot do. Once again we find the neural computer acting independently of the subject, obeying its own biological laws, and perhaps undergoing some sort of technical difficulty.

The neural computer's mental translations

There are three types of translation that the neural computer, aided by the sensory antennae and laboratories, presents to the subject: sensory, mental and emotional translations. The three are different in nature, although their interconnections make it difficult to distinguish them. The neural computer of a dog can offer its owner, a particular dog, a visual translation of the Union Jack – an organic photograph of this flag. However, it is genetically prevented from translating this image into the sphere of ideas. The hardware of a dog's neural computer permits it to translate an external object, the Union Jack, into an organic photograph, but it does not allow a translation of this photograph into an idea: 'This flag represents my country, Great Britain, and all the members of this territorial community.' The neural computer of a British child, on the other hand, can simultaneously translate an external object, the Union Jack, into a photograph, and this, in turn into a precise idea: 'This is my country's flag.'

The neural computer automatically transforms a sensory translation into a mental translation, as long as such a transformation is allowed by its hardware, and the relevant software has been acquired. This law applies to all sensory translations.

The neural computer's emotional translations

Suppose I take my dog out for a walk. It stops here and there, sniffing at various places. Suddenly, it begins to wag its tail and sniff a particular tree with heightened interest. My dog's neural computer has in this case carried out a triple translation: a sensory translation (a particular smell), a mental translation (this smell belongs to its mate), and an emotional translation (the activation of erotic pleasure). The hardware of a human being's neural computer is incapable of carrying out this triple translation: his olfactory antennae cannot detect such a smell, and even if they could, this smell could not be transformed into an idea (to whom does this scent belong?), nor into an erotic sensation (if anything, it would be translated into one of repugnance).

The hardware of a human being's neural computer allows it to acquire software for the complex sensory, mental and emotional system of the 'tribe' or 'territorial society'. If the brain of an American, for instance, has acquired this program and if he were to observe a group of foreigners carrying rubbish in his country's flag, his neural computer would automatically translate these images into feelings of indignation and desires for vengeance (with the intensity specified by the software).

The Five Systems of Communication

There are, in my view, five systems of communication, which can be referred to as the natural, the cultural, the somatic, the imaginary and the social.

The natural system

The natural system of communication is the one we have just analysed, where the sender is always a tree, or some other external body.

The cultural system

Here, the sender is culture. We can define culture as 'a system, a series of systems, or a set of products created by a human society'. A bee is born into a natural world of flowers, rain, wind, aggressive animals and so on, but it is also born into a cultural world: the beehive system, which includes rules that determine who is who (citizens of the beehive, as opposed to foreigners; male bees and female bees; the queen bee and subordinate bees; soldier bees and explorer bees), and which also manufactures certain products: wax and honey. The latter is not the product of an individual, but of a society. Human beings are also integrated into both a natural and a cultural world. They find themselves in a natural world with certain characteristics and particular laws (oxygen, bacteria, the law of gravity, and so on), as well as in a cultural world composed of elements such as the English language, religions, ethical systems, aesthetic codes, and so on. English is not the product of an individual. It is the product of a society. Honey is to the beehive what English is to England. (I shall later consider the contribution of a Shakespeare to English or of a Cicero to Latin – in other words, the contribution of an individual to the development of a cultural system.) The neural computer of a human being is equipped to acquire, store, and reproduce the cultural systems of any human society. In this case it is human society which sends messages to the brain.

The somatic system

In the somatic system of communication, the sender is one's own body. In this case the messages are sent neither by a tree – the natural world – nor by the English language – the cultural world – but rather by the individual's body itself. The stomach, for instance, may inform the brain that it is completely empty. The neural computer then consults the relevant program, and sends the subject the following message: 'The stomach needs food.'

The imaginary system

The sender in the imaginary system of communication is neither nature, nor society, nor the body, but merely the imagination. The neural computer, as we have seen, has the capacity to reproduce 'filmed' scenes for the subject. In this case the sender is the world of the imagination. (I shall, for the moment, leave aside the creative process by means of which the subject, aided by his neural computer, creates new worlds of fiction, thought, ethics, politics, and so on.)

The social system

The social system of communication is that in which the sender is either a human being or some other animal. These are the different phases of the social system of communication conceived by the genetic plan:

(1) Subject A wants to communicate his thoughts and feelings to subject B.

(2) The neural computer of A translates these ideas and feelings into images and sounds, in accordance with the software of laughter, crying, speech and other codes.

(3) The neural computer of A sends these translations to the visual and phonic somatic instruments, via the postal service provided by the nerves.

(4) The phonic somatic instruments (vocal chords, mouth, tongue, teeth and lips) begin to move and emit the sounds required by the neural computer. The face, eyes, eyebrows, lips, hands and body make the required visual signs.

(5) These images and sounds travel through various natural and cultural physical channels situated between the sensory instruments of A and the sensory antennae of B.

(6) The sensory antennae of B – eyes and ears – perceive these images and sounds, and transform them into biological photographs and sounds.

(7) B's laboratories send these biological photographs and sounds to B's brain via the postal service provided by the nerves.

(8) B's neural computer consults the diverse programs installed in its software and in accordance with these programs, translates these sounds and images into ideas and feelings.

(9) B's neural computer finally presents these mental and emotional translations to the subject.

(10) B, the subject, understands and feels as soon as he receives the final mental and emotional translations.

Nine 'metaphors' take place during the course of this process, if we employ this term according to its original meaning in Greek, Μέτα φέρειν, 'to take something further, to take something from one place to another'. There are nine transformations, or translations:

1. SENDER: Subject A
   GOODS: Metaphysical reality: ideas and feelings

2. TRANSLATOR: A's neural computer
   TRANSLATION: Ideas and feelings into biological images and sounds

3. POSTAL DELIVERY: A's nerves
   GOODS: Biological images and sounds

4. TRANSLATOR: Face, mouth and other somatic instruments
   TRANSLATION: Physical images and sounds

5. POSTAL DELIVERY: Light and air
   GOODS: Physical images and sounds

6. RECEIVER: Eyes and ears
   PROCESSED GOODS: The images and sounds are perceived and processed into biological photographs and sounds

7. POSTAL DELIVERY: B's nerves
    GOODS: Biological images and sounds

8. TRANSLATOR: B's neural computer
    TRANSLATION: Biological images and sounds into ideas and feelings

9. RECEIVER: B, the subject
    GOODS: A's ideas and feelings after having passed through this whole complex process of transference and translation.

During the course of these 'meta-phors', transfers, transformations or translations, the original message might have been lost, altered or distorted. Subject A's objective might have been to deceive subject B (deliberately misusing the communicative codes for this purpose). In such a case the neural computer generally obeys his wishes like a humble slave.

It might, however, give away the deception, as Freud revealed in his *Psychopathology of Everyday Life*. The neural computer of either or both of the subjects might have made mistakes during the course of a translation due to the incompleteness or inaccuracy of its programs, or perhaps due to a temporary breakdown. Their visual and phonic instruments (vocal chords, face, and so on) might have manufactured images and sounds with the distinct clarity prescribed by the brain, but alternatively, they might have produced a much lower standard. The instruments themselves might have been damaged or deteriorated.

For instance, the vocal chords of A might have been in poor condition, due to a viral infection. The light that is necessary to transport A's facial gestures might have been either too bright or too dim to do so properly. The transmission of the sound emitted by A's mouth might also have been deficient. The nervous systems of either or both of the subjects may have been faulty. B's neural computer might have committed major errors of translation due to the inadequacy of its software, and so on.

You, the reader, or I, the author, do not have direct access to the reality of a tomato, of our bodies, of our imagination, or of the thoughts and feelings of another human being. The original messages sent from these five different worlds arrive to us across all these labyrinthine channels and by means of all the various translations I have described. (These, however, are relatively insignificant difficulties which cannot overshadow the marvellous communicative relationship that is established between the different worlds and yourself, or myself, in that complex physical, metaphysical, natural, cultural and biological reality where light, air, sensory antennae, brains, nervous systems and that mysterious entity we call 'you' or 'I' all play an indispensable role.)

The Emotional World of the Human Being

René Descartes is renowned for having discovered the continent of doubt (although in this he was preceded by Socrates and other earlier thinkers). Any kind of informer can deceive us. Descartes demonstrated, with impeccable logic, that the external world might be nothing but an illusion. We might see our in-laws riding winged horses through the sky, only to wake up and realize that we have merely been dreaming. Such a terrifying reality, we then discover, does not actually exist. But even so, says Descartes, 'cogito ergo sum', 'je pense donc je suis' (I think, therefore I am).[6] Although the object of my thoughts might be a non-existent winged horse, a mere illusion, as long as I think, I must be something. Descartes realized that there are two types of being: mental beings (my thoughts) and real beings (a horse that exists outside my thoughts). He concluded that for us the most real, authentic, and reliable beings are our own thoughts. Whatever the reality of the external horse may be, nothing can deprive me of my mental reality of the horse: my idea of the horse.

As I pointed out earlier, Descartes was unable to grasp the importance of feelings, excommunicating them from the church of knowledge for being 'confusi status menti' (confused states of the mind). He failed to discover the continent of feelings, which is evidently different from that of ideas, and which is, in my view, the most important, intimate and vital one for the human being. I may be capable of seeing, hearing, thinking, imagining and dreaming; but if I am incapable of feeling, I am still nothing to myself.[7] Descartes, Kant and other philosophers distinguished the *ens rationis* (a mental being, or idea) from the *ens reale* (a real being, or one which exists independently of thought: a real stone, a real tree, a real horse, and so on). These thinkers, however, missed out a third, entirely independent category: the *ens sentimenti, ens sentimentale*, the emotional beings, or feelings: the pleasure we experience when we make love, when we win, when we find a lost child, or the pain we experience from a toothache, or when we break a leg. 'Sentio, ergo sum' (I feel, therefore I am). What matters to the human being is how he feels. Whatever the original cause of his feelings may be (a real, imagined, or dreamed thing, or a real, imagined, or dreamed person), what matters is whether those real or mental existences are translated into pleasant or unpleasant feelings by the processes of his neural computer. Neither real objects nor ideas constitute the most important reality for a human being. What matters to him are the feelings he achieves, independently of where he derives them from.

Let us try to imagine what our world would be like without feeling. If a young man saw an attractive young woman, he might be able to see her and touch her. He might be able to think: 'This young, sweet, affectionate girl is someone I could get along with brilliantly.' However, without feeling, these images and thoughts would not produce any pleasant sensations or emotions in him. Were we unable to delight in the exquisite flavours of a gourmet meal, or in the company of close friends, or in the contemplation of a beautiful landscape, were we unable to feel anything, we would have become stones, machines or computers. We would cease to be what we are, for our one true reality – the reality of our feelings – would have evaporated. A tape recorder can record sounds, a video can reproduce films, a computer can carry out quasi-mental operations, but these machines cannot feel, while the human being can (although not what he wants to feel, but what his neural computer compels him to feel). For the human being, the ultimate relevance of all sounds, images or thoughts, and of all external realities (objects and people), is defined for him by his own feelings. What really matters to the human being are the feelings that his neural computer hands over to him, along with every image, taste, colour, smell or sound derived from a given object or person.

According to the genetic plan which governs the world of feelings, a real object or person (in the external world) is usually translated into a more intense emotional reality than an imagined one. If a thirsty man slurps up a plentiful quantity of fresh water from the fountain of his imagination, the neural computer will pay him a meagre amount of satisfaction. If instead he drinks it from a real fountain, the neural computer will punctually pay him a high dose of pleasure. It is for this reason that St John of the Cross, the mystic poet and writer of sixteenth-century Spain, wrote that:

> The infirmity of love cannot be cured
> Without our loved one's tangible presence.

St John of the Cross was referring to the physical presence of God. He confessed to having been 'entranced' by divine love, to having derived an exquisite pleasure from the invisible presence of God. But he also confessed – noting the difference between the pleasure derived from real objects or persons, as opposed to that derived from imaginary ones – that these 'raptures' could be nothing compared with the infinite pleasure he would experience if he really saw God (although God, presumably, is invisible).

A human being, under the influence of certain drugs, or owing to some pathological condition, may believe that he is really seeing, hearing, smelling, tasting and touching what are in fact imaginary objects and persons. In these cases such purely fictional beings can be perceived as real, and since this is the case, the neural computer pays the subject the emotional salary normally reserved for pleasures derived from real objects and persons.

We may observe that if a drugged male obtains the same pleasure for making love to an imaginary woman which he would obtain for making love to a real woman, he receives an illicit emotional payment from his neural computer. With the aid of drugs, a human being can delight in pleasures that are genetically reserved for sensory perceptions of real objects and persons.[8] The human being can learn to play tricks on his neural computer: he can receive an emotional salary without 'earning' it – in other words, without carrying out the relevant task for his body or for his society. Nature seems to be omniscient, however, and has reserved severe punishments for such trickery. A subject who repeatedly defies these laws will be forced to pay a number of genetically foreseen penalties (the inevitable consequences of alcoholism and drug addiction).

My point is essentially that for the human being, the reality that ultimately matters is the reality of his feelings. Irrespective of whether or not the ghost he sees is real or not, what matters to one who has such a vision is his anguish or his terror. Whatever the real state of a subject's tooth (whether or not it is actually infected), if he feels an intense toothache, this is the reality that matters to him. If all objects and persons were to leave us indifferent, how could their reality matter?[9] The acclaimed Spanish novelist José María Gironella has written about the depression he suffered at a given point in his life, explaining that during this time, neither his wife's presence nor the success of his books provided any relief whatsoever. The nature of the objects and persons of the external world had not changed in any way, but for him this reality had in some sense disappeared, since his neural computer was now incapable of translating this reality into pleasant feelings. His neural computer translated the physical reality of his wife into a visual, phonic and tactile one: he could see her, hear her, embrace her or kiss her. But his neural computer was incapable of translating this mental, sensory woman into an emotional one. He knew that she was his wife. He knew that his latest books had been extraordinarily successful, but this knowledge was not translated into any pleasant sensations or emotions. Images, sounds and even ideas are not ends for the human being; they are merely means to emotional ends. 'I feel, therefore I am': this is the key to understanding our truth, our being, and our happiness. What difference does it make if we stand before a natural spectacle such as the Niagara falls, or enamour the most desired 'sex-symbol', or win millions of pounds in a lottery, if our neural computer has for some reason broken down, and is unable to pay us the appropriate emotional salary?

Ideas themselves are programmed in the brain along with pleasant and unpleasant feelings. The idea that an inevitable death awaits us is translated by our neural computer into a disagreeable emotion which Unamuno referred to as 'the tragic sentiment of life'. The idea that we may survive death in another world may console us to a greater or lesser degree. (We know we are going to die. We believe, if we have faith, that we will survive in another world. To believe is to know with doubt.) John Locke said that 'there is no one in the commonwealth of learning who does not profess a love for the truth'.[10] What, then, came first: the chicken of feeling or the egg of knowledge? Both are causes and effects. Ideas are governed by feelings, and feelings by ideas. The emotional system is an informative system (the urges to eat inform me about something of which I was unaware), but at the same time, the system of ideas is translated into a system of feelings within the complex laboratories of the neural computer. Locke, and any other citizen of the '*commonwealth of learning*', would be completely indifferent to the discovery of new ideas were it not for the urge to do so released in him by the neural computer. When Gironella writes his books he is manipulated by emotional mechanisms (the urge to write and to be successful): one cannot eat or write without the urges to do so. When this same author was depressed, the books he had written, or those he was to write, 'left him cold' (an interesting, revealing metaphor).

Blaise Pascal famously said 'je suis un roseau, mais un roseau pensant' (I am a reed, but a reed which thinks).[11] Thought thus becomes an existential frontier between two categories of being: those who think and those who do not. 'The universe can crush me, but it does not know that it can, while I do.' Here is the basis of our superiority, according to Pascal and other thinkers. However, it is not the fact that we are aware of knowing which makes us superior to the stone. What matters is that this thought ('I think, but the stone does not') makes us feel superior. Thought, once again, is the means, while feeling is the end. If a great writer is suffering from a depression, he may know that he is superior to a stone and to other writers, but he does not feel superior, and nothing makes any difference to him.

The end is not sex, or money, or even God. The end is what we feel when we come into contact with any of these realities. If a subject's neural computer translates money into agreeable feelings, it has significance for him. If not, it makes no difference to him at all. The *Homo rationalis* is not as important as the *Homo sentimentalis*, the emotional animal. It may be true that our knowledge is superior to that of the monkey and the stone, but this can only constitute an advance for us if our awareness of this superiority is translated into an emotion of satisfaction.

The human being is an animal that frantically employs its intellectual faculties to attain pleasure, or pleasant feelings. Both St John of the Cross and Don Juan can be seen as explorers searching for the same precious pearls of pleasure[12] (on a broad meaning of this term). They differ only in their strategies, but not in the ultimate objective of their pursuits. St John of the Cross decides to forego the carnal pleasures which Don Juan relishes, in order to attain sensations which are more agreeable to him: those that emanate from the love of God both on earth and especially in the heavens. Don Juan, on the other hand, much prefers the worldly pleasure of sexual conquest to St John's mystical ways. It should hardly surprise us, then, that Christians, Muslims and other religious groups define Heaven as a place of infinite pleasure, and Hell as a place of uninterrupted pain.

What ultimately matters to the human being are the emotional translations that his neural computer makes of the world as it is in itself, for it is on this that his happiness depends.

3
Biosocial Laws

Laws, Exceptions and Infractions

Sir Edward Evans-Pritchard, my Oxford 'tutor', devoted much time and effort to a fundamental issue in the social sciences: whether or not there are any demonstrable laws that govern human society. Evans-Pritchard undermined the work of Comte, Montesquieu, Ferguson, and all those who maintained that there are social laws as rigidly precise as the law of gravity, and that they had discovered some of them. He then reached the socratic conclusion that all we really know about social laws is that we know nothing about them. 'Comte,' says Evans-Pritchard, 'provided us with some excellent guidelines for discovering social laws, but he failed to discover any of them himself.'[1]

The attempt to find a gold mine or the abominable snowman is one thing, while the existence of such a mine or of such a creature is quite another. This abominable gentleman may not actually exist. Evans-Pritchard was rather sceptical about the very existence of social laws, although he did not actually deny it, and admitted that only the discovery of such laws would allow social anthropology and sociology to gain a position of dignity and respect in the commonwealth of learning. One of the fundamental points made by this eminent anthropologist was that whenever we believe we have discovered a social law, we soon find an exception to it, and thus realize that there is in fact no such law. Evans-Pritchard rejected Durkheim's view that an exception reveals something 'atypical or 'residual', and argued that either a law has no exceptions, such as the law of gravity, or there is in fact no such law. 'Therefore,' concluded Sir Edward, 'even if sociology were to successfully discover certain general principles about its subject-matter, these would always have an inferior level of generalisation compared to the organic and inorganic sciences.'[2]

I am academically indebted to Evans-Pritchard for having posed this crucial problem from diverse angles in his books and articles, as well as in numerous conversations[3] (from 1968 to 1973, the year of his sudden death, I engaged in dialogue with him on an almost daily basis). I have ultimately reached the following conclusions: (1) an exception does not invalidate a law; (2) an infraction does not destroy a law; (3) social laws do not have a lower level of generalization, nor are they less precise or rigorous, than those of the organic or inorganic sciences.

In a series of courses I taught at the University of Southern California, I used the following example to approach the problem of laws, exceptions and infractions. Let us suppose that a martian attempted to discover the rules of the traffic code in one of the earth's cities. After numerous observations, he might believe he had discovered the following law: 'Whenever a traffic light is red, the driver must stop his car.' Let us suppose that another martian discovered an exception to this rule. An ambulance, sounding its siren, passed through a red light, and a police officer, far from attempting to detain it, co-operated so that no one could prevent it from doing so. If this second martian employed Evans-Pritchard's reasoning, he would declare that the first martian's discovery had been undermined: 'I have found an exception to the rule; since there is an exception, there is no rule.' However, it is said in English, in Spanish, and in other languages that 'an exception confirms the rule'. This seems to me a scientifically accurate observation: if there is an exception to a law, this implies that the law exists. There cannot be an exception without there being a law. Furthermore, an exception can benefit a law in various ways: it can contribute to the discovery of its existence, its strength, its rigour, and its related penalties. An exception publicizes a law.

We must also consider the infraction or violation of laws. Let us suppose that the second martian observed that, although most cars stopped when the lights were red, others speeded through with total indifference. This martian concluded that we cannot call something a law unless everyone abides by it. However, this reasoning is similarly flawed. Neither an exception, nor an infraction, can invalidate a law. An infraction, like an exception, presupposes the existence of a law: if something is not a law, there can be no infractions of it. Furthermore, as with exceptions, infractions reveal the existence of laws and publicize them. The neural computer automatically assimilates a program and discovers the existence of a law in three phases: (1) the discovery of a penalty; (2) the discovery of the infraction which corresponds to this penalty; (3) the discovery of the law which corresponds to this infraction. Certain biosocial laws, though not all of them, require the possibility of infractions.

There are various independent and competitive biological systems. The digestive system is genetically programmed to function partly on its own, and partly by seeking the subject's collaboration. The neural computer might have been programmed to expel solid, liquid and gaseous substances without asking for the subject's permission and co-operation. This is precisely what occurs in the case of water, salts and other substances which are expelled through minute pores in the skin, without asking for the subject's permission and co-operation. A baby's neural computer expels organic excretions (solids, liquids and gases) without consulting the subject. The genetic plan, however, has established that a system of cultural laws will gradually enter into his neural computer, and that the latter will inform the subject about when, where and how he is to expel these organic solids, liquids and gases. The neural computer, by means of two different, conflicting programs, may inform the subject about two opposed actions he must perform: the digestive system may threaten to flog him with the whip of pain if he does not immediately expel a particular gas, while the biocultural system which governs the public expulsion of gases may threaten to punish him with shame and ridicule if he dares to give way to his bodily needs. Both systems inform, pressure and threaten the subject with emotional rewards and punishments.

The emotional system is composed of a series of laws which in the case at hand, as well as in many other cases, presupposes the election of the subject between two rival actions, and hence not only the possibility, but even the need, of violating the laws of one of the two systems. The subject has to violate certain laws in order to obey others.

The Precision, the Rigour and the Inevitability of Unwritten Biosocial Laws

It is widely held that 'customs' are less precise and less rigorous than 'laws', if by customs we mean unwritten laws, and by laws we mean those that are written. Once it is recorded by the neural computer, a custom, although it may not be written anywhere, can acquire the precision and the vigour of a written law. A custom, once it has become a biocustom, can even function with greater precision, rigour and inevitability than a written law. A criminal may evade the penalties of the written law by evading arrest. However, his neural computer may seize him immediately, condemn him, and begin to torture him with the emotional whip of guilt. An individual may also dare to commit serious infractions against the written law (rape, treason, and so on), but he might never dare to violate a custom, an unwritten law, such as breaking wind in public.

Seneca the Elder pointed to the power and the rigour of biosocial laws when he said that 'certain laws which no one has written are more inevitable than any written ones'.[4] The Spanish novelist Benito Pérez Galdós also hit the nail on the head when he referred to the 'empire of custom'.[5]

Exceptionless, Inviolable Laws

Although it is true that an exception does not invalidate a law, and that the same applies to an infraction, I also believe that there are social and biosocial laws which admit of neither any exceptions nor any infractions. If a subject jumps off a ten-storey building, he will find himself simultaneously governed both by the law of gravity, and by the emotional law of vertigo. Whether he knows it or not, and whether he likes it or not, the law of gravity will make his body fall towards the ground at a mathematically precise speed. Similarly, whether he knows it or not, and whether he likes it or not, when he looks down from the edge of the roof, and as he begins to fall, a feeling of anguish established by the genetic plan and installed in his neural computer will be triggered with the same rigour, precision and inevitability as the law of gravity: the emotional penalty of vertigo. A subject feels something whenever the neural computer, upon being informed about a particular organic occurrence (a hair trapped under the eyelid, a finger exposed to a temperature which could burn it), finds a program that prescribes the activation of a given feeling with a particular intensity. The emotional system functions by means of laws that allow the subject to commit infractions, but it also functions with other laws that do not allow him to escape their inevitable, mathematical rigour.[6] No other legal system is in this sense either as powerful or as effective as the biosocial system of the brain.

The Law of Conflicting Laws

Laws and systems are forces of energy that conflict with others both in the physical and in the social world. 'What would happen,' I once asked my students at the University of Southern California, 'if we dropped a metal container with the volume of this lecture hall from an altitude of eleven thousand feet?' They all agreed that it would fall to the ground. I disagreed with them, pointing out that the law of gravity is one force, but not the only force. It might come into conflict with other forces and lose out to them. An opposed energy can defeat the law of gravity. I referred to the anecdote Kant employs to criticize Plato: 'The innocent dove, upon encountering the resistance of the air, imagines that it could fly with greater ease if space was empty, without any air.'[7] The innocent dove does not realize that in order to fly, it is necessary for a particular energy – that which is generated by the movement of its wings – to conflict with the wind – an energy which pushes it in the other direction – and with gravity, an energy which pulls it towards the earth. A jumbo jet that ascends and flies at an altitude of eleven thousand feet demonstrates with its own weight that the law of gravity is not always the only, or the strongest, energy acting on an object. In the same way it is true that laws in the physical world are energies which conflict with one another, it is true that laws in the biosocial world are programs which often strive with one another and pull the individual in opposite directions.

The Law of Genetic or Involuntary Infractions

Within the emotional world, governed by biosomatic and biosocial laws, the genetic plan allows for the occurrence of involuntary infractions, or organic breakdowns: certain ab-normalities are in fact normal. A normal kidney – governed by its own laws – is not supposed to manufacture stones. However, kidney stones represent a normal organic breakdown: they can occur. Similarly, certain irregularities may occur in the emotional system (malfunctions in the hardware, the software, the organic laboratories, the nervous system, and so on). As a result of this, a subject may be compelled to laugh, cry or suffer a toothache not when he ought to, but only because some part of him is not in working order. During my childhood there was a young man in Pamplona, the city I went to school in, who became notorious for his unstoppable laughter. He would walk up and down the streets of this small city, laughing constantly for no particular reason. Everyone knew that his laugh was abnormal, that it had been caused by an attack of meningitis he suffered when he was a child. Here we must again notice that we are aware of an ab-normality. We are aware that a law is being violated and hence, we are aware of the law itself.

The Genetically Determined Limits of Chance

Chance is the opposite of law. The Arab word for chance signifies 'dice': the number which someone 'rolls' is not determined by a law. Chance, like the roll of dice, is not controlled by some plan, system or law. However, in every game there is also a rule that specifies which elements in the game are subject to chance, and which are subject to rules. A law specified in the genes similarly determines which elements are subject to chance and which are subject to biosomatic and biosocial laws.

As in every other game, in the genetic and biosocial game chance is not entirely subject to chance: its influence is limited.[8] We should avoid falling into the logical (or perhaps illogical) trap of thinking that because certain things are determined randomly, everything must be. In any human action, such as the writing of Hamlet, we ought to distinguish between the following five different factors: human action (e.g. Hamlet) = nature + culture + a neural computer + chance + a particular individual (William Shakespeare). Hamlet is a consequence of: (a) oxygen, potatoes, water, etc. (products of nature which are regulated by natural laws); (b) the English language and English culture (the cultural products of a particular territorial society – England – which are regulated by social laws); (c) the neural computer which receives, processes and presents all these natural and cultural products to William Shakespeare (an individual); (d) chance: the fact that Shakespeare was born and raised in England during a particular period of time (the sixteenth century), was endowed with a very special neural computer, and so on; and (e) the influence of the subject (the genetic plan allows for the individual's decisions and actions to have a particular degree of influence). We could therefore say that the copyright of Hamlet belongs to the oxygen Shakespeare breathed, to the potatoes he ate, to the English culture he acquired, to the neural computer which processed bread and adverbs, and which informed and pressured him in relation to what he should do or refrain from doing by means of the emotional system, to the natural and cultural influence of chance, and finally, to the influence of William Shakespeare himself.

Biosocial Laws

In an article published in *ABC*, a Spanish daily newspaper, Dr José Botella-Llusia, an eminent Spanish physician, spoke of the 'movement founded by Alexis Carrel, and recently developed both by the Oxford school (for instance, by Jáuregui), and by the Harvard school (by Wilson), which centres on the idea that sociology is a branch of biology, and obeys the same laws as the latter'. Dr Botella-Llusia was referring to my book *Las Reglas del Juego: Las Tribus* (The Rules of the Game: the Tribes) – published in Madrid in 1977 – where I claimed that to be English, Spanish, French, Nuer, Apache or Chinese is not only a physical reality (that of a precisely delimited territory located in a particular part of the planet Earth), but also a biological one (that of tribal or territorial ideas and feelings). I argued that in the same way a human being feels a toothache if he has a cavity, he feels both humiliated and enraged if a group of foreigners invades his territorial society. Botella-Llusia understood one of the fundamental claims of my theory: that society, if by anything, is governed by biological laws. To be Spanish or English is not a purely external, political or cultural fact: it is also a biological one. It may be true that we are not born Spanish or English; we are not genetically endowed with the Spanish or the English culture. We are not born with patriotic feelings towards Spain or England. A human being, however, is born with a biological constitution (his neural computer's hardware) which determines that he will become Spanish or English, and, once this occurs, that he will be governed by biological laws or mechanisms (such as tribal or territorial urges and feelings).

In 1982 I published a second book in Barcelona entitled *Las Reglas del Juego: Los Sexos* (The Rules of the Game: the Sexes), in which, along similar lines, I attempted to discover the natural and cultural rules of the games played by the sexes – rules which, once installed in a neural computer, govern its subject through biological mechanisms. This study endeavoured to prove and analyse the existence of certain biosocial laws which govern the functioning of human society through the neural computers of its members.[9]

Conscious and Unconscious

Freud was a true pioneer in the study and exploration of the brain. There is still much to be said about what is conscious and what is unconscious, but we are all indebted to Freud in this field. He made the illuminating discovery that an error which may appear to be completely random could have been brought about, in fact, by unconscious laws. Freud pointed out that when a given gentleman was making love to his wife and called her by the wrong name, this was not actually an error, or the result of some accidental factor. It was rather a logical act of the unconscious, which was aware of the fact that he was passionately in love with Petra, his lover, rather than with Paula, his wife. He did not call the latter by any name (which would have been an accidental mistake), but by the name of his lover. It was an error of his conscious self, but an accurate statement of his unconscious brain.

In my two earlier works, I employed the term 'abulic' (from the Greek ά-βουλειυ, 'involuntary') to refer to what is unconscious, in order to stress that unconscious ideas and feelings function with complete independence not only of the subject's consciousness, but also of his will.

Only the individual sees, hears and touches (subjective, conscious actions), but he sees, hears and touches what the neural computer allows him to see, hear and touch by means of a completely unconscious, independent process. Only the subject thinks (a subjective, conscious action), but he thinks what the neural computer allows him to think, in accordance with unconscious, independent laws.

Feelings, which are the most subjective experiences imaginable – since my toothache is exclusively mine, and no one can share it with me – are also partly unconscious and independent of the will: we are compelled to feel whatever the neural computer, a biological machine, makes us feel by means of an unconscious process that takes place independently of the will. Not only ideas, but also feelings, are partly unconscious, although Freud was of the contrary opinion.[10]

In this work, conscious and unconscious are thought of as adjectives rather than as nouns. Freud, a member of the culture in which nouns are all written with capital letters, while adjectives are written with small letters, turned two adjectives, conscious and unconscious, into nouns, having failed to discover the nouns and their relation to these adjectives. In this work the nouns are the brain, the programs, the feelings, and the subject or individual (what we call someone, a person, you and I, that 'thinking and feeling entity'). The brain and its programs are unconscious by nature: the brain cannot feel pain when it tortures the subject with a cruel headache, or with the urge to commit suicide. The subject can be conscious or unconscious; he may be in the process of feeling or not feeling to certain quantitative and qualitative degrees (the consciousness and the feelings of a baby do not have the same quantitative and qualitative degrees of consciousness as that of a child, an adult, an elderly person, a drunk, a drugged person, Einstein, Bach, a mentally handicapped person, someone who has been administered a local anaesthetic, and so on: this issue requires another book).

Feelings can be inactive or unconscious, or they can be activated to different quantitative and qualitative degrees. The subject is then obliged to feel them or to receive them in his consciousness. Only the subject can be conscious and feel, but the brain has exclusive control of both consciousness and the release of each feeling. This whole book is, to a certain extent, an analysis of the nouns 'brain', 'programs', 'feelings', and 'subject', and the adjectives 'conscious'/'sentient', 'unconscious'/'insentient'.

4

Human Society

Human Society, Human Culture and Human Nature

The emotional system governs the respiratory and the digestive systems (somatic systems), as well as the erotic, the linguistic and the religious systems (social systems). Very often a somatic system and a social system within the same neural computer pressure or threaten the subject with opposed emotional currents. It is thus highly useful, and perhaps even indispensable, to study the inter-relation or simultaneous opposition of both systems, in order to gain a better understanding of how a social or biosocial system functions. Biosocial and biocultural systems intervene, or interfere with, the functioning of somatic systems, since all are governed by the same emotional republic of the brain.

Edmund Leach appears to have fallen into the same theoretical trap into which Rousseau and Hobbes both tumbled: the opposition between nature and society.[1] According to Leach, what is innate, biological and natural is something physical, 'such as the colour of the skin', while 'the manner of dress' is 'purely cultural'.[2] Something which is cultural or social (such as a dress code) does not fall within the bounds of nature or biology, is variable (there is no single code which regulates the manner of dress of all human beings), and is therefore not natural. However, when a person's brain assimilates a dress code – the rules that govern the use of clothing – this code becomes something as biological as the colour of his skin (and in some ways even more so). We may be mistakenly led to believe that a person's skin is something natural and biological, while his society and culture are external, variable, and therefore not natural or biological. Rousseau held that Man, in his natural state, was noble, pure and innocent until society corrupted him:

> The horse, the cat, the bull, even the donkey, have a higher stature, a more robust constitution, more vigour, more strength, more courage in their jungles than in our homes; they lose half of these advantages when they are domesticated: it seems as if, while we strive to make their lives more pleasant, we only accomplish their ruin. The same happens to man. To the extent that he becomes a social animal he becomes the slave of others, he becomes weak, cowardly, despicable, arrogant . . . ; since nature has measured both man and beast by the same standard, every comfort that man procures for himself becomes a cause of his degeneration, an even greater degeneration than that of the animals he has domesticated.[3]

Thomas Hobbes held the contrary view: before the advent of society, in a state of nature, 'every man is every other man's enemy' and the life of man was 'solitary, poor, evil, brutish, and short'.[4] In Rousseau's view, society represents the worst possible domestication of man, while for Hobbes, society is the origin of his security, his creativity and his happiness. Although these two thinkers defend opposed points of view, they both agree on a crucial point: society is not natural; society is something added on to nature, something that changes nature, something opposed to nature; society appears during a second phase of the course of Man's history (he first lived in a state of nature – when he was savage – and afterwards in society).

A human being's body, as well as his society, is governed by nature, by genetic laws, by biological laws installed in the brain. No human society could function without the systems of crying and laughter. Both of these systems are as biological as the digestive or respiratory system. Nature is indeed the tamer and man the tamed or domesticated animal – to a very great extent – but this applies as much to his social actions (laughing, speaking, and so on), as to his somatic ones (eating, breathing, etc.).

By employing the emotional whip, Nature pressures the human being to work for his body and for his society. This whip is always biological and emotional. Leach justifiably complained that while social anthropologists are primarily engaged in the study of human society, no social anthropologist has dared to provide a definition of such a thing.[5] This, as a working hypothesis, is my definition of human society: 'A structured, unique community made up of de-individualized individuals, which functions by means of the software installed in their neural computers, and which constitutes a team that competes against other teams with the aim of producing culture and a dynamic hierarchy.' I shall now offer a brief sketch of its principal elements:

A community

A community is a unity representing all: one identical thing for all members. Human society is, above all, a community. The motto of the American coat of arms, which appears on every bank note, as well as on every coin, is 'E pluribus unum': 'Out of many, one.' The Latin preposition '*e*' refers to two periods of time: during the first there are many, and during the second, these many become one, one single thing. There are various mechanisms that transform many individuals into one society. Some of these mechanisms are physical, while others are sensory, mental and emotional. There are more than two hundred million Americans ('*pluribus*', many). One territory (one, not two) is one of the physical elements that transform all of these individuals into one society, one community, one being. This physical element becomes biological when it is installed in the brains of these two hundred million Americans as one identical biological possession – one which is sensory, mental and emotional. The territory of the United States of America is located in a particular part of the planet Earth, but also in the brains of all its inhabitants. The United States does not and cannot signify anything to a dog which lives in this particular territory (its hardware does not allow for this).

Structured

The human body functions as a unity, although it is composed of numerous parts which play different, complementary, hierarchical roles. In my earlier book *The Rules of the Game: the Sexes*, I attempted to demonstrate that men and women, like sperm and ova, have been designed by nature as incomplete parts which play different, complementary roles. Culture adds new elements to this complementary differentiation. The breasts are a female flag, while the penis is a male flag: both contribute to differentiate men and women, who play incomplete, complementary roles in the production of a human being. A brassière is a cultural device which covers the female's natural flag: her breasts. But is this its only function? The brassière is in fact a cultural flag of the female. Female apes do not possess this cultural mechanism of differentiation, since they do not wear brassières.

In a territorial society such as England or the United States, the difference in cultural roles, as well as the divisions between them, is immense. The different positions are complementary and generally hierarchical. There is perhaps no other society as hierarchical as that of human beings. At the same time, as we shall see in a later chapter on shame, bees do not feel ashamed of the hierarchy or the monarchy of their hives, while in our species even societies such as Great Britain refer to their society as democratic, rather than monarchic. The President of the United States is as much of a monarch as a queen bee, but in spite of this fact only perceptive cartoonists, such as Conrad of the *Los Angeles Times*, dare to portray this figure as a monarch (the implication being that a particular president has usurped the powers that were never conferred upon him by the people).

Today we know that sperm, those minute big-headed creatures with long tails, take part in a presidential race – the vaginal marathon – with the aim of attaining a monarchic throne (the female ova). The game is a deadly one, for all losers die. It would be mistaken to affirm that the constitution of this particular society (that of sperm) is a democratic one. It is partly democratic and partly egalitarian in its first phase: all sperm are created equal (as the American 'Declaration of Independence' states: 'all men are created equal . . . endowed by their Creator with certain unalienable Rights'). All sperm are manufactured with the same care in the genital mass-production factory (about two hundred million sperm are produced every twenty-four hours). All sperm are stored in the same genital refrigerator. All take part in the same vaginal race and have the same chances of winning this particular 'gold medal'.

However, this is only the first phase. In the second phase, the constitution is clearly hierarchical: the sperm become rivals in a deadly game. *Aristos*, in Greek, signifies 'the best', and *cratein*, 'to rule'. As in any other game, the objective is to eliminate equality and create a dynamic, 'aristocratic' hierarchy. In the last phase, the constitution finally becomes a monarchic one: only one, the best, the sperm that wins the race against two hundred million other 'runners', will be able to crown itself monarch and sit on the throne of the only available ovum. *Monos*, in Greek, means 'one': only one rules.

A scientific parallel can clearly be drawn between the constitution of 'sperm society' and that of the United States of America (and of other human societies): all Americans are born equal, and any of them could conceivably become senator, secretary of state or president. However, various games or political competitions transform this initially egalitarian society into a hierarchical one: only a minority actually become senators or congressmen, and an even smaller minority attain the post of secretary of state. Finally, the constitution and society of the United States of America is partly monarchic: only one, whoever wins the presidential race (like the sperm who wins the vaginal marathon), becomes the monarch: only one rules. Only one decides if and when the Vietnam war is to begin, if Hiroshima is to be bombed, or if tariffs are to be raised so that British products will not pose a threat to the sale of items 'Made in USA.'

The difference between human beings and sperm, or wolves, lies in the fact that only the first is pulled by opposed biological and emotional currents: one that pressures him to defeat, to win, to climb the hierarchical ladder, and to enjoy the sight of all the humiliated, dejected losers he has defeated; and another derived from the ethical and/or religious systems that pressures him with the mechanism of shame to resist the hierarchical and monarchical urges to win, or at least to hide those urges in public, in the same way he hides the 'shameful parts' of his body. Communists would be reluctant to admit that their society is hierarchic and monarchic, but it seems evident that a secretary-general such as Mao or Khrushchev is a fully-fledged monarch. Catholics, whose creed recommends Christian humility, refer to their monarch, the Pope, as the *servus servorum*, the slave of all slaves. This is one of the most fascinating contradictions of the human species: to fight for hierarchy in the name of equality. When Reagan won the presidential race for the first time, his first words were: 'This is the most humble day of my life.' Had a sperm heard this remark, he might have told Reagan: 'Oh, come off it. Why, then, does Carter look so depressed, and you so satisfied? Don't tell me you didn't get a thrill out of defeating two hundred million others. Why else would you have put yourself through the presidential race, which can be a truly deadly game?' Human beings are pulled by opposed emotional currents, on the one hand to play and win, and on the other to hide such 'lowly instincts'. It is not easy for the anthropologist or the philosopher to discover what is human, especially in the case of digging out the 'dirt' swept underneath the semantic, ideological, ethical, aesthetic or religious carpets. This tendency to conceal is one of the genetic frontiers that distinguishes human beings from apes, and which the anthropologist must discover in all its dimensions.[6]

Unique

England, or any other human society, must necessarily be a single entity (were there two, they would two societies: to be and to be one necessarily go together), but it must also be unique – in other words, different from all the rest. Any mechanisms of unity (the flag, the name or the territory) and any kind of system (such as the system of currency) needs to be unique. We must take note of two social laws of tremendous interest: 'the more unique or different a society, the more solid a society it will remain', and 'the more united a society, the more solid a society it will remain'. When guineas and shillings were taken out of circulation in order to adopt the decimal system, Sir Edward, my Oxford tutor, told me that 'today England has died a little'. This is a scientifically accurate statement.

De-individualized individuals

The label 'de-individualized individuals' may seem absurd or contradictory. It is evident that a human society is composed of individuals, but there is more to it than that. In order to function as a component or as a social cell – as a part of a whole: *e pluribus unum* – an individual has to be de-individualized. The identity of an individual, such as William Shakespeare, evaporates, and is replaced by a social identity: that of an Englishman. Common images and sounds which correspond to common ideas and feelings, and which are installed within the neural computers of a society's members, de-individualize and socialize each individual.

An Englishman once killed a Frenchman at a football match. These two men never knew each other as individuals. The Englishman had no complaints about this Frenchman as an individual. He knew nothing about his personal life (not even his name). However, they recognized each other as members of rival societies – England and France – through certain visual and phonic mechanisms (their respective flags and languages). They saw, heard, recognized and emotionally responded to each other as rival social cells. One of them killed the other due to a purely social or biosocial rivalry: for being the member of a rival hive. It is interesting to discover how often, and to what extent, human beings think, feel and act not as particular, unique individuals, but as members of some social group: as Englishmen, Marxists, Catholics, and so on.

Software

(I have already defined this concept, and shall examine it in detail throughout this anthropological excursion.)

Team

A human society functions and exists as a team. The motor of human society is the game. Eric Berne employed the game as a scientific concept in his famous best-seller *Games People Play*.[7] I discovered this work when I read the preface written by the distinguished Spanish psychologist José Luis Pinillos for the paperback edition of my book *The Rules of the Game: the Tribes*. Dr Pinillos mentioned the fact that there was a precedent for the analysis of something apparently frivolous – games – in a scientific work. This reference piqued my curiosity, and eventually I read the work. In Dr Berne's use, 'game' has negative connotations, as is evident from expressions such as 'she played games with me'. This relates to only one aspect of my definition of a game: the element of cheating. There can be no cheating without rules (see the points made earlier about laws and infractions).

I define a social game as 'any rule-governed competition which occurs between two societies with the aim of winning and producing hierarchy'. According to this definition, the Olympic games are social games, as are all wars, 'Miss Territorial Society' beauty contests, and the duel between the yen and the dollar. Since it is being employed as a scientific metaphor, one must precisely delimit its use or meaning. The concept of a 'game', as it is popularly employed, has childish or frivolous implications. My definition of game does not have such connotations. These are the principal ingredients of the concept as I see it:

(1) *A team is made up of players and fans.* A society such as Spain becomes unified each time that Spanish players compete against players from other territorial societies. In any given team, the fans are as important as the players. The game of war unifies a territorial society more than any other game – as I explained in my book *The Rules of the Game: the Tribes* – in three phases: before the war (inventing and manufacturing new military weapons and devices, and training the players, or soldiers, to kill more efficiently); during the war; and after the war (more than any other social event, wars are commemorated in monuments, books, stamps, coins, street names and elaborate annual rites).

(2) *A game takes place between two societies.* The key word here is 'between', which in this context also means 'against'. No game can be played without a rival team to play against. Great Britain became unified as a team when Argentina 'reconquered' (according to the Argentinians), or 'invaded' (according to the British) the 'Islas Malvinas' (according to the Argentinians) or 'Falkland Islands' (according to the British). The Argentinians, both the rich and the poor, the ideological right and left, felt Argentinian in the face of the British, whose class and ideology were also diluted by this military game. When the Nazis attacked the Jews, all those Jews who were in the diaspora became unified, felt Jewish, began to communicate with each other, became a team, and eventually founded the state of Israel in 1948 (twenty centuries after being expelled from their own land). In his autobiography, Albert Einstein confessed that the persecution of his people led him to feel truly Jewish and to become a Zionist, although previously he had thought of himself as a 'citizen of the world' and had condemned all forms of nationalism. When one team challenges another to an economic, military, athletic, ethical or religious confrontation, it unifies the members of the opposing

team. Without the Nazis, the State of Israel might not have come into being when it did.

(3) *The rules of the game.* Every game, including war and the economic game of exporting and importing, must necessarily have rules which can be broken and rules to punish those who cheat. As in every other human game, each society tends to interpret the rules in its favour, but the rules themselves (including ethical and legal norms, as well as ideological and religious ones) must always exist. Those who violate the rules can be punished. (For instance, many Nazis were imprisoned for breaking the rules of the game of war. The victors of a war are generally the ones who point to the abuses perpetrated by the losers. Had the Japanese won the Second World War, they might have accused the United States of the 'crimes' of bombing Hiroshima and Nagasaki, by which thousands of civilians, including many women and children, were executed.)

(4) *Players aim to win and produce hierarchy.* Games manufacture hierarchy. All competitors begin a game on an equal footing, and all finish in some hierarchical position. All games eliminate equality: the winners are superior to the losers. Every game has three phases: *before the game*, when all the competitors are equal; *during the game*, when the hierarchy fluctuates between the different teams; and *after the game*: the equality is transformed into a hierarchy. If the game ends in a tie – in other words, if the equality is not broken – the game has not served its purpose (another proof of the hierarchical function of a game). Chess, like war, is designed to turn those who play it into winners and losers.

(5) *The emotional mechanisms of playing, winning and losing.* For centuries numerous thinkers have become engaged in an apparently endless debate over what ultimately motivates human beings to toil, slave and sweat. Some have held that money is the essential factor, others that it is God, and still others that it is sex or power. In my view, however, the key concept lies in the word '*more*'. I would argue that the neural computer is governed by an innate law that allows neither exceptions nor infractions: the emotional law of the winner and the loser. In accordance with this law, the neural computer punctually pays a specific pleasure to anyone who wins a game, anyone who puts himself in a superior hierarchic position. In the economic game played by the different social classes, a person who lives in a middle-class neighbourhood, in a middle-class flat, with middle-class furniture and a middle-class car (and

perhaps with a middle-class dog), receives an emotional payment (the pleasure reserved for winners according to the genetic plan) when he compares himself with the blue-collar worker who lives in a 'humble' neighbourhood, and in a poorly decorated one-bedroom flat. However, the same middle-class gentleman has to suffer the unavoidable emotional penalty reserved for losers by the despotic rule of the genetic plan, when he compares himself with members of the upper class who live in luxurious palaces and mansions with dogs of aristocratic pedigree. If a prisoner looks through the bars of his cell window at those who are free to walk the streets, his neural computer will compel him to suffer the pain reserved for losers (this man has lost in the game of freedom). However, if this same prisoner compares himself with another inmate condemned to life imprisonment, his neural computer will then reward him with the pleasure reserved for winners. 'Poor devil,' he may think to himself. 'He is going to spend his entire life in this unbearable place.'

The fundamental aspect of the innate game program is winning or losing, having more or less, being more or less. The same money, the same car, the same freedom can generate either pleasure or pain, as the preceding examples show. The genetically implanted law of the game is as follows: 'The neural computer will pay a degree of satisfaction for every degree of superiority obtained by the individual over other individuals.' The complement of this mathematically rigid law is therefore, 'The more a player loses by, the lower his position on the hierarchical scale, the greater the emotional penalty he will be compelled to suffer by his neural computer.' Consequently, there can be no winners without losers. The innate law of the game – of winning and losing – is cruel in its nature: the pleasure achieved by the winner is mathematically proportional to the pain suffered by the loser.

The aim of producing culture

The honey and the wax of the human beehive is culture. The game is the fuel, the energy of the social motor, but the product is culture. Without Spain there would be no Spanish, and without England there would be no English. Rousseau exaggerated the price that human beings have to pay: 'born free in the state of nature', while 'chained from all sides in the state of society'. Apparently, he was not aware of what human beings obtain in return for paying this price: culture. Rousseau fell into the 'Tower of Babel' trap: to show only one side of the social and cultural coin (the confusion created by the many languages spoken). This is the price, but it is not the whole coin. The other side reveals the rich cultural variety which anthropologists have shown to be a priceless treasure owned by the human family. A cultural Esperanto would be unbearably monotonous. It would constitute a tremendous loss for the human race. Although an individual can make his own particular positive or negative contribution to his culture, a software version of which is held by his neural computer, culture is a social product. Every human society occupies a place in the hierarchical scale of creative cultural contributions to humanity. Culture is both a cause and an effect of any given society: the more original and varied a society's culture, the greater this society will be. Shakespeare is the father of his plays and, at the same time, their effect: without *The Complete Works* there would be no Shakespeare (the Shakespeare who wrote such impressive works). England creates the English language, and the English language contributes to the creation of England.

A dynamic hierarchy

Another function of the social game is to create a dynamic hierarchy. When we refer to nations and their political systems as democratic, we leave out something crucial: the fact that each human society – particularly those we call nations – struggles and competes against all others in order to attain a greater piece of the world's cake: the cake of fame, of power, of wealth, of culture. As a result of this, some nations become planets, while others become their satellites. The fascinating program of human shame leads to the use of social cosmetics (an issue I shall deal with later) which disguise and conceal the ugly political realities, and hence officially all nations are said to be equal and equally sovereign. Although we may confidently speak of the equality and the sacred sovereignty of each nation, we soon find ourselves referring to 'superpowers', to the 'third world', and to 'spheres of influence'. In the past, a 'superpower' was known as an 'empire', and 'spheres of influence' were known as 'colonies'. This is semantic make-up.

The anthropologist must discover, explore and analyse the use of political cosmetics as conscientiously as the reality which such make-up aims to disguise or conceal. This much seems to be clear: according to the genetic plan, sperm, human individuals and human hives are created equal, but they are programmed to play and to become winners and losers, 'superpowers' and 'spheres of influence', planets and satellites. The hierarchy is dynamic in the sense that it is neither genetically predetermined (as in the case of the queen bee), nor permanently established. A new game can radically alter the hierarchy: Rome falls, Britain erects the British Empire, Japan loses the 'game' in 1945, the United States becomes the planet around which all other nations revolve, and so on.

Types of human society

There are various types of human society. I shall briefly mention some of the types I have identified (this issue, which to my knowledge no one has even attempted to deal with, would require a separate book).

(1) *Humanity*. Humanity as such is a human society with its own culture and its own biosocial systems, as I am attempting to demonstrate in this work.

(2) *Kinship societies*. These include the family, the lineage and the clan. A kinship society is one of descent: the common element is ancestry and/or an alliance.

(3) *Territorial societies*. Another type of human society is what in the past I have called 'the tribe', and which I now prefer to label with a more neutral term, 'territorial society', or *geopolis*, if we wish to translate this concept into Greek so as to give it a 'more scientific' name. A territorial society is a community of land: the common element is a delimited territory. (My book *The Rules of the Game: the Tribes* primarily addresses this issue.)

(4) *Class societies*. In *The Communist Manifesto*, Karl Marx asserted that 'workers do not have a fatherland'.[8] Marx argued that humanity is divided into two antagonistic classes: the bourgeoisie and the proletariat. In his view, this is the key to understanding society, and everything else is irrelevant. Marx was a pioneer in that he discovered the world of social classes. According to Marx, who in this instance shows himself to be a sharp, original thinker, these may adopt various forms or names, and they may wear different collars,

but they are always essentially the same. Furthermore, he continues, this antagonism between the different classes is the motor of history. As pioneers who have made important discoveries are prone to do, Marx went too far when he claimed that this particular struggle is the motor of history. It is not the only or the most important motor – but it is undoubtedly *one of the* motors of human society, since the desire to win, to defeat or to ascend is installed in the brains of those who are members of an inferior class.

Karl Marx was entirely mistaken, however, when he confidently affirmed that 'workers do not have a fatherland'. Even those who adopted Marxism fought on different, rival territorial teams (for instance, the Chinese, the Soviet or the Yugoslav teams). Territorial societies as a whole are the most complex, complete, sophisticated and dynamic of all human societies (although not in all circumstances). A class society, or class, is a community of material goods.

(5) *Ideological societies.* To be a Marxist is not the same thing as to be a member of the bourgeoisie or of the proletariat. We may find Marxists, socialists, anarchists, conservatives and extreme right-wingers amongst the 'working' class, as well as amongst the middle class and even amongst the 'aristocratic' class.

If a class society is a society of material goods, an ideological society is a community of beliefs and/or ethical and political ideas. Which of these is the society that matters most to a human being, which is the most important to him: to be British (his territorial society), to be a multi-millionaire (his class society), or to be a Marxist (his ideological society)? This is a complicated scientific question, and one which cannot easily be answered.

(6) *Religious societies.* Perhaps nothing is as exclusive to our species, and nothing as alien to that of apes, as religious societies such as the Catholic, Muslim, Jew or Hindu communities. A religious community is a community of theological beliefs. (It should be noted that even the beliefs of atheists are theological beliefs. The relevant concept is God, whether it is accepted or rejected.)

(7) *Professional societies.* Bees can be classified into soldiers, workers, drones and queens. In a similar manner, although in a more elaborate form, human beings can be classified into doctors, shoe-shiners, government ministers, clowns, astronauts, grave-diggers, and all the other professions one could find in the 'yellow pages'

or elsewhere. A professional society is a community of workers: its members have the same jobs or professions.

Two brothers may belong to the same kinship, territorial, class, ideological, religious and professional societies: two English brothers who live in a luxurious neighbourhood in London may be practising Catholics and members of the Labour Party. In the majority of cases, however, human beings belong to some of the same 'teams' as other human beings, while not to others. For instance, one could conceive of the following case: two English brothers, from the same kinship and territorial societies – one of them is a millionaire, while the other is a blue-collar worker (two different, opposed class societies); one of them is a fervent Marxist, while the other is a convinced fascist (two different, opposed ideological societies); one of them is a militant atheist, while the other is a devoted Catholic (two rival religious societies); and one of them is a punk rock singer, while the other is a baker. Both ridicule and look down on the other's profession. 'Look at my poor brother, dressed in that preposterous outfit, jumping up and down like a monkey and howling like a lunatic!', the baker might say. 'Look at my poor brother, sweating like a slave, baking the same bread day after day, imprisoned by that monotonous, routine existence!', the punk rock singer might say.

Part II
Emotional Control of the Body

5

Emotional Control of the Digestive System

The emotional control of entrances and exits of goods (solids, liquids and gases) from the exterior to the digestive system and from the digestive system to the exterior.

Emotional Control of Nourishment

The entrance of solid or liquid nourishment into the body is controlled by an emotional code co-ordinated by a partly bionatural and partly biocultural program installed in the brain. During the period when a human being lives inside the maternal womb, the entrance of nourishment through the umbilical cord is not controlled by any emotional mechanisms. From the moment of birth, however, a human being is governed by the emotional 'dictator' every time he needs a meal.

The Law of Hunger: a Bionatural Program which Regulates the Time and the Quantity of Nourishment

The stomach is a digestive laboratory in communication with the brain twenty-four hours a day. By means of the nervous system, the stomach has the brain fully informed about the quantity of food it is processing. The brain automatically releases a particular degree of the urge to eat (what we refer to as hunger or appetite), which is mathematically proportional to the amount of nourishment required by the brain. If the stomach is completely empty, the brain will trigger one hundred degrees of hunger; if the stomach is half empty, the brain will trigger fifty degrees of hunger; if the stomach is full, the brain will reduce the densitometer of hunger to zero degrees. The neural computer will pay the subject one hundred degrees of pleasure when he ingests a roast beef sandwich, if his densitometer of hunger was peaking at one hundred degrees, but it will only pay him twenty degrees of pleasure for the same sandwich if his densitometer only registered twenty degrees. For this reason, he enjoys the beginning of a banquet more than the end.

When a baby begins to suckle, it anxiously tries to find its mother's nipple, and sucks on it at an accelerated rhythm. After a while, this velocity diminishes, and when it is almost full, it begins to play with its mother's breast. It sucks a little, then stops, smiles and strokes the breast, until its mother, who probably has a million other things to do, decides that it has had enough. We can observe how this law functions in a baby who suckles or in any one of us, every single day. We are all humble slaves of our digestive laboratories. This law is as rigid, inevitable and precise as any physical or biochemical law.

The Bionatural Program of Prescribed Foods

Every species is governed by a genetically installed program which admits the entrance of certain foods, and forbids that of others. A vulture is programmed to ingest decomposing corpses. This animal's neural computer encourages it to look for and eat a dead meat: 'If you find and eat the decomposing corpse of a dog or a sheep, I will pay you a precise quantity of pleasure.' The vulture's neural computer may then have this animal imagine itself finding, looking at, smelling and thoroughly enjoying a meal consisting of the dead body of a horse. A human being's neural computer, however, will discourage its subject from looking at, smelling and particularly eating a decomposing corpse, by means of emotional threats. Each species 'likes' to eat not what its members choose, but what its innate program specifies. All species, including that of human beings, are governed by a bionatural program of prescribed foods.

The Bionatural Law of Suckling

During the initial months after birth, a human being is programmed to enjoy the ingestion of only his mother's milk. We could carry out an experiment to prove the validity of this emotional law. If, instead of milk, we gave a baby wine or beer, its face would express disapproval. It would begin to cry and would do everything it could to reject this liquid. The biochemical laboratories installed in the mouth inform the brain about the chemical properties of all solid or liquid nourishment. The brain then consults its digestive programs – which in this case are bionatural – and consequently informs and advises the subject to either swallow or reject the substance in question, by activating pleasant or unpleasant emotional mechanisms. The human digestive system is composed of various genetically designed labs and mechanisms.

The maternal milk factory

A biological timer set by the neural computer orders the breasts to begin manufacturing milk. Breasts are bionatural factories which are perfectly equipped to produce, store and administer a specific product. When a woman's reproductive system informs the neural computer that a sperm has fertilized an egg, the neural computer automatically orders these milk factories to begin their work. The pregnant woman, who notices these changes, is now 'ready for action', like an aircraft before it takes off. When the reproductive system informs the brain that the baby has been born, the brain, without consulting the subject or asking for her permission, orders the breasts to begin functioning.

The lacteal system has the brain informed at all times about the amount of milk produced and stored. When the neural computer learns that the milk level has reached a certain limit, it informs the woman in question that her 'natural milk bottle' is ready to be fed to her baby, by setting off the urge to breast-feed. At the same time, the neural computer offers this woman a specific emotional salary – the pleasure of breast-feeding – a pleasure which a man can evidently never have access to. If the milk level rises up to its maximum capacity, the neural computer will increase the urges to breast-feed to their highest intensity. I remember taking my wife to see Verdi's *La Traviata* at London's Covent Garden, shortly after our third child had been born in 1974, and how during an interval she told me that the pain in her breasts was becoming too unbearable to be able to listen to further opera. We had no choice but to return to our home in Oxford, due to the strictness of this bionatural law.

The bionatural milk bottle

A woman's breasts are genetically conceived, designed and installed milk bottles. No artificial milk bottle can equal their softness, malleability and compatibility with the baby's mouth. A baby is programmed to enjoy ingesting his mother's milk, and also to enjoy sucking on his mother's breast. The neural computer pays the baby pleasure for ingesting the prescribed substance through the prescribed instrument.

It is said that a given saint, I cannot recall which, never suckled on Fridays in honour of Christ's Passion. If this really occurred – and it seems scientifically improbable, to say the least – this baby's brain must have somehow acquired a cultural program – which would therefore be biocultural, and thus biological – that led him to obey this precept, or bioprecept. On Fridays, according to this hypothesis, the brain's digestive program would entice him by saying: 'If you suckle now, I shall pay you an emotional salary.' At the same time, its biocultural program would sway him in the opposite direction by saying: 'If you give up the worldly pleasure of suckling today, I shall pay you a superior emotional salary in another life, some of which I shall advance to you now in this life.'

Cultural suckling instruments

Female apes do not feed their offspring artificial milk from artificial bottles. The *Homo sapiens*, during the course of a rational process of acquiring knowledge and passing it on, has discovered the chemical properties of maternal milk, and has manufactured an artificial breast with a rubber nipple. This is one of the genetic frontiers between human beings and apes. It is also an instance of culture working as a slave of nature both in the manufacture of milk and of suckling instruments. However, an imitation hardly ever displaces its original, and the milk bottle is no exception to this rule. The rubber teat has not displaced the mother's nipple, and artificial milk has not displaced maternal milk. The baby's neural computer consults the bionatural program, and realizes that the milk bottle does not quite fit the genetically prescribed model. The baby's neural computer pays it fewer degrees of pleasure owing to the incongruity between the milk bottle and the innate program's model. Were we able to interview the baby, it might say: 'There is nothing like my mummy's breast. I much prefer to suck on her nipple. It's so soft, so delicious. Why are you giving me this awful bottle? Why don't you give me my mother's milk instead of this disgusting stuff? It's like trying to replace fresh salmon with the tasteless frozen type.' Cultural milk is also inferior to natural milk. The baby's neural computer pays it fewer degrees of pleasure owing to the incongruity between the chemical properties of artificial milk and those of the genetically prescribed model. The greater the incongruity, the more degrees of pleasure the baby is deprived of.

Artificial milk may in certain special cases be superior to a particular mother's milk. This, however, does not invalidate the law of the superiority of maternal milk generally. What happens in these cases is that an exception confirms the truth of the law: this particular woman's bionatural system has broken down. Either she produces no milk, or insufficient milk, or deficient milk. A milk bottle may in certain special cases also function more effectively than a particular woman's breasts. However, the law of the superiority of natural milk bottles still stands. Once again, an exception confirms its validity: the breasts may be damaged due to cancer, leprosy, or some other cause.

Can it be possible for a given baby's neural computer to acquire a new program (the taste of artificial milk and the use of artificial milk bottles), and for this biocultural program to replace the bionatural one? It is indeed possible and even probable. The neural computer acquires a new program by means of numerous, cumulative recordings. If someone drinks an alien liquid substance that clashes with the relevant program installed in the software, the neural computer dissuades him from drinking further by triggering unpleasant sensations. However, if the person ignores the emotional pressure and insists on drinking the substance in question, the brain may eventually incorporate this drink to the relevant program, and even create an addiction to it.

Numerous anthropologists and missionaries have told me how a tremendous effort had to be made initially to gulp down the typical alcoholic drink of a given 'primitive' society, but how upon returning to Europe after several years, they longed for the drink which had initially seemed so repulsive to them. This suggests that the neural computer, obeying its own laws and independently of the subject's will, can acquire a new program, and also increase, decrease or cancel it.

Bionatural and Biocultural Laws of Temperature Control

The neural computer is bionaturally programmed to control the exact temperature of both food and drink. The taste laboratories located in the mouth inform the brain, via the postal service provided by the nervous system, about the precise temperature of a sip of coffee or a swig of beer. The neural computer consults the bionatural program of temperature control, and triggers pleasant or unpleasant sensations depending on the extent to which the temperature of the drink agrees or disagrees with the temperature required by this program. The subject is entirely unaware of the many complexities of this law. Fortunately, the neural computer performs this task for him.

The temperature of maternal milk is perfectly regulated by the neural computer. When the baby suckles its mother's breast, it receives pleasure not only from ingesting the right milk through the best possible channel, but also because the milk has the required temperature. I once overheated a milk bottle I was preparing for one of my children. As soon as I began to feed it to him, he stopped sucking and started crying clamorously. In the dramatic language of crying, he was in effect saying, 'Look, Daddy: the milk tastes all right, but try not to burn my tongue the next time!' The law of temperature control governs us from the moment we are born to the moment we die, always according to a genetic program which is common to the whole species.

The installation of biocultural programs concerning the temperature of certain foods and drinks is also allowed by the genetic plan. 'How can these people like their beer so warm?', I have often heard Spaniards complain when they are served this alcoholic beverage in England. If a Spaniard has acquired a program for drinking beer at a very cold temperature, his neural computer will punish him with an emotional penalty for every degree of incongruity between the temperature of the beer he is drinking and that which is installed in the program.

The Interference of Reason

'I like my beer cold, extremely cold. However, I am convinced that drinking beer, or any other beverage, at extremely cold temperatures leaves one at the mercy of bacteria. It does not allow the immune system of the throat to function properly.' This confession was made to me by Dr José Ramón Mozota, a nose and throat specialist, as we drank beer together in a Spanish bar. In this case, the Spanish biocultural program regulating beer temperature, which has been acquired by Dr Mozota's brain, subtracts a few degrees of pleasure for drinking beer at a lower temperature than that which is prescribed by the program ('I like my beer cold, extremely cold'). However, before drinking, another program derived from the rational faculty of the *Homo sapiens* threatens him thus: 'If you drink extremely cold beer, I shall torture you with the uncomfortable sensation of anxiety. I shall disturb you with the fear that you are developing throat cancer, and shall not allow you to live in peace. You know very well what throat cancer is like, so beware!' This Spanish physician has acquired two conflicting programs concerning beer temperature: one of them as a Spaniard, and the other as a physician. Once installed in the brain, both programs will advise and pressure him with contrary emotional whips. If he drinks extremely cold beer, he will receive an emotional salary from the Spanish biocultural program, but he will have to suffer the emotional penalty of the medical biocultural program: a feeling of anxiety. If he drinks beer at a higher temperature, he will have to pay an emotional penalty for disobeying the Spanish biocultural program, in order to free himself from the anxiety with which his medical biocultural program has threatened him.

Unlike apes, human beings often find themselves crucified no matter what they ultimately decide to do, because of different conflicting programs installed in their brains. For this reason we could say that in one sense human beings are less free than apes, because they are governed by more laws, and are therefore liable to suffer more penalties. Reason – another genetic frontier between human beings and apes, although not the only one, as many have claimed – creates new biocultural programs, to which an ape's neural computer has no access. Once installed, these programs function automatically, like any other program contained by the neural computer, through the automatic, mathematically precise activation of emotional mechanisms.

The Bionatural Law of Nourishment in Relation to Age

The human brain – and that of other animals – is programmed to inform and persuade the subject about what to ingest, and even about how to ingest it, depending on the phase of development he is going through. The brain of every human being possesses precise information about his age. During the first phase of his life, maternal milk is the substance required by the brain, and suckling the genetically prescribed mode of ingesting it. As the brain learns about the child's growth, it orders the manufacturing and installation of teeth, and gradually begins to trigger the urge to chew and to ingest solid foods. If a 40-year-old man still enjoyed suckling his mother's breasts, we would infer that the law of nourishment according to age was being seriously broken. As a human being grows, his neural computer, according to a genetic plan, advises him, by triggering pleasant and unpleasant sensations, to change from liquid to solid nourishment; from suckling to chewing; from more to less sweet flavours; from lesser to greater quantities.

The Bionatural Law of Nourishment in Relation to Sex

When a woman becomes pregnant, and as soon as her neural

computer receives this information from the reproductive system, it triggers unusually intense urges to eat. This was always one of the clues which made my wife and myself suspect that 'the stork' was planning to pay us a visit. The brain is programmed to demand more nourishment for a pregnant woman by triggering a more intense sensation of hunger. We can, therefore, speak of a particular densitometer: the densitometer of pregnant women. (This issue is dealt with more extensively in my book *The Rules of the Game: the Sexes*.)

The Bionatural Law of Nourishment in Relation to Health

The neural computer is punctually informed at all times about the physical state of each organ and of the body as a whole. My father, a man who always enjoyed a hearty appetite, lost it completely during a given period of his life. We could not understand why it was that he did not even feel like having a little wine. A small stone had apparently clogged up the tube which transports bile to the stomach. What we call 'loss of appetite' is a symptom of the brain's decision, after becoming aware of an organic breakdown, to cancel the urges to eat. Before triggering the desire to eat, the brain consults the program concerning health – among others – and, depending on what it discovers there, may increase or diminish the intensity of the densitometer of hunger, and may even cancel the subject's appetite entirely. My father would have given anything to recover the desire to eat and drink, but the neural computer makes concessions to no one. Once again we can verify how feelings, pleasant or unpleasant, function with complete independence of both the subject's conscience and his will, in accordance with biologically rigid, inflexible and mathematical laws.

The Emotional Customs Department

The genetic plan has conceived and installed an ingenious customs department designed to inspect any goods that reach the 'borders' of the digestive system. The customs officers which first perform this task are the eyes. These organic cameras send the brain an initial inspection of the substance in question: a visual or photographic inspection. If a vulture's eyes send images of a dog's decomposing corpse, its brain will approve of the sight and pay the vulture an emotional payment in advance. An eagle's brain, however, would wholly disapprove of these images and dissuade it from sending any more by activating a sensation of repulsion. The brain always contrasts the images filmed, developed and sent by the photographic labs in the eyes, with the contents of bionatural and biocultural programs. It then accepts or rejects these images by activating pleasant or unpleasant sensations.

Once a given food specimen has passed the scrutiny of the brain's visual customs, it must pass the control of a second department: the olfactory customs. A piece of fish might be approved by the brain's visual customs, but subsequently be rejected by its olfactory customs. 'Ugh! This fish reeks. It's rotten,' the individual might then say. A person's penetrating olfactory antennae pick up olfactory data, process it in the labs installed in his nose, and send the results to his neural computer. The latter contrasts this olfactory information with the biocultural and bionatural programs found in the customs department, and triggers off pleasant or unpleasant sensations depending on the extent to which the smell complies or fails to comply with the requirements of these programs. The brain will trigger off sensations of repulsion if a human subject sniffs a decomposing corpse – in accordance with an innate program common to the whole species – or similarly from the smell of a characteristic dish from a foreign culture which clashes with the biocultural program registered in a particular subject's brain.

The third customs department is constituted by the taste buds installed in the mouth. These tasting antennae pick up taste data, process it in the relevant labs, and send the results of this analysis to the brain, via the nervous system. A particular dish which has passed through the visual and the olfactory customs of the brain is finally subjected to the rigorous scrutiny of the taste customs.

Here we find the emotional law of the quality of nourishment. The brain pays the subject a precise, mathematically calculated salary depending on the extent to which the quality of the nourishment analysed by the taste customs fits the requirements of the bionatural and biocultural programs installed in the brain. Nature astutely pays the subject a meagre advance for looking at and smelling the food that has been approved by the neural computer, but this reward is nothing compared with the salary it would pay him for ingesting the food. (This situation resembles the meagre advance payment that it pays the male for looking at and touching the female – in some species for smelling her as well – compared with the much larger amount it pays when the goods have been deposited in the place prescribed by the neural computer.) The emotional payments provided by the neural computer are never late, but nature only pays a substantial emotional salary when the assigned task has been performed – in this case, when the nourishment has been ingested.

The Bionatural Law of Hunger in Relation to the Subject's Emotional State

A human being's neural computer is always informed about the physical state of the left hand's little finger (which may suddenly be stung by a scorpion), of his pancreas (which may become inflamed due to a viral infection), of his five children (one of whom may be about to undergo a surgical operation), of his mother (who may be extremely ill), and of many other possible circumstances, such as being about to receive the Nobel Prize. A Spanish gentleman once related the following incident to me: 'I was thoroughly enjoying a delicious seafood entrée, when suddenly the phone rang. I was told I had been fired. From that moment, I was unable to have another bite. Even when a sumptuous roast lamb was served, I couldn't even try it. I had completely lost my appetite.' This illustrates how the genetic law of hunger is related to the subject's emotional state. The neural computer is programmed to diminish or cancel the desire to eat if the subject feels deeply grieved or anguished. The neural computer may also increase the intensity of the hunger densitometer if the subject is feeling overjoyed as a result of winning some particular game. Before activating the mechanism of hunger, the neural computer always takes account of the subject's emotional state. During my childhood, I heard the story of a dog which unearthed its owner, recently executed during the course of the Spanish Civil War. When they buried him again, the dog continued to keep his master company, remaining next to his grave during the next few days. People brought him food, but he would not eat and soon died of grief. This is undoubtedly another example of how the neural computer can cancel the individual's appetite due to his emotional state.

Emotional Blackmail

The neural computer of each species is programmed with bionatural software which forbids the ingestion of certain harmful substances by means of the emotional system. It is bionaturally programmed to impede the entrance of food that has been processed in the stomach and evacuated. The emotional mechanisms that the neural computer has at its disposal are so powerful that no subject can easily disobey them. I do not know of any biocultural system (religious or otherwise) which attempts to persuade the subject to ingest his own faeces.

It is extraordinary to discover how the neural computer informs the subject about the importance of a particular task that has to be performed, by triggering off an intensely pleasurable feeling such as the sexual orgasm, or how it warns him about the danger which an action such as ingesting his own faeces represents, by threatening him with an intensely unpleasant sensation which cannot easily be ignored.

I have been told that in India the prime minister who succeeded Indira Gandhi in 1976 drank his own urine for breakfast. There is apparently a cultural program in this country which for health reasons, or due to certain religious beliefs, advises or orders the subject to transgress the bionatural law which prohibits him from drinking this liquid excretion. If this, which I have not actually confirmed, is true, it would imply that a biocultural program can offer the subject an emotional compensation which allows him to infringe a bionatural law as strict as this one.

Amongst the types of emotional blackmail the neural computer can employ in order to impede the ingestion of processed (and hence harmful) foods, the most powerful one is that which can be triggered off for ingesting vomit. I have never heard of a cultural infraction to this extremely severe law (it is said that certain saints dared to violate it for the love of God, but this sounds like popular fantasy in bad taste).

The neural computer also penalizes the subject with less severe emotional penalties for merely looking at solid or liquid bodily wastes (urine, faeces or vomit). But here we can again admire the skilful wisdom of nature. A baby's faeces are not as revolting to its mother as they are to other people. The neural computer pays a mother an emotional salary for cleaning her baby. It is also worth noting how doctors and nurses can develop a biocultural program which allows them to perform certain repulsive tasks on their patients. We could also consider the case of a mother who helps her son to vomit. Such a woman is pulled by two opposed emotional currents: the law of visual and olfactory repulsion pressures her with highly unpleasant sensations to abandon her son, and with the law of maternity, which moves her to help him by activating an extremely intense feeling of maternal care. Biosocial laws often have more powerful emotional mechanisms at their disposal than biosomatic ones.

The Bionatural Law of Vomiting and its Emotional Mechanisms

Once the stomach has received sufficient food, the neural computer lowers the densitometer of hunger to zero degrees, thus informing the individual that he has finished the task. The subject can now concentrate on other activities: driving, reading, milking cows or conducting an orchestra. Meanwhile, the stomach sends the brain information about the chemical properties of the food that has been ingested. The neural computer, in the light of this, orders the different tanks that contain gastric juices to transmit the quantities prescribed by the digestive program. The neural computer does not inform the subject about this state of affairs, since it does not need his co-operation during this phase of the digestive process. All of the highly sophisticated digestive labs – the stomach, the pancreas, the liver, the kidney and the intestines – work together like an orchestra conducted by the neural computer, transforming roast beef and Yorkshire pudding into different components, which in turn are converted into the different cells that make up the body. Some of the food, however, becomes waste which is of no use to the body.

To the extent that the subject complies with the requirements of the different bionatural and biocultural programs, the neural computer activates the mechanism of satisfaction. This feeling can help the individual to confront the miseries of life. It is said that Schopenhauer, the celebrated German philosopher, found it extremely difficult to deliver a lecture on the dark apocalyptic future of the human race, because immediately before doing so he had enjoyed a luxurious banquet. A human being tends to have a different view of life and destiny on an empty stomach than on one which has been filled with the food required by the brain. We have already seen that sometimes the emotional state of a human being can interfere with the law of hunger. It is also true, however, that the satisfaction provided by 'a good meal' can improve the subject's emotional state, and that 'an awful meal' (an infringement of various laws of the brain's digestive program) can irritate him severely.

If the brain receives a telegram from the stomach informing it that an excessive amount of food has been ingested, the brain will activate an uncomfortable sensation proportional to the excess. The brain, with its emotional language, had warned the individual in the following terms: 'You have had enough. Forget the cake and the cheese. There is no room for them.' The subject ignored this warning, having received an opposed emotional message from another program: 'If you do not eat the cake, you will be being extremely rude to your hosts. I shall punish you with feelings of shame and ridicule.'

If the brain calculates that due to an excess of food or to some other infraction, the stomach will be unable to process all of the food properly, it will automatically and unconsciously resort to an emergency procedure: the vomiting mechanism. This is an extreme measure foreseen by the admirable genetic machinery of the human body. The brain activates an extremely unpleasant sensation proportional to the gravity of the situation. By making the subject pay this emotional fine, the neural computer has sent the subject the following message: 'I warned you not to eat that cake. Now I have no choice but to put you through this torture. Listen to me next time, and I won't have to punish you again.' By activating this extremely disagreeable sensation, the brain also pressures the individual to stay away from food in general. The same brain which triggered off pleasant sensations for looking at, smelling and ingesting that roast beef and Yorkshire pudding when the stomach was empty, now dissuades him from doing so by activating extremely unpleasant feelings.

The brain then activates one of the most violent and irresistible emotional mechanisms: the urge to vomit. As always, a contract is drawn up – *do ut des* – in which the neural computer unilaterally imposes its conditions: 'If you co-operate by making a muscular effort to expel what I tell you to expel through the mouth, until I tell you to stop, I shall cease to disturb you with this horrific sensation.' The subject has little choice, or perhaps no choice at all. The neural computer pressures the subject with such an emotionally intense force – the densitometer of vomit at one hundred degrees – that before he knows it, he is co-operating with the brain like an obedient slave, expelling the unwanted goods through his mouth. The subject may make a strenuous effort to resist this emotional hurricane which the brain has activated, if he is threatened by the penalties of shame and ridicule: 'Restrain yourself, run, and don't make a fool of yourself in front of all these people.' However, in spite of his efforts to comply with this biosocial and biocultural precept, the subject may be unsuccessful.

The neural computer gradually prepares the subject to carry out any particular task, whether it be to make love or to vomit, by progressively increasing the relevant densitometer until, at a certain point, it unleashes a practically, or wholly irresistible mechanism: the final, massive urge to vomit or ejaculate. During the various phases of sexual intercourse and digestion, the co-ordination and the harmony between the physical world (the hardening of the penis, the tensing of muscles, and so on), the biochemical world (the precise combination and the mixture of numerous chemical substances), and the emotional world (the pleasant and unpleasant sensations which are automatically activated), each controlled by the unconscious functioning of the brain, are wonders of creation we should not fail to notice (Descartes, unfortunately, discovered the headache but not the head).

One of the occupational hazards of being a mother (a profession which is in many other ways extremely rewarding) is that the new 'tenant' often interferes with the work of the digestive labs. Consequently, the brain activates different degrees of the unpleasant urge to vomit. The motion of the seas can also disturb the delicate tasks of the digestive labs, and compel the neural computers of sea travellers to feel nauseous.

Biocultural Programs which Partly Govern the Digestive System

Although there is a bionatural program common to every member of the species, there exists also a wide variety of opposed cultural systems which help to delimit the territory of different human societies. Every time a particular culinary system is registered in the neural computer's software, it becomes biocultural and functions autonomously by informing and pressuring the subject with powerful emotional mechanisms.

Biocultural Additions to the Culinary System

Every human infant is a bionatural addict to maternal milk. The neural computer, however, is programmed to create certain addictions to particular dishes and drinks elaborated by a given culture. 'I am dying to eat some proper English bacon,' I was once told by an English lady in Los Angeles. I have often heard Spaniards say in Oxford or Los Angeles how much they long for the traditional 'tapas' served in Spanish bars.

Once the characteristic dishes of a particular culture – such as English bacon, or Spanish 'tapas' – become part of the bioculinary programming of the neural computer – by means of a cumulative process – a biocultural addiction to them is created. An Englishman is an addict of the dishes of the English culture registered in his brain. From then on, the brain will lobby the subject to ingest the dishes in question with emotional pressures mathematically proportional to the degrees of addiction, as well as to the time elapsed since they were last consumed.

Biocultural Taboos of the Culinary System

Every biocultural system prohibits the ingestion of certain plants, animals, spices, oils or dishes. By a 'biocultural taboo of the culinary system', I mean anything that has been registered in the neural computer's software as a substance forbidden by the digestive laboratories through emotional mechanisms of punishment. In his autobiography, Mahatma Gandhi confesses that at one point in his life he believed that if the British had conquered and subjugated India with what was in his opinion a more refined culture, it may have been due to the fact that they ate red meat. He then attempted to defy an Indian culinary taboo which had been registered in his brain since his childhood: the taboo on eating meat, and particularly red meat. His neural computer, however, made him pay a severe emotional fine for infringing this bioculinary taboo. In the end, he decided to give up the attempt.[1]

The pig is a taboo animal in various culinary systems, while in others it is a fundamental element. Europe, as a cultural community, hinges on two important figures: Christ and the pig (*servatis servandis*) – and I say this with all due respect. The architectural, musical, religious, ethical, and other systems of Europe are largely centred on the figure of Christ. If we were to wipe out all the Romanic, gothic, Renaissance, baroque and modern churches of Europe; if we were to wipe out the Gregorian chant, the motets by Victoria and Palestrina, Bach's Mass in B Minor, and all the music inspired by the figure of Christ, the culture of Europe would be substantially impoverished. In the culinary system of Europe, the pig is king. What we could call the 'culinary baroque of Europe' has developed from this animal. Its head, ears, legs, tail, blood, ribs, intestines and tongue have been transformed into smoked and cured hams, sausages, steaks, bacon, salamis, pates and so many other culinary variations on the same porcine theme. The pig is a cultural frontier between religious societies – Christians, as opposed to Jews or Muslims; and territorial societies – European, as opposed to non-European nations. The pig, furthermore, has penetrated into the territory of the brain, becoming a strong addiction for Europeans, and a severe taboo for Muslim or Jewish brains.[2]

Biocultural Laws of Fasting

Various cultural systems include certain rules about fasting on particular days. Muslims cannot ingest anything in the daytime during the month of Ramadan. Christians are obliged to fast on certain days during Lent. A neural computer that has registered rules of fasting such as these acts like a judge, policeman and executioner who warns, threatens and punishes the subject with a severity that is mathematically proportional to the importance of the program. A Muslim whose brain has recorded this rule with all its strictness will be pulled by two opposed emotional currents: firstly, the bionatural law of hunger, which will address him in these terms: 'If you insist on not eating, I shall continue to disturb you with the uncomfortable sensation you now feel. If you eat, I will reward you with satisfaction'; and secondly, a biocultural, biosocial law which pressures him to do the opposite: 'You know very well that a good Muslim must obey this law of fasting. If you respect it, these will be the compensations: a pleasant feeling of hope (of reaching an afterlife of happiness and unimaginable erotic pleasures), and the pleasant feeling of being admired by the Muslim community. If you dare to infringe this sacred norm, I shall make you pay the following severe fines: you will feel condemned by God and by your parents, who live in you, and by the whole of the Muslim community, who you will imagine looking down on you contemptuously. If anyone discovers the truth, you will be scorned, ridiculed and eventually ignored by any Muslims who discover your sin.' It is rare for a Muslim to violate this rule.

A monkey is governed by the law of hunger, but not by any laws concerning fasting, or by any other biocultural laws. We can see how a biocultural law of a social kind can defeat a bionatural law of a somatic kind. The emotional laws and mechanisms which defend the beehive are more powerful than those which defend one of the cells that make up the beehive. The confrontation between the good of a particular subject, and that of his society, can be extremely intense. A human being who decides to fast is always pulled by two opposed emotional currents: that of his life, and that of his society. One case that received much media coverage was that of the Irishmen who held a hunger strike and died after a long, painful agony ('agony' can also be understood to mean 'struggle', the meaning of the original Greek word from which it derives). In such a situation, a young man is subjected to the powerful emotional mechanism of hunger. After a few days of fasting, when food is brought to his cell, his neural computer, in the powerful, eloquent language of feelings, speaks to him thus: 'I am torturing you with these cruel sensations because you stubbornly insist on fasting. Look at that sausage. It smells so good. Come on, take a bite, eat everything you've got in front of you. I will then gradually cease to torture you. You'll never feel better. But if you continue to fast, I shall intensify the torture.' At the same time, however, a biosocial and biocultural program installed in this same neural computer pressures him to do the opposite by employing the same language of feelings: 'If you continue your fast and die like a hero, you will be admired and idolized by Irishmen today and forever. You can feel these profound emotions already. Imagine what it is like to be admired by all your countrymen. You will be on the front page of every single newspaper. Isn't this pleasant feeling of fame worth all the pain you are going through? In any case, if you give up, I shall have to punish you with extremely severe penalties. I shall not only deprive you of all the pleasant feelings of fame you are now relishing, but I shall also subject you to the tortures of shame, ridicule and disdain. The Irish people will despise you for deserting them, for being a coward, for being someone not worthy of calling himself an Irishman.' After several days of 'agony', some of those who began to fast decided to start eating. Others, however, died, sacrificing themselves on the altar of their society. The emotional mechanisms designed to defend the life of an individual are extremely powerful, but they can be defeated by those designed to defend and protect the life of his society.

The Biocultural Structure of Meals

Human societies distinguish themselves, among other things, by their wide variety of culinary structures. By this I mean 'the code which regulates the number and the order of daily meals, defines which meals are sacred and which are profane, and sets out the order of each meal'. In Europe, daily meals are structured into breakfast, lunch and dinner. However, this is not the division made in other cultures. All societies make a distinction between ordinary meals and special occasions, such as wedding banquets and other social rites. Spaniards have a special dinner on Christmas Eve, and Americans have one on Thanksgiving Day. Thanksgiving Dinner is meticulously designed: the turkey is cooked in a special way, on a particular day, and only certain kinds of guests are invited. A neural computer which has been programmed with this biocultural code will punish an American individual if for whatever reasons he does not comply with these precepts of his territorial society. 'When I spent Thanksgiving Day in Moscow,' an American student of mine once told me, 'I had a really awful time. I was unable to eat the traditional turkey with anyone. It was one of the worst days of my life.'

It is also common among the practices of the *Homo religiosus* to find two types of meals: profane and sacred meals. Passover Supper is a sacred meal for all Jews (even for many of those who are agnostics or atheists). This meal is regulated by a detailed code that specifies what is to be eaten, how it should be eaten, what is to be worn, how everyone is to be seated, who is to be invited, what is to be said and sung, what passages are to be read from their holy books, and so on. Christians have converted the Jewish Easter celebration into a mass, which is essentially still a sacred feast where, at least according to the Catholic faith, the body of Christ is eaten. A Catholic whose brain had registered this program would be disheartened if he were deprived of participating in this sacred banquet.

The structure of a meal is also meticulously defined by a society's culture. When it is registered within the neural computers of its members, it becomes a biocultural program in their software. The neural computer will pay the subject an emotional salary if he respects these rules, and will penalize him if they are violated. If an Englishman were to be served salad and cake, followed by coffee and chips, roast lamb and finally soup, his neural computer would be unable to pay him the emotional salary it would have given out if these dishes had been served in the prescribed order.

No one can break the rules registered in his neural computer without being compelled to pay the emotional fine proportional to the infraction. The subject can violate certain biocultural or bionatural laws – within certain limits established by the genetic plan – but neither a dictator, nor a multi-millionaire, nor any other human being can escape this innate law, to which there can be no exceptions or infractions: the immediate, automatic, unappealable payment of an emotional fine for every infraction that is committed.

The Biocultural Code of Locations

Human societies have also created a code which defines the locations where human beings can eat and drink. This is a cultural code to which an ape is not subjected. What human beings refer to as their 'homes' are the only territories where they are allowed to eat without having to ask for permission to do so, and without having to pay for every meal or dish. If a husband had to pay his wife for every dish she served him, the ridicule provoked would reveal the fact that this law was being violated. This is precisely the frontier which divides the community of the family from those who have no right to eat in that home, unless they are 'guests'.

Another elaborate code prescribes the rules which regulate the behaviour of the hosts and the guests. It would surprise an ape to discover the cultural rules of the human beehive, which make practically every single human action (no matter how trivial it may seem) fall under the regulation of some particular code registered in the brain. The rights and obligations of hosts and guests do not have to be learned in school. This is unnecessary, for the neural computer is programmed to decipher and register this code by means of purely unconscious observation, in the same way it deciphers and registers the grammatical rules of a language. The Gospel relates the case of a guest who was thrown out of a wedding for infringing one of the rules of this biocultural code, by not wearing the appropriate clothing. After any given banquet, the hosts, as well as the guests, often discuss and criticize everyone's behaviour, comparing and contrasting every single gesture, outfit, comment and dish with the cultural code in use.

Restaurants, taverns, pubs, coffee shops and bars also constitute a human monopoly. An eagle must hunt in order to eat. A wolf pack attacks its prey in an organized hunt, and afterwards all its members take part in a banquet, according to a bionatural code which determines the amount of food each of them can eat, depending on their hierarchical rank (human beings are not the only animals whose access to different qualities and quantities of food is conditioned by their hierarchical status). Neither an eagle nor a wolf can occupy themselves with other activities and then go to eat in a restaurant, without having to worry about hunting. In any given home the members of the family can eat without having to pay,

and without having to be invited; those who are not members of
the family can eat without paying, as long as they are invited; in
any given restaurant people can eat without having been invited,
as long as they pay. A meal shared between hosts and guests ought
to be a ritual translation of friendship (although, as with any other
language, all kinds of abuses may occur). In a restaurant, however,
the transaction is a purely economic one: certain dishes are served in
return for a specified amount of money. It would be very awkward if
a guest asked his hosts: 'How much did this salmon cost you?' If this
occurred, one of the rules of the culinary code of hosts and guests
would have been infringed.

A territorial society is partly defined by its restaurants, its pubs
and its bars. The British landscape is characterized not only by its
green meadows and by the River Thames, but also by its pubs. Each
pub has its name, its symbol, its decoration, its history, its anecdotes,
and even its style of serving. Furthermore, these pubs are registered
in the brains of the British people. A particular pub is located not
only in Soho Square, but also in millions of brains. Once this pub
has been installed in the brain of an Englishman, the latter will be
pressured to visit this pub by the emotional mechanisms of addiction.
An Englishman who lived in Los Angeles once related the following
event to me: 'I hadn't stepped on English soil for three years. When I
saw a pub, I almost started to cry. I went inside and asked for a pint.
I felt like embracing the bartender and everyone else who was there. It
was such an extraordinary feeling to be myself again! I felt more like
an Englishman than ever before. I told myself: Thank God I'm in a
pub! I was overjoyed.' The neural computer of this Englishman paid
him an emotional salary proportional to the urges he felt for going
to a pub, urges which had accumulated in the relevant densitometer.
This affective and addictive programming of pubs is one which occurs
in a particular territorial society: England.

The restaurants and bars exported to foreign societies can perform
a function which we could refer to as a mechanism of geopolitical
preservation. A Chinese restaurant in the United States contributes
to maintain the cultural and social identity of the Chinese people
who live there. Many English people frequent a pub in Santa
Monica, California, in order to meet other English people and
'feel at home' ('home' in this case refers to their territorial home,
England). Mexicans who live in the United States preserve their
ethnic identity by eating 'carnitas', 'burritos' and 'fajitas' in the

many Mexican restaurants around the country. When a Mexican enters one of these restaurants, his neural computer rewards him with an extremely pleasant feeling for entering his cultural territory.

Another cultural invention that belongs to a society's culinary world is the market, the supermarket, or the delicatessen. A territorial society may be characterized by its fish stands, its butchers' shops, its open-air or covered markets, and many other establishments which distinguish themselves by the type of products they sell, their manner of selling, their design and their mode of presentation. A Spaniard whose neural computer has been programmed with buying characteristic Spanish products such as 'chorizos', cured ham, sardines, red beans, chickpeas, and so on, will be lobbied by his neural computer to search for them if he finds himself in a foreign country. When a Spaniard leaves Spain, he leaves his land, but he carries it with him in his brain. 'Thank goodness! I have finally found a shop that sells all kinds of Spanish products: from olive oil to chickpeas', a Spanish lady triumphantly said when she found a shop in Oxford that sold products from her land. In Los Angeles I have seen Germans who meet at German delicatessens, where they can 'feel German' when they find the sausages and the bread that their brain pressures them to eat with its usual system of promises and threats: pleasant or unpleasant feelings. These shops are, like restaurants, mechanisms of social and cultural preservation and communion. Shops and restaurants are, like culinary products, physical entities, but their installation in the brain is metaphysical, mental and emotional.

The Biocultural Code of Utensils

Each culture has invented utensils with which to cook food, receptacles in which to serve it, and tools with which to eat it. Europe is in this sense the culture of forks and spoons, whereas China or Japan are chopstick cultures. In India, as well as in Arabic countries, the norm is to eat with one's fingers, while in Western culture this would constitute a grave violation of the culinary code. All of these culinary tools are geophysical elements which become geopsychological when they are installed in the brain. Forks and spoons are for a European as biological as hands and fingers. Forks and spoons are not only on the table, but also in a subject's brain.

During the annual festivals of a Spanish village near my own native one, a group of young men went around offering girls hot chocolate, which they served from a bedpan. Everyone knew that this bedpan was new, and hence as clean as any ordinary cooking receptacle. However, the neural computer of a Spaniard, especially during that rural period, had associated that object with other substances, and hence immediately activated an unpleasant feeling and an emotional threat when the hot chocolate was ingested. An English bishop, however, related to me how he once saw a group of children in an African school cheerfully eating their breakfasts out of bedpans. These African children had never seen such receptacles, and thought that they must be one of the great European culinary inventions. Their brains contained no biocultural taboos on bedpans, unlike the brains of those Spanish girls, whose cries of disgust still echo in my mind – 'Get away from us, you revolting pigs!' – while their faces translated the feelings of repulsion that their neural computers had activated. The programs which enter a neural computer's software govern the subject through the precise, automatic release of pleasant and unpleasant feelings.

The Biocultural Code of Etiquette

Each culture has created a more or less elaborate code of rules which regulate table manners: where and when people may sit down and get up; who can speak when and how; the hierarchical order in which dishes are to be distributed; the outfits, the make-up and the jewels which are prescribed and proscribed; how people ought to eat and drink. All of this constitutes a complex grammar which the brain assimilates unconsciously by means of observation and practice. The neural computer automatically deciphers the rules of this code without consulting the subject, and compels him to respect it by means of emotional promises and threats. It is said that a given aristocrat once married a girl of 'humble' origins, and that during their first public banquet, she infringed a basic rule of the biocultural code of high society etiquette, by getting up and saying: 'Excuse me, I have to take a . . . ' (here she employed the proscribed noun which refers to the act of urinating). After the banquet, her husband instructed her tactfully on how not to make the same mistake again. Nevertheless, during the following banquet, this young lady, whose brain had not been programmed with the code of high society etiquette, got up and said: 'Excuse me, ladies and gentlemen, I must absent myself momentarily and visit the powder room, and while I'm at it, I'll take a . . . ' (here she employed the taboo noun which refers to the human task of eliminating solid waste from the digestive system).

This anecdote, undoubtedly exaggerated in the letter, though not in the spirit, would have amused Freud. The young lady made a conscious effort to comply with the rules of high society etiquette, but her neural computer revealed in several ways that she was unfamiliar with the grammar of the aristocratic code. In the first place, her pedantic language ('Excuse me, ladies and gentleman, I must absent myself momentarily and visit the powder room . . .') is like an old woman's excessive use of make-up: the excessive use of linguistic make-up reveals, rather than concealing, the idiomatic wrinkles. In the second place, this young lady's neural computer betrays her by allowing her to utter a taboo word. A person can change his social status overnight by inheriting a vast sum of money. However, the cultural schemes – of the aristocratic class or of a territorial society – are programmed in the brain over the course of a slow, lengthy, repetitive process. Even rules of etiquette taught in school, including those taught in specialized schools – the tea ceremony of the Japanese upper class requires five years to be learned – eventually pass from the conscious subject to the unconscious brain. Any Japanese adult who attends one of these tea ceremonies can placidly converse, walk around, and contemplate the elegant kimonos, without having to worry about the rules of this elaborate rite. In the same way he can direct his conscious attention to the topics of conversation without having to concern himself with the rules of grammar; his neural computer, which has already registered the code of this tea ceremony, allows him to unconsciously comply with all of its rules. The brain of this Japanese individual would unconsciously detect, with the swift accuracy which characterizes the neural processor, an infraction of any of the rules which regulate this extremely complicated rite.

The Meal: an Egalitarian and Hierarchical Mechanism

A territorial society, or geopolis, can also be a culinary community: a territory delimited by the frontiers of a common culinary system, or one where the common biological denominator is the biocultural program of nourishment itself. China, Japan or Europe are culinary communities. One Chinese individual identifies himself with another Chinese individual in relation to a European for, among other things, belonging to the same culinary system, and for being governed by the same culinary brain program.

Within Europe, different territorial communities and their members possess different culinary systems. All Frenchmen share the same culinary system, and consider themselves members of the same beehive in relation to Italians – in this sense it is true that '*l'égalité*' exists. In Italy, Communists and fascists, millionaires and beggars, atheists and Catholics, all belong to the same culinary and biological republic: the republic, or the biorepublic, of lasagna, brodo and fettucine. All Mexicans are similarly governed by the same biocultural parliament: that of 'carnitas', 'enchiladas', and 'tortillas'.

However, although the members of different ideological, religious, and economic (or class) societies are reducible to the same cultural and biocultural common denominator – the same culinary system (*e pluribus unum: una manducandi forma*) – there is also a sense in which they are hierarchically divided and classified by culinary criteria. All Indians (i.e. from India) are governed by the same common culinary system, one which is opposed to that of Europe or China. However, the traditional hierarchy of castes is defined (or at least used to be defined) by a precise hierarchy of foods and manners. Each caste possesses a hierarchically defined culinary system: 'the higher the caste, the more refined the food, and the more elaborate the manners'.

The social classes in Madrid, Los Angeles or Moscow are defined and maintained by a hierarchical culinary code: who you are depends on what you eat, where you eat it, and whom you eat it with. Meals act as a frontier between classes among wolves, bees and human beings. The brains of Englishmen are programmed with roast beef and fish and chips. This is the physical and mental frontier between an Englishman and a Swede or an Indian. However, only the members of the English upper class dine in extremely expensive restaurants and exclusively with members of this particular social class, savouring the exquisite dishes which the members of the middle or lower classes only know about through hearsay. The privilege of dining in first-class restaurants, and in the first-class compartments of trains and aircraft, distinguishes and divides one social class from another. The members of different ideological societies (Communists, socialists or conservatives) identify themselves as members of one common society when they meet each other in exclusive, luxurious restaurants.

Members of the same ideological group who belong to different classes may exceptionally sit together at the same table (an exception which confirms the rule). For example, once a year all Spanish Communists, both rich and poor, partake of the same 'paella' at the party reunion organized annually in Madrid's 'Casa de Campo'. However, on any average day, the upper-class Communists and socialists drink the same Dom Perignon champagne, fly first class, and eat in lavish restaurants with members of a rival ideological beehive, though of the same social class, while those who wait on them reveal, by the very fact that they cannot enjoy the dishes which they serve, their inferior class (although among these waiters we may find some who profess faith in right-wing ideology, and others who sympathize with the left wing). A Communist who lives in Beverly Hills and drives a Rolls-Royce may invite a member of his own social class to dinner, although the latter may be on the opposite side of the political spectrum, but he would never invite a member of his ideological society who did not own a Rolls-Royce, or at least a Mercedes (I have witnessed affairs of this kind among the Californian upper class). I have never found an exception or an infraction to this culinary class rule.

Catholics also refer to their equality – one of a religious kind – when they share the same sacred banquet at the same table and with the same beliefs. Outside the walls of the church, however, upper-class Catholics share their table with atheists, agnostics or Jews, as long as these are members of their class, but never with Catholics of an inferior social class. The Spanish director Luis García Berlanga explores this issue in one of his acclaimed films, in which a group of wealthy individuals decide to invite a few beggars to dinner on Christmas Eve. This apparent act of equality is in fact a ritual proclamation of hierarchy: only the rich can allow themselves the luxury of inviting beggars to dinner, but not the other way around.

The rules of class equality require that guests should be capable of inviting their hosts in turn. Furthermore, since these beggars are unfamiliar with the rules of upper-class etiquette, the Christmas Eve dinner merely serves to widen the gap that divides the two classes. The culinary frontier – which is both physical and mental – is like a Berlin Wall that divides men into territorial and economic divisions of class.

Even if all of those who partake of a meal define themselves as equals in relation to those who serve it and to those who cannot partake of it because they do not possess the right religious, territorial, ideological or economic passport, beneath the apparent equality one may still discover a hierarchical reality. Among those who participate in the same Catholic 'Communion' – in this case a scientifically accurate expression – the priest appears to be the leader or 'number one player' of this community. The host he eats is larger; he is the only one who drinks from the chalice (although today there are exceptions to this rule); he is the first to receive Communion. These are all ritual affirmations of hierarchy. At a solemn banquet of Communists, in spite of the fact that equality may be the fundamental element of their ideology and the central theme of their sermons, the leader – or 'Secretary General' – will sit in a special place; he will be served before anyone else; he will sit and get up before anyone else; and he will deliver the address to which everyone else will be forced to listen and applaud (no matter how dull) like good, humble and obedient subjects.

The Culinary System: an Ethical and Philosophical System

The culinary system is frequently the stone which a culture transforms into an ethical statue. In Spain the traditional 'cocido de garbanzos', a chickpea stew, has become a fundamental element of its culinary system, as well as a biological possession common to all Spaniards, independently of where their political sympathies may lie. One can find chickpeas in Spanish fields, supermarkets, people's kitchen pantries, and in the pantries of their brains. Inside a sack of chickpeas one can sometimes find a chickpea that distinguishes itself from the rest in both its colour and its taste: the black chickpea. The Spanish people have turned the black chickpea into an ethical symbol: it stands for the heretic, the revolutionary, the one who does not accept his society's norms and intends to change them. The neural computer of an Englishman is not programmed with either the culinary or the ethical chickpea of Spain, nor can it decipher the meaning of this sentence: 'siempre fui el garbanzo negro de mi familia', of which the literal translation would be 'I was always the black chickpea in my family'. The philosophical, ethical, sociological and psychological symbol into which the Spanish people have transformed the black chickpea is installed in the software of every Spaniard's neural computer.

The omelette, another basic component of the Spanish culinary mosaic, has also become a political and ethical symbol: a symbol of revolution. When a Spaniard speaks of 'el día que dé vuelta la tortilla', which literally means 'the day the omelette flips over', he is referring to the overthrow of the current political authorities. The Spanish people thus transmit a political lesson which would have amused Machiavelli: firstly, that human society, like an omelette, is made up of two classes: those who are on top, and those who are at the bottom; secondly, that those who are at the bottom are in an inferior, unpleasant position; thirdly, that someday society will be flipped over like an omelette: those who are on top will find themselves at the bottom, and those who are at the bottom will occupy positions of power, prestige, wealth and fame; fourthly, that human society, like an omelette, is always hierarchic: the individuals that make it up may exchange their positions, but the hierarchical structure remains. Although those who preach revolutionary sermons generally affirm, maintain and swear that hierarchy will come to an end and that a paradise of equality will be accomplished, the Machiavellian Spanish people suggest that society will always be divided into those who rule and those who are ruled, into the top and the bottom, just like the omelette.

I have mentioned these two examples to illustrate the existence of a world waiting to be discovered: that of the ethical and political symbols which different territorial societies derive from their culinary systems, and which govern any given society's members from the biocultural parliament in their brains.

The Culinary System: a Vehicle for the History and Culture of a Society

It is not merely coincidental that there exist in the world brands of alcoholic beverages such as 'Beefeater', 'Charles III' and 'Napoleon'; there exists a brand of biscuits from Avila called 'The Yolks of Saint Theresa' and a brand of chocolates manufactured in Salzburg, Mozart's birthplace, called 'Mozart Kugeln'. The word 'sandwich' is derived from the name of an English city where a given lord had the idea of placing a bit of meat between two pieces of bread; the hamburger indirectly publicizes a particular German city; and in Los Angeles one can find restaurants with names such as 'Toledo' and 'Madrid'. Through their respective culinary systems, all territorial societies enrich the programming of their members' brains with the geography, the history and the culture of their nations. If certain dishes and drinks transcend the borders of their own territory, they become genuine ambassadors by exporting to other countries a lesson in history and culture.

Could one ever come up with a better publicity campaign for Yorkshire than that provided by its 'Yorkshire pudding'? 'I would forgive the Italian people for anything, had I anything to forgive them for, if only because they invented pizza,' an American professor once told me as he bit into a slice of 'pizza napolitana'.

It is probably accurate to say that Italy does not have a more popular ambassador in the United States than pizza, nor does the United States have a more popular one around the world than Coca-Cola. The United States quietly slips into the brain of a Russian, not as a result of the work of CIA spies, but as a result of the seemingly irresistible flavour of Coca-Cola. When the neural computer of a Russian rewards him with a pleasant sensation for drinking Coca-Cola, it generates unconscious feelings of affection towards the land where this soft drink comes from.

Bionatural and Biocultural Systems of Evacuation

Let us recall the three phases of the digestive process. During the first, the neural computer solicits the subject's co-operation, by pressuring him to ingest certain foods and drinks. During the second, the neural computer ceases to disturb the individual, allowing him to occupy himself with other activities, while the digestive labs function autonomously. During the third, the neural computer is programmed to avoid eliminating solid, liquid and gaseous waste without informing the subject and asking for his authorization.

The incredibly sophisticated digestive labs of the human body, always under the supervision of the brain, process and deposit solid, liquid and gaseous waste in the appropriate tanks (the bladder or the intestines), in accordance with the genetic plan. Each of these tanks has the brain continuously informed about the amount of waste contained in them. The brain, according to the innate program regulating the evacuation of solids, liquids and gases, and depending on the amount of waste that has accumulated in these deposits, informs the subject of the task that has to be performed: solid or gaseous waste may have to be expelled, or the urine tank may have to be emptied. By activating one of these three distinct urges, the neural computer informs the subject about which of these chores must be done. He knows nothing about what particular waste has accumulated, nor when, nor why it must be eliminated. Only his neural computer 'knows' – unconsciously, of course, like all other computers – and informs him about what to eliminate and through what channels.

The genetic plan has foreseen three qualitatively different feelings – the urges to urinate, defecate and expel a gas – which allow the neural computer to tell the subject which of these three different tasks he must perform. We should not fail to notice and admire the ingeniousness of these qualitatively different emotional mechanisms, which can be compared to a set of traffic lights. Each different colour lets the subject know what operation has to be carried out. Furthermore, the different intensities of each of the colours, as well as the different intensity of each of these feelings, indicates the urgency with which the job needs to be done. The neural computer activates an emotional intensity of urges mathematically proportional to the quantity of solids, liquids or gases that has accumulated. Anyone can verify the considerable variations in emotional intensity which are experienced before and after carrying out any of these three operations. 'Ahh, I really needed that!', the subject may exclaim after relieving extremely intense urges to urinate. The neural computer had pressured and threatened the subject to empty his tank by activating the maximum emotional intensity of this densitometer. However, if a doctor instructs a patient to urinate when his tank is practically empty, the neural computer will merely pay him a token salary for performing this task. The amount of emotional satisfaction the subject experiences for carrying out any of these three operations is mathematically proportional to the intensity of the urges accumulated in the relevant densitometer. Anyone can verify the workings of this emotional law, to which we are all subjected.

The Bionatural Program of Emergencies

The digestive labs can inform the brain about any incidents or accidents which upset the 'normal' absorption and accumulation of faeces. The brain then contrasts this information with its digestive program and automatically activates an emotional emergency mechanism. The brain alerts the individual about the situation with an emotional siren, by triggering off extremely intense, painful urges. Its message could be translated as follows: 'Run. There is no time to lose. This is an emergency. If you do not attend to it immediately, I shall continue to torture you with this pain.' ('Diarrhoea' comes from a Greek word which means 'to run across a field'.) The intensity of the brain's emotional mechanisms is mathematically proportional to the urgency with which the harmful waste must be eliminated. The brain allows the subject to resist for a time, but if he insists on disobeying its orders due to opposed emotional pressures of a social kind (let us suppose, for instance, that these emergency mechanisms are activated by the brain of an orchestra conductor who finds himself conducting Beethoven's *Eroica* at New York's Carnegie Hall), the brain, according to the genetic plan, can ultimately force the subject to expel this waste, which will announce its exit with a loud warning (a sort of phonic alarm foreseen by the genetic plan to inform both the protagonist and the spectators of the event: the phonic alarm of diarrhoea). Emergency situations can also occur in cases of gas or liquid elimination, each having its own emotional mechanism of high intensity (the expulsion of urine with kidney stones, for instance, is accompanied by one of the most unpleasant sensations in the whole of the brain's emotional repertoire).

The Bionatural Program of Evacuation in Relation to the Subject's Emotional State

All human beings occasionally experience alterations in the process of evacuation due to external emotional reasons (external, that is, to the digestive system). 'When exam time comes around, I suffer from diarrhoea year after year,' a student recently confessed to me. 'I became so nervous during the interview, that I could hardly resist the urge to urinate while we were still on the air,' a Spanish television personality once admitted to me. We could almost say that faeces are like a barometer which reflects the emotional state of the subject: normal faeces indicate that all is well, while painful diarrhoeas are often a sign of some sort of emotional unrest. All organic and social systems are autonomous and regulated by their own particular laws (for instance, the digestive system and the kinship system). However, it is also true that one system can influence and alter the proper functioning of another (for instance, a social system which requires a student to undergo the torture of an exam can disturb the normal process of digestion by setting off the mechanism of diarrhoea, or even that of vomiting).

The innate alarm system, which is designed to prepare the subject for any dangers that may threaten his life, unleashes a particular emotional alarm – that of fear, which I shall discuss later – and may also trigger the urge to evacuate.

'To evacuate out of fear' is an expression employed in numerous languages (I use 'evacuate' here as a euphemism for the usual taboo words) which echoes this sophisticated defence program. Hospital patients who are about to be operated on, as well as women who are about to give birth, are often forced to evacuate waste by means of an enema. This is a wise measure which liberates the patient's body of an organic burden. The objective of the genetic plan, which compels the endangered subject to rid himself of this load (in every sense of the word), seems to be the same.

Biocultural Programs of Evacuation

The culture of the *anthropos* species includes, among other things, a code of precise rules which regulate evacuation: when, where and how this task must be performed. An ape is subjected to a bionatural program of evacuation similar to that of a human being, by means of a comparable system of emotional mechanisms. However, unlike his 'descendant', an ape does not seem to be subjected to a biocultural code which can conflict with the bionatural one.

The Biocultural Code of Gas Elimination

Every human society has created a cultural code which regulates the evacuation of organic gases. By means of a cumulative process of observations and recordings, this code is installed in the software of every human being's neural computer, from the time of his childhood. Anthropologists have not discovered any 'primitive' societies that are not governed by this code. The neural computer, as I pointed out in an earlier chapter, informs a human being, as well as an ape, about when an organic gas has to be expelled, what the urgency of the operation is, and what the emotional terms of the contract are. However, unlike the case of an ape, the hardware of a human being's neural computer is genetically designed to assimilate a code which regulates the expulsion of organic gases.

This biocultural code is made up of very precise rules concerning the moments when this particular 'freedom of speech' is permitted. The rules specify in front of whom the expulsion of gases is wholly forbidden, and the emotional fines that would have to be paid if the code was violated. The general rule in all cultures is that this organic act, independently of how useful or indispensable it may be for the digestive process, can only be performed in private. The emotional penalties codified by the neural computer are extremely severe and unappealable: the highest degrees of shame and ridicule are inevitably triggered off. The American people may have allowed or forgiven a President such as Kennedy for having engaged in an occasional erotic escapade, but had this Head of State ever broken wind during a public ceremony, such an action would have destroyed his political career, his good name, and perhaps even his sanity. Let us suppose that the President, after this faux pas, addressed his audience as follows: 'Excuse me, ladies and gentlemen, but I had beans for lunch, and well, you know how it is . . . ' Such an excuse or justification would of course only bring about more severe social and biosocial penalties.

Suppose that a human being finds himself in a public situation. A professor, for instance, may be delivering a lecture in a university hall. If the digestive laboratories inform the neural computer about the presence of a certain gas in a particular place, the relevant emotional densitometer will be immediately activated. One could translate the brain's message to the subject as follows: 'Expel this gas and I shall pay you an emotional salary. If not, I shall continue to disturb you with this uncomfortable sensation.' The biocultural program of gas expulsion, however, also warns and threatens this same subject: 'Don't you dare allow this gas to exit. Every student is familiar with this organic melody. Imagine the shame and the ridicule you would be forced to feel.' Both the program which defends the organic republic and the one which sides with the social republic are biological, both inform the subject about something he should do or avoid doing, and both pressure him with very powerful emotional mechanisms. The social program, however, is stronger. A university professor, even a fervent supporter of political liberalism or anarchy, would never dare violate this extremely severe social and biosocial law. This is one of the strictest taboos in every human society (next to incest and illegitimacy of birth, although it is more widely respected).

Hollywood films, which today attempt to shock the spectator by violating the norms of good taste, have rarely dared to break this taboo. My children laughed uproariously when they heard this unexpected sound in Ingmar Bergman's *Fanny and Alexander*. Laughter reveals the infraction, as we shall see later when I discuss the ingenious genetic mechanism of laughter. This biocultural rule cannot even be violated in front of close relatives, friends or colleagues. Even a parent who accidentally allows the escape of a gas may excuse himself in front of his children, who will have to make an effort not to punish him or her with laughter. This biocultural prohibition is usually lifted only in nuptial territories.

In Delhi I discovered that the supreme religious leader of the Jain, a multi-secular religious society, is exempt from this rule. As I interviewed this figure for a Spanish television series in front of a distinguished audience, he raised his right buttock and began to play a unique fanfare recital which resounded loudly in the room. We could not believe our own eyes, or ears (not to mention our noses). Our neural computers pressured us to laugh with the highest emotional intensity. The mechanism of shame – which I shall discuss later – made our faces blush. It was one of the most difficult moments of my entire career. I later discovered that only this supreme religious leader is exempt from this prohibition. He is also exempt from wearing any clothes (during the interview he was completely naked). This exception is an important mechanism of hierarchy and monarchy (in the Greek sense of the word: monarch = number one, or supreme leader). Such an exception does not undermine the rigour of this social law. We can also discover a hierarchical element in this other rule: 'the higher the position on the hierarchical ladder, the greater the infraction and its corresponding penalty'. The feelings of shame and ridicule would be greater if someone violated this taboo in front of the Queen of England, than if he did so in front of the porters of Buckingham Palace. The Queen of England herself would be subjected to more severe emotional fines if she infringed this rule in the middle of an address, than a porter who did the same.

In 1979, a rumour circulated in Spain according to which the Spanish Nobel Prize Winner Camilo José Cela, who was then a member of the senate, gave his opinion on another senator's speech by breaking wind (the renowned novelist denied the truth of this incident at a dinner party he attended at my home in Los Angeles). The immediate reaction set off in all of the brains which registered this sound reveals the gravity of this infraction and, therefore, the rigour of this taboo. During the course of the same year, a court battle took place in the city of Pamplona over this same issue. During a political demonstration, when a policeman asked one of the participants a question, the latter raised his leg and gave the officer a resonant organic answer. The judge heard the professional opinion of a physician, who as an expert witness was asked whether the action was an uncontrollable bodily one, or whether it was a deliberate insult against an agent of the government. All of these facts reveal the gravity of a law which may appear to be frivolous, but which uncovers one of the genetic frontiers between human beings and apes.

Some cultural anthropologists confidently affirm that this social norm and all other social norms are not registered in a human being's DNA, or in his genetic code, and that therefore it has nothing to do with the biological world. However, this is in my view a very serious error, although it is thought to be a self-evident truth. A human being's DNA includes a genetic program which is responsible for creating a neural computer with a particular hardware that can decipher the cultural law of gas expulsion which exists in his society. Such hardware can accommodate this law within the brain's software, and hence the law can govern the subject whose brain has registered it through the rigorous dictatorship of feelings (which include emotional penalties such as shame and laughter, which I shall discuss later). An ape's DNA cannot generate a neural computer with the hardware that makes possible the installation of this kind of software.

A friend of mine once said to me: 'Do you want to know my definition of Heaven? It's a place where you can (...) whenever it pleases you' (I prefer to censor the verb he employed here to refer to the act of expelling an organic gas). In spite of its vulgarity, this definition is interesting from an anthropological point of view. Human beings are social animals which are subjected to significantly more social codes, laws and penalties than bees within their hives or wolves within their packs. Every single human action, no matter how trivial or frivolous it may seem, falls under some social and biosocial code.

The Biocultural System of Evacuation

All human societies have created a code which regulates where, when, and how, solid and liquid waste may be evacuated. I have never heard of a dog who has been taught the biocultural program of gas expulsion, and it seems probable that this animal's hardware (as well as that of any other animal) cannot assimilate such a program in its software. This is clearly one of the genetic frontiers between a human being and an ape. However, a dog's brain can assimilate, at least partially, the biocultural code of evacuation of solid and liquid waste. A dog is, like a human being, governed by the emotional mechanisms of its neural computer (although emotional mechanisms such as that of laughter, shame, religion, magic, and so on, are genetically excluded). I was once told about a German shepherd dog who always complied with this rule, which he had been taught when he was a puppy, but who one day soiled the living room carpet. This dog found itself at the mercy of two powerful emotional mechanisms: a bionatural one and a biocultural one. An emergency undoubtedly made it impossible for the poor animal to resist the emotional pressure, and thus he failed to go out into the garden as he should have. His owner reprimanded him severely, although he refrained from hitting him. Nevertheless, this emotional penalty must have been so unbearable for the dog that it became depressed and died of sorrow, according to the veterinary surgeon.

During the first two years of infancy, a child is only governed by the bionatural system of elimination of organic waste. His mother or parental guardian soon attempts to introduce the first rule of this code into his little brain: 'You must tell mummy when you want to take a pee; a good little boy does not wet his nappies.' The child's neural computer gradually assimilates this first rule: waste can only be evacuated in certain prescribed rooms and receptacles. In this domain, as well as in others, the more 'civilized' a society becomes, the more rules are established in it. For instance, separate rooms labelled 'Ladies' and 'Gentlemen' are created, representing a new cultural and biocultural frontier between the sexes – the inequality between the sexes is currently increasing in numerous ways, although many defend the contrary view. If a gentleman who found himself at the theatre were to be pressured by his emotional mechanisms to evacuate solid waste urgently, and found that the 'Gentlemen' toilet was occupied, while that of 'Ladies' was not, he would find it very difficult to enter the foreign territory. The emotional penalties of shame and ridicule with which this man's neural computer would threaten him would not make it easy for him to take such a dangerous step and invade a place his society and his sex forbid him from trespassing.

This cultural code has also designed certain devices which are adapted to the bodies of each sex, such as male urinals. Culture, once again, acts as the 'servant of nature'. When a man urinates in a public toilet, he complies with two different rules: an organic one (the elimination of waste) and a social one (respect for the place and the manners prescribed by his society).

Other hygienic norms are also regulated by and installed in the software of the neural computer, such as the use of toilet paper, as opposed to the use of water. If a human being has been programmed to use toilet paper, his neural computer will punish him with uncomfortable feelings if he fails to find paper after the organic task has been performed. This issue, like so many others, can become coloured by cultural and territorial pride. I remember hearing a European lady say to an Arabic woman in Oxford how she found it rather odd that people in Arabic countries do not use toilet paper. 'This is because the Arabic people are very civilized,' she proudly responded. 'We use water, rather than the paper Europeans use. If you think you are the most hygienic and civilized culture in the world, think again.' Nothing is more 'natural' to a human being than his culture, once it has become his biological property. A European's urge to defecate is as biological as his desire to use toilet paper.

6

Emotional Control of Entries to the Body

In the same way that every substance which enters the digestive laboratories is rigorously scrutinized by the biological and emotional 'border patrol', every particle that attempts to penetrate the human body through one of the many possible channels (eyes, ears, nose, anus, arms, legs, or any other part of the body through which a bee's stinger, a mosquito's poison, or a fatal bullet can squeeze) is meticulously examined by other 'agents' of the brain who are no less competent than those which inspect all nourishment.

The Emotional Control of Entries to the Lungs

A human being is an automobile which runs on oxygen rather than petrol. A brand new Rolls-Royce, as well as an old, beat-up Vauxhall, cannot be driven without petrol. If the petrol in either of these vehicles runs out, it inevitably stops. A human body that fails to receive oxygen, whether it be the body of a king or that of a beggar, also stops. The sophisticated machinery of an automobile needs to consume petrol in order to move, and the sophisticated machinery of a human body needs to consume oxygen in order to move. Oxygen is the indispensable fuel of the human body. An automobile depends on petrol as much as a human body depends on oxygen.

> What difference does it make to be a king
> Rather than one who goes from door to door?

asked the Spanish poet León Felipe in one of his celebrated laconic poems. With regard to oxygen, there is evidently no difference whatsoever. A human being has to suckle uninterruptedly on the breasts of this invisible, ethereal mother from the moment of birth to the moment of death. In fact, the human body depends more on oxygen than a car does on petrol. An automobile has a tank that allows it to become temporarily independent from the source of fuel. Nature, however, does not provide a human being with an oxygen tank. He has to be permanently connected to the fuel station. Hence, unlike a human being, an automobile can run out of fuel, remain immobile for days, months and even years, and still be capable of moving again as long as it is refuelled. If a human body is deprived of its indispensable fuel for a short time – not years, days, or hours, but merely minutes – it will stop for good. Unlike the case of the car, this human stoppage is irreversible. A human being is designed to 'de-compose' once the labs in his respiratory system have ceased to function.

As soon as a baby comes out of the maternal dwelling, its neural computer becomes aware of this event. In accordance with a genetic program, the neural computer then orders the lungs to begin absorbing oxygen uninterruptedly at a particular rhythm. From this moment onwards, the highly sophisticated labs of the respiratory system, always under the supervision of the brain, begin to suck in oxygen through the nose and/or mouth, to process it, and to expel waste through these same channels. The neural computer does not need the co-operation of the subject to acquire, process or expel the gases consumed by the respiratory process. With the aid of the breath laboratories, it takes care of providing the individual with all the fuel he needs, and of expelling the gases consumed. The neural computer regulates the quantity of fuel, its quality and the respiratory rhythm. The individual can drive, write, make love, pray or sing without having to worry about the highly complex workings of this process. The neural computer is wholly and uninterruptedly informed about everything that occurs in the respiratory system. The subject is entirely ignorant about all of this, since the neural computer does not share any of this information with him.

The Law of Oxygen Quantity

The respiratory labs inform the brain, via the nervous system, about the quantity of oxygen that is being received from the outside. The subject knows nothing about this law, nor does he know how to measure the amount of fuel that silently penetrates the human body. The respiratory labs, however, are equipped with a sophisticated system of detection that measures the quantity and the quality of this colourless, odourless, tasteless fuel. If the quantity of oxygen received is inferior to that required by the bionatural program of the brain, this program, in accordance with another innate program, will activate an uncomfortable feeling proportional to the degree of oxygen insufficiency. The neural computer, which thus far has not interrupted the subject's activities, now triggers off a mechanism of alert comparable to the flashing red light which warns a driver that his car is almost out of petrol. The brain's emotional message could be translated as follows: 'Look out! The oxygen you are receiving is adequate, but the quantity is insufficient.' As always, the neural computer invites the subject to remedy the situation by making him an emotional offer: 'If you do something about this, and breathe sufficient oxygen, I shall cease to disturb you.' If the quantity of oxygen received is minimal, the neural computer, in accordance with an ingenious program designed by nature, activates a truly 'alarming' alarm system: an intense feeling of suffocation. This is one of the most distressing sensations designed by the genetic plan. The neural computer polarizes the whole of the subject's attention on one issue: more oxygen must necessarily be breathed. A subject who is undergoing this emotional torture is evidently unable to drive, write poetry or make love. If the neural computer learns that no oxygen is being received – either because of the place where the subject finds himself, or because the respiratory channels have been obstructed – it activates the highest possible degree of suffocation in this particular emotional densitometer. A person who dies of suffocation must necessarily undergo this gruesome torture. Those who do not breathe in a sufficient quantity of oxygen, because some part of their respiratory system has broken down, are relentlessly subjected to the emotional penalty that the neural computer, a merciless automatic machine, makes them suffer.

The Law of Oxygen Quality

When a car runs out of petrol, it stops; when a human being runs out of oxygen, it also stops. If we filled a car's petrol tank with a combination of petrol, water, wine and other chemical substances, the motor would probably stop, break down, or not function properly.

In a similar manner, not merely the quantity of oxygen breathed in, but also its quality, makes a difference to the human body. What happens when the oxygen that enters the lungs is combined with organic gases, with gaseous waste from automobiles or factories, or with any other gases that are harmful to the human body?

Nature has foreseen this problem and included an ingenious system to confront it in its providential genetic plan. The subject is not an expert in chemistry or biochemistry, nor does he know what the chemical composition of an organic gas is, nor what gases are beneficial to his organism, nor for what reasons they are either vital or hazardous. The neural computer, aided by the respiratory system, not only measures the exact quantity of oxygen that is breathed in from the outside, but also detects the presence of nearly every gas that tries to infiltrate into the body, even if it is combined with many other gases. It is also equipped to analyse the exact composition of every one of these gases.

If the quality of the oxygen breathed is adequate, and if it is not combined with harmful gases, the neural computer does not provide the individual with the report it has received from the olfactory 'customs officers', and leaves him alone. However, the neural computer will inform the subject about the entrance of any furtive gases or harmful 'visitors' by activating the emotional mechanisms devised by the genetic plan. If the olfactory antennae detect an organic gas which has illicitly penetrated the body, the neural computer will trigger off an unpleasant feeling of low intensity, since the damage caused to the respiratory republic is minor. However, even in this case we should not fail to notice the infinite wisdom and prudence of nature. The emotional fine is greater if the organic gas has been expelled by another person. If the gas has come out of the exhaust pipe of an ageing bus and it penetrates the body, the neural computer activates a more severe emotional penalty. And if the car in front of us expels a sickly bluish gas that reaches our lungs, the neural computer triggers off an even more unpleasant sensation. As an extreme case, if the biological 'customs officers' of the pulmonary republic detect the presence of terrorist gases that may destroy the entire machine, the neural computer activates an emotional mechanism which constitutes a truly unbearable torture. The brain's message could again be translated as follows: 'If you escape these gases, I shall cease to torture you in this manner.'

This law of oxygen quality may conflict with other biosocial laws. If a mother breathes in lethal gases during a fire in her own home, she will be impelled by the ghastly emotional mechanism of suffocation to abandon the house immediately. However, if her baby is still trapped inside, the biosocial law of maternity will pressure her with other equally irresistible emotional mechanisms to rescue him at all costs.

The Law of Respiratory Rhythm

The marvellously ingenious government of the respiratory republic also regulates the rhythm, or speed, at which oxygen enters the body. The neural computer alters the rhythm of the pulmonary 'bellows', according to two laws established by the genetic plan: the law of wakefulness and sleep (two different rhythms) and the law of the energy required at any particular moment. The neural computer is fully informed about the energy required by the diverse ministries of the organic republic. If a person begins to climb a steep hill, his legs will ask the neural computer for supplementary energy in order to compensate for this special effort. The neural computer will then accelerate the rhythm of the pulmonary 'bellows' and increase the quantity of fuel received. If the stomach needs extra energy in order to carry out a difficult digestion, the neural computer will also increase the rhythm of the lungs. This also occurs during sexual intercourse, in order to compensate for the amount of energy that is consumed. It is noteworthy that the neural computer automatically alters the rhythm of the lungs, without ever consulting the subject. However, when the rhythm changes from a normal velocity to a higher one, the neural computer begins to disturb the subject as follows: 'For every degree of excess speed, the subject will feel a higher degree of unpleasantness.' The cyclist, or the marathon runner, is pressured by this emotional law, and their neural computers punish them for infringing it. 'Stop running,' the brain commands the marathon runner, 'and I shall cease to disturb you with this unpleasant sensation.' The subject understands this message perfectly, but is also pressured by more powerful emotional mechanisms of a biosocial kind: 'Continue running. Make an even greater effort. If you give up, you will be forced to suffer shame and ridicule. You will also be deprived of the pleasure of victory.' Marathon runners have to pay this high emotional price for infringing the law of respiratory rhythm, in order to purchase the sweet compensations that the neural computer sells to the winner.

The margin of liberty the genetic plan has reserved for the subject in this domain – that of the law of respiratory rhythm – is extremely limited. The subject can stop breathing for a few seconds or augment the respiratory rhythm for a while, such as when the doctor orders him to hold his breath, or to breathe faster. However, the marathon runner cannot diminish the accelerated respiratory rhythm triggered off by his brain. I have never heard of anyone who has died after going on an 'oxygen strike'. In other words, I have never known of someone who, for whatever reasons, was able to defeat the emotional law of suffocation by voluntarily obstructing the entrance of oxygen until causing death.

We can now, from a new perspective, discover the rigour, the precision, and the purpose of the emotional laws, which function with the same independence from the subject as biochemical laws. The respiratory system is not only a biochemical system, but is also an emotional one. Were it not for the brain's warnings of all infractions of certain biochemical laws, and of the gravity of such infractions – the lack of oxygen, the entrance of harmful gases, or the excessive rhythm of the organic bellows – and were it not for the brain's ability to pressure the subject by means of emotional threats, promises, punishments and rewards, the organic machine would inevitably and irreversibly break down (in other words, the individual would die). Every human being is a slave who works twenty-four hours a day for the respiratory system, from the cradle to the grave, inhaling and exhaling under the emotional supervision of his neural computer. If he keeps the rhythm of his pulmonary bellows steady, if he breathes in the required quantity of the prescribed fuel, and if no forbidden gases creep into the body, the neural computer will allow him to live in peace. However, if he violates any of these laws, this processor in his head will compel him to suffer emotional penalties.

Emotional Control of Coughing and Sneezing

Nature has foreseen the possibility of foreign bodies and of dangerous microscopic animals which can obstruct the respiratory process by surreptitiously entering the body. Having anticipated this problem, Nature has designed an ingenious biological system to expel all *personae non gratae*, or dangerous foreigners who may invade the respiratory republic.

One of these mechanisms of expulsion is the cough – a biophysical, biochemical, emotional mechanism. The subject is never aware of the fact that a given noxious item has penetrated a particular organ of the respiratory system – a fish bone in the trachea, millions of bacterial organisms in the olfactory channels, or water in the lungs – nor does he know how much harm it can bring to the system. The neural computer, however, is an expert in all of these highly complex scientific issues. All of the organs, bellows, channels and laboratories of the respiratory system are endowed with a system that can detect the furtive entrance of any physical or chemical body (a bacterial organism or an apple pip). These sophisticated systems of detection, via the nervous system, keep the brain informed at all times about the entrance of any foreign bodies, about their physical and chemical characteristics (the size of a pip and its chemical composition), and about their precise location (a given section of a particular channel).

The neural computer, according to the guidelines set by the bio-natural program on invasions of foreign bodies, informs the individual about the presence of a particular body that has infiltrated into the respiratory system, and incites him to expel it by automatically activating a particular emotional mechanism: the urge to cough. The neural computer triggers off the emotional densitometer of these urges at an intensity proportional to the degree of danger the intrusion of such a foreign body represents, by calculating the number of bacterial organisms or the quantity of water that has invaded the lungs, the importance of the affected organ, and the general state of the entire organism.

Anyone can verify the varying intensities of the urges to cough: minor, intense, extremely intense or truly 'irresistible'. By means of these diverse emotional commands, the neural computer orders the subject to carry out a specific task for the respiratory republic: to repeatedly activate certain muscles at a prescribed rhythm until the neural computer cancels the urges. The same neural computer which, according to the bionatural program on expelling foreign bodies from the respiratory system, advises the subject to cough, also automatically consults its biocultural programs. If any of these programs prohibits the activation of these muscles in public, the same neural computer will advise the subject either to resist the urges to cough, or to perform this organic task somewhere else, by activating emotional threats proportional to the gravity of the infraction. The penalty of shame and ridicule can be extremely severe, for instance, if a subject dares to cough during a classical guitar recital inside a concert hall.

These two conflicting laws – that which protects the interests of the somatic republic and that which defends the cause of the social republic – can put the subject in extremely difficult situations. A typical example – often employed in films, novels and situation comedies – is that of the man who, due to the sudden arrival of his mistress's husband at two o'clock in the morning, jumps out of bed and hides in a wardrobe fulls of coats and hangers. As soon as his neural computer learns of the invasion of dust, fluff and other foreign particles, it activates the urge to cough at 80 or 90 degrees. At the same time, however, the neural computer threatens this lover with severe emotional penalties due to the danger which being caught in such a situation represents for him. The subject will do his best to resist the urge to cough, but his will may succumb to the unrelenting emotional pressure of his neural computer. The mechanism of sneezing is comparable to those of vomiting and diarrhoea. All three are biological emergency mechanisms. The neural computer suddenly unleashes such a powerful emotional mechanism that before the individual has any time to think about it, he has performed the task demanded of him. In principle the subject has the last word, and the neural processor asks for his authorization. However, the brain subjects him to such emotional pressure that, in spite of his efforts, he may be unable to prevent the occurrence of this sonorous organic expulsion. The invention of the handkerchief, an instrument employed to muffle the blaring sound of a sneeze, is one of the many cases in which we discover reason working as a slave for culture: *ratio ancilla culturae.*

Emotional Control of Scratching

Throughout the layer of skin that covers the human body, nature has installed biological 'customs officers' which detect the presence, and particularly the entrance, of foreign bodies. Whether it be on the big toe of the left foot, on the end of one's nose, or in the crevices of other more 'private' parts, these biological 'customs officers' are on the alert twenty-four hours a day. If a mosquito silently lands behind someone's left ear, injects its minute organic syringe, and begins to dine at the 'host's' expense, the latter, who at that very moment is reading the newspaper, can neither see nor smell this mischievous bug. His biological 'customs officers', however, are capable of detecting its presence and informing the brain about where the invasion has taken place, about the seriousness of the wound, and about the biochemical characteristics of whatever the mosquito takes and leaves (perhaps some extremely dangerous bacterial organisms).

The neural computer, after consulting the bionatural program on this sort of invasion, activates an emotional mechanism that is different from all the rest: the urge to scratch. When the neural computer triggers off this sensation, it achieves the following two objectives:

(1) It informs the subject about the presence of this treacherous insect and about the fact it has bitten him in a particular zone of his corporal geography; (2) it advises the subject to scratch the area that has been invaded, offering him a particular emotional salary in return (proportional to the seriousness of the bite). Thanks to this ingenious biochemical and emotional mechanism, the subject can send the mosquito away, although this stubborn animal may attempt to land in other parts of the body and continue its dinner.

If Descartes had read the previous paragraph, he might have insisted on denigrating all feelings for being deceptive informants, in an attempt to defeat me in the emotional game of 'being right' (a favourite, rather irrational sport all thinkers practise). He might have said: 'Can't you see that the information feelings provide us with is always faulty? They are unable to prevent the mosquito's attack. They only inform us when it is already too late. The mosquito wins out.' My response to this Cartesian objection would be that here we can detect a small flaw in the emotional system as an informative system, but that it is unjust to present only one side of the coin as if it was the coin in its entirety. Thanks to the amazingly efficient functioning of this ingenious mechanism of scratching, the subject is able to know when and where a flea is dining at his expense, to get rid of this impertinent little animal, and perhaps even to catch it after a prolonged hunt.

One should also say that according to the general plan which regulates the whole of the animal kingdom, each species is programmed to surprise members of other species, to suck some of their blood, and often to kill and then eat them. Nature seems to have distributed the possibilities of winning and losing this game in a democratic manner. The flea and the mosquito risk their lives when they land on and introduce their organic syringes into the human body, and their neural computers undoubtedly warn them about this risk. However, their minute bodies, and their ability to fly, in the case of the mosquito, and to jump, in the case of the flea, permit these insects to outsmart even an Einstein's neural computer, and to enjoy a banquet at the expense of his blood and his patience. Whenever we see a cow employing its tail to get rid of the flies that have landed on its posterior, it is evident that this cow's neural computer has informed it of the presence of these insects by activating a similar emotional mechanism, since no other sensory antenna (visual, phonic or olfactory) could have done so.

Sometimes the invasion of cutaneous zones comes from the inside, such as in the case of measles. What purpose does it serve to scratch oneself in such cases? Does scratching interrupt the interior invasion of bacteria? Considering what we know about the function of the emotional system, it seems evident that if the neural computer offers the subject an emotional salary for performing this task, then for some reason it benefits the parts of the body that have been invaded by internal or external enemies.

Occasionally, certain articles of clothing disturb a person's skin cells. These cells then send their complaint to the neural computer, and the latter informs and bothers the subject by activating an uncomfortable itch. The brain's message could be translated as follows: 'Remove that article of clothing and I shall cease to annoy you.' However, the neural computer also unconsciously assimilates the cultural code prevailing in the subject's society which regulates the act of scratching. It may be permitted to scratch one's hands or face in public, but not other more 'private' parts of the body. The neural computer may activate an irresistible itch in the 'private' parts of a university professor while he lectures in front of three hundred students, due to the fabric of his new pair of underpants. 'Scratch yourself,' his neural computer insists. However, this same neural computer, according to the biocultural program which regulates the manual action, also sends him the following warning: 'If you scratch that somatic zone, I shall punish you with shame and ridicule.' Here we can again point to a hierarchical law: 'The higher the position of the person who infringes this law, the greater the infraction and the corresponding penalty.' If the Pope or the Queen of England violated this cultural law in public, they would be punished with a much higher degree of shame and ridicule than an ordinary citizen who did the same.

Scratching one's head or other parts of the body can develop into a habit or a nervous tic. Such occurrences constitute minor breakdowns of a person's neural computer. With age, some of these extremely sophisticated biochemical or emotional mechanisms become deteriorated. When it 'becomes nervous', the brain activates an irresistible itch, when in fact it should only do so during a flea invasion or an attack of measles.

Human beings have discovered that if they scratch the spots brought about by chickenpox, the scars that remain will permanently disfigure their skin. This can provoke a fierce emotional battle between a somatic program and a social one. The former can increase the scratching densitometer to its highest intensity: 'If you do not scratch yourself now, I shall continue to torture you with this irresistible itch.' The social/biosocial program, however, strikes back: 'Scratch yourself now and ridicule awaits you tomorrow. Everyone will pity your scarred face.' The subject, after a harsh, prolonged struggle against the itching mechanism, finally gives up and begins to scratch himself.

Here we can observe a new biological law of the emotional system, which we could refer to as the 'law of the emotional vent'. Once the subject begins to scratch himself, the neural computer will activate a new densitometer of irresistible urges: 'the densitometer of the open emotional vent'. If a subject who has been resisting intense urges to scratch himself – in order to avoid leaving permanent scars on his face – suddenly gives up and begins to do so, he will continue to scratch himself anxiously. The same occurs with the opening of the physical and biochemical emotional vent of the urges to urinate, ejaculate, eat, hit, evacuate and other urges which I shall discuss later. When the subject has resisted the pressure of an emotional current, if he ultimately gives in and opens an emotional vent, the latter will overflow by order of the neural computer. The subject then urinates, ejaculates, kisses, hits or scratches himself like a puppet manipulated by the emotional strings of his brain.

If the biological 'customs officers' of the skin inform the neural computer that the intruder which has perforated the skin is considerably more dangerous than a mosquito and that the poison that has been deposited is significantly more harmful (such as that of a bee, a scorpion, a tarantula or a snake), the brain will let the subject know about the gravity of the invasion by activating substantially more painful emotional mechanisms than the minor itch triggered off by a flea bite.

The neural computer, after taking into account the seriousness of the invasion and the bionatural program that stipulates which emotional mechanisms are to be activated, may release an intense pain in the affected area. In this way, it will advise the subject to cancel the use of his hand, if this is where the snake has bitten him, and warn him not to allow any objects to touch this part of his body. It may also make the subject feel queasy, and hence advise him not to consume any energy with other activities, so that it may all be employed in the struggle against the pernicious invader, which could irreversibly destroy the whole of the organic republic.

The Emotional Control of the Contact and Penetration of Clothing, Needles, Knives, Tubes and Other Objects

Human beings are the only animals that wear clothes and cosmetics. No animal other than the human being is subjected to a biocultural code that obliges him to dress or make himself up according to extremely precise rules, the violation of which can be punished with severe emotional penalties. Certain articles of clothing, cosmetics, earrings, metallic objects, ropes and other items can damage the somatic republic. Tightly fitting clothes can interfere with the circulation of the bloodstream, while certain cosmetics can obstruct the millions of cutaneous channels on the surface of the skin, and hinder the excretion of sweat and other particles which must leave the body. Nothing escapes the attention of the unconscious neural computer, always aided by its incredibly efficient 'secret service'. The biological 'customs officers' of the skin punctually inform the neural computer about the amount of damage that is being done to the body, and about the precise location where this is occurring. The brain then informs the subject about this state of affairs, and pressures him to remove the article of clothing, or the cosmetic, by means of an emotional mechanism of an intensity mathematically proportional to the damage the object in question is causing.

During the traditional Holy Week processions which take place in Spain, numerous penitents walk for hours wrapped up tightly in layers of rope. These men are forced to pay an extremely severe emotional fine for damaging their respiratory, circulatory and cutaneous systems. Their neural computers, however, have been programmed from childhood with the biocultural code of Holy Week penitence, and hence pressure them with even stronger emotional mechanisms to suffer this torture. A monk, whose brain has been programmed with biocultural norms that require the wearing of hair shirts and the use of other instruments of penitence, pays the emotional price imposed by his neural computer for damaging the somatic republic in order to buy other 'superior' pleasures: intimacy with God, the admiration of the faithful, and the hope of limitless happiness in the afterlife. A woman who tortures herself with a pair of shoes she can barely squeeze into is pressured by her feet's bionatural defence lawyer as follows: 'Take these shoes off immediately and you will be able to walk and live in peace.' The biocultural defence lawyer, however, strikes back: 'These shoes make your feet look elegant. Imagine the shame and the ridicule you would feel if everyone saw the bunions on your unattractive feet. Imagine their laughter!'

Here lies one of the genetic frontiers between human beings and apes. An orang-outang would never place shackles on its feet for religious reasons, nor would a female gorilla injure herself with an extremely tight-fitting corset in order to make herself look more attractive. As in other domains, the emotional mechanisms that defend society are often more powerful than those which support the somatic republic or the life of the member of a species, which is not merely the *Homo sapiens* (the thinking animal) but also the *Homo emotionalis* or *Homo sentiens* (the feeling animal).

Pins and needles

I was once about to take part in a televised debate in Los Angeles, when suddenly I felt as if someone had pricked my genitals with a needle. As soon as I crossed my legs, this sensation became more painful. I politely excused myself, got up from my seat, and walked towards my dressing room fretting about what could possibly be happening to me. A brief investigation revealed that a pin had somehow found its way to this private, delicate area of the male anatomy. We all ought to marvel at the amazingly sophisticated system of biological detection and information which has been invented, manufactured, installed and maintained by Nature. I, the subject, was occupied and preoccupied by the debate in which I was about to take part, and had no idea about what was happening in a particularly sensitive part of my body. My visual, phonic or olfactory antennae could not have detected the presence of a needle in this private zone. The biological 'customs officers' located there, however, detected the invasion of this minute lance and immediately informed the brain of its presence. After consulting the relevant program, the neural computer then informed me about the incident and advised me to do something about it unless I wished to continue receiving its emotional pricks.

A needle's invasion of any part of the body is immediately detected by the biological 'customs officers' of the skin, who relay the exact results of their investigation to the neural computer; the latter consults its bionatural and biocultural programs, and then informs the subject about where, how deeply, and when the sharp end of a needle has pierced the left foot's little toe. It also advises him to remove it by activating an emotional mechanism proportional to the damage done (calculating the extension and the depth of the incision and the importance of the affected organ: less intensity for the sole of the foot than for a testicle or an eye), and may advise him to continue pricking himself in accordance with another program. Such is the case of the insertion of a syringe's needle. The brain advises the individual not to allow the doctor to prick him, and punishes him with an emotional penalty corresponding to a bionatural law;

but it also advises him to let the doctor do his job by pushing him with opposed emotional pressures that a monkey would not be able to decipher. An ape would also be incapable of understanding why a shaman, a wizard or a witch should introduce long, sharp needles into his face and body during the course of a magical or religious ceremony.

Emotional pressures of a biosocial and biocultural kind allow these human beings to withstand the pain triggered off by their brains (which may also be softened by the effects of certain drugs).

Knives and swords

The brain contains a pre-installed plan of accident prevention. If the ocular cameras inform the neural computer about the presence and the nearness of a sharp knife, the biological processor will make the subject visualize an imaginary documentary warning him that if this instrument penetrates his body, he will experience severe pain of varying intensity, depending on the importance of the affected zone (higher for the lungs, lower for a leg). However, in spite of these cunningly designed mechanisms of prevention, a human being can commit the ritual suicide known in Japan as *seppuku* (also known outside Japan as *hara-kiri*) by stabbing his own heart with a sword. This sacrifice, dedicated to Japan and its emperor, is traditionally looked upon by Japanese society as a noble, courageous act. It is not spontaneously performed, but requires several years of training. It is not a typical act of suicide, but an elaborate ceremony during which special garments are worn and in which several officiants take part, a particular recitation is pronounced, and a sword is introduced in a ritual manner. With his own blood, the protagonist must then write 'Long live Japan!' on a silk canvas. This demonstrates that after a long period of training, the brain can acquire a biocultural program of this nature – the *seppuku* program – which can move a human being to stab himself with a sword by means of certain emotional mechanisms that can defeat the conflicting feelings which attempt to dissuade him from committing such a crime against his own body.

The members of numerous human religious and/or territorial societies take part in ritual ceremonies where tattoos, incisions and deep cuts are made on their bodies. Jewish children are circumcised for various social reasons (the hygienic motives adduced are not the genuine reasons, or at least not the only reasons for carrying out this operation). Circumcision is like a three-pronged social label which is attached to the body of a child: it is a label which denotes his sexual, his religious and his territorial identity. Furthermore, it is a visual, a mental and an emotional mechanism. It is a flag placed on an organ which is constantly looked at, touched, and, above all, stored in the biocultural files of the brain. Whenever this flag is seen, the emotional flag in the brain is strengthened. Numerous tribes have placed this kind of sexual or territorial flag of identification on the body by means of tattoos or cuts which can never be removed. When male adolescent members of the Nuer – a territorial society in Sudan – are initiated and ritually transformed into virile adults, they must lie down and remain immobile with their arms folded and their mouths shut, while the master of ceremonies cuts open five grooves on their forehead with a sharp knife that is sunk in until it makes contact with their skulls (without employing any kind of anaesthesia). These five scars adorn the forehead of a male Nuer adult until the time of his death. One of the worst ways of insulting a member of this society in public is to say that his or her brother, boyfriend, father or husband cried when these grooves were cut open. When the neural computer of one of these Nuer adolescents is informed about this injury by the biological 'customs officers' at the forehead, it activates an extremely painful emotional mechanism. The brain's message could be translated as follows: 'Shout, run, avoid this pain at all costs, or you will continue to receive an emotional stab every time the knife makes an incision.' However, the biocultural code of Nuer virility strikes back: 'Do not move a muscle; do not scream; do not cry. Be a man. Be a Nuer. Otherwise, you will be the laughing-stock of the village. You will be too ashamed to even show your face in public.' Once again, we find human beings caught between opposed emotional forces. Shame and ridicule are even more powerful emotional mechanisms than the extremely intense pain with which the neural computer attempts to defend the life of the subject's body.

The Organic Cameras and Photographic Laboratories

All photographers and photographic lab technicians know how to take proper care of cameras in order to ensure that they stay in good condition, and they also know how to repair them if they break down. The marvellously sophisticated genetic plan, which has designed the photographic cameras and laboratories of the human body, has also established a series of laws and biochemical emotional mechanisms which warn the subject about any hindrance to the functioning of these organic instruments, and about any type of damage to them.

The emotional law of light intensity

A biological 'cinematographer' measures the intensity of the light which enters a person's organic cameras at all times, and immediately communicates this information to the brain. If the intensity of the light exceeds the limit foreseen by the relevant program, the neural computer informs the subject about this infraction by means of an emotional penalty proportional to the seriousness of the infraction. If the driver of a car approaching us from the opposite direction flashes its powerful headlights in our eyes, we can verify the workings of this biochemical/emotional law. In such a case, we are punished with an uncomfortable sensation advising us to avoid the excessive intensity of such a light for the benefit of our organic cameras. People who work in television studios are forced to pay this emotional price – in return for other emotional benefits – because they constantly have to face extremely powerful lights. If we look directly at the sun on a clear day, the neural computer activates an extremely unpleasant sensation which pressures us to focus our organic cameras elsewhere. Our brains thus warn us about the dangers of looking at solar light. It is also worth noting that powerful lights are often employed as instruments of torture.

The emotional law of fatigue

Like film cameras, our eyes are equipped to take different types of shots. The muscles which activate the focusing mechanism inform the brain of each shot, or change, and of the time that passes during each of these takes. If the neural computer discovers that a particular shot exceeds the time of duration prescribed by the relevant bionatural program, it warns the subject about this infraction and advises him to change the shot by activating a painful sensation (a discomfort in the eyes), which will be intensified if he fails to obey the command. The writer/reader may insist on maintaining the same shot due to opposed emotional pressures of a social kind, and this may provoke the gradual deterioration of his organic cameras (progressive myopia and other irreparable injuries).

The emotional law on the intrusion of foreign bodies

Like both photographic and film cameras, our eyes are equipped with a 'cap' that can prevent the intrusion of foreign bodies. These unwanted objects could impede accurate shots of the selected visual field or damage the 'lens'. Once again we discover an ingenious mechanism which protects these fragile instruments. If the biological 'customs officers' in the eyes inform the brain that a foreign body is about to crash into them, the neural computer will activate an emotional mechanism of emergency: 'Look out! Cover your organic cameras, or you shall pay an emotional fine.' This emotional mechanism is comparable to sneezing, diarrhoea and vomiting. Although in principle the subject has the last word, before he can think about it he has placed the 'lens cap' on his organic cameras. This emotional mechanism is as wonderfully agile and efficient as the instantaneous mobility of the 'lens cap' devised by nature, which is always within the subject's reach.

If, in spite of all the genetic mechanisms of prevention, a minute grain of dust or sand slips through and lands on the organic cameras, it cannot be detected by the ocular, phonic or olfactory antennae. The biological inspectors installed by nature to detect the intrusion of these particles inform the brain about its presence, and the neural computer then lets the subject know about the incident, advising him to carefully rid himself of the invader, by triggering off an uncomfortable sensation proportional to the seriousness of the damage. The emotional penalty reserved for the slicing of an eyeball by a razor blade is one of the most horrific mechanisms the neural computer has at its disposal. The mere sight of such an occurrence in *Un Chien Andalou*, the celebrated short by Luis Buñuel and Salvador Dali, is penalized by the neural computer with a feeling of severe disgust. The first time I saw this film several people in the audience screamed with terror.

The emotional control of the organic microphones and sound laboratories

The delicate organic microphones and the sophisticated sound laboratories which nature has designed and installed on each side of the head measure the precise intensity of the sounds that reach them, and immediately send the results of this investigation to the brain. The neural computer then consults the law of phonic intensity and warns the subject about any infractions, advising him to obey by activating an uncomfortable sensation proportional to the seriousness of the violation. Anyone can verify the rigour and the mathematical precision of this physical, biochemical, emotional law. If the volume on a television set is a little too loud, the enjoyment of whatever we are watching is disturbed. If the volume is turned up to its maximum, the noise becomes unbearable. We should notice that none of us knows what volume best suits our organic sound labs, nor can we measure loudness in the way that a sound technician could by employing the appropriate equipment. It is the 'technicians' which work within our organic labs that measure the intensity of all incoming sounds. The brain unconsciously 'knows' what volume is best for us. It continuously contrasts the information received from the sound labs with the intensity prescribed by the relevant program. If the volume of the incoming sound fully coincides with that which is registered in the program, the neural computer allows the subject to enjoy the film he is watching. However, as soon as this law is slightly infringed, the brain immediately whispers an emotional message into his ear: 'Turn the volume down a little.' If the volume greatly exceeds the intensity prescribed by the genetic plan, the neural computer will prevent the subject from enjoying the film by flogging him with the emotional whip.

Aided by the different organic labs and antennae, the neural computer pressures us to obey all of the laws that regulate the use, as well as the maintenance, of our eyes and our ears. Were it not for the emotional system, this would be impossible. Our eyes and our ears could be destroyed without us ever taking any notice.

Certain biocultural programs conflict with this bionatural law of sound intensity. In contemporary Western society, adolescents are pressured to infringe this law by a severe generational precept. In rock concerts, as well as in night clubs, musical quality is equated with sound intensity: 'the higher the volume, the better the music'. (The renowned classical guitarist Andrés Segovia thought that the correct equation was precisely the opposite: 'the lower the volume, the better the music'.) Most adolescents do not question this cultural, generational precept, as is usually the case when it comes to social precepts. An adolescent who dared to publicly question the validity of this equation ('the more noise, the better') would be penalized with shame and ridicule, and excommunicated from his generational society like a 'heretic' from a religious group or a 'dissident' from an ideological sect. Adolescents sacrifice both the damage done to their ears and the corresponding emotional penalty they suffer on the altar of their generation. Do the brains of these adolescents eventually acquire this program and create an emotional addiction to this excessive volume? Indeed, their neural computers eventually pressure them to listen to excessively loud volume even when they listen to it in their cars or through their headphones. The brain continues to penalize them for infringing the bionatural law of sound intensity. However, once again, the emotional mechanisms of a biocultural program, which upholds a series of social norms (the generational society is particularly strict), defeat the emotional mechanisms that defend the poor, ill-treated somatic republic. A new ailment has developed as a result of this: the partial deafness provoked by repeated infractions of the bionatural law of sound intensity (another variation of the *cultura inimica naturae* theme).

In numerous societies certain cultural precepts require that people's ears be pierced, and that earrings be hung from them. The same neural computer that pressures a subject to wear these adornments by means of emotional threats, also warns him that he is causing minor damage to these organs. Nothing that invades the human body and causes damage to it, no matter how minor the injury may be, can escape the notice of the biological secret service agents of the brain; nor do the latter ever fail to inform the neural computer about the intrusion; nor does the brain ever cease to warn the subject about it. This triple biological law admits no exceptions or infractions.

The Emotional Control of Phonic Monotony

There is a bionatural law installed in the brain which we could refer to as the emotional law of phonic monotony. A musical phrase we may find agreeable, such as 'Yesterday, all our troubles seemed so far away', can become unbearable if the record breaks and we are forced to hear it over and over again. Here lies a clue that can help us to discover the law. The biological 'customs officers' of the auditory system control the intensity of incoming sound, its quality, and also its variety or monotony.

A two-year-old child does not seem to tire of hearing the same phrase, the same song, or the same story. As soon as a father has finished singing a particular nursery rhyme for his two-year-old daughter, the latter removes her pacifier and says: 'Again! Again!' The child continues to ask for more repetitions, while the father begins to lose his patience. Freud noticed this curious phenomenon, and treated it as a mysterious enigma.

Here we can discover the astuteness of nature and its ingenious genetic plans. The cultural files of this two-year-old child are practically empty. Her neural computer is programmed to gradually acquire a biological library, a dictionary and a record collection. A biocultural program is acquired through practice or repeated listening. For this reason the neural computer of the two-year-old girl pressures her to listen to the same song over and over again. The child is unaware of this law (not even Freud became aware of it, although he was very close). Her small brain, however, pressures her to listen to the tune repeatedly, by activating emotional mechanisms. The neural computer is programmed with a law of phonic variety or monotony according to the age of the subject and the amount of acquired recordings contained in the brain's archives. Neither the two-year-old girl, nor a forty-year-old woman, knows how many times she ought to listen to a particular melody, symphony, popular tune, phrase, sound or series of sounds. She does not have to worry about this. Her neural computer, in accordance with this precise law, will tell her when to stop by sending her an emotional message: for every degree of excess, the emotional penalty will be raised by one degree.

Whenever we listen to a melody that we like, the brain pays us an emotional salary for contributing to enriching its biocultural record collection. We may then listen to it again: *Bis repetita placent.* The brain pays us another amount of pleasure. Suppose we listen to it a third time. The brain may then send the following message to us: 'All right, one last time.' If we listen to it a fourth time, the brain will warn us: 'If this continues, you are going to be punished with an uncomfortable feeling.' If we are forced to continue listening to the tune, the brain will gradually increase the emotional fine. It is noteworthy that this genetically designed emotional punishment has been exploited to torture people both in medieval and in modern times.

In this, as in so many other domains, there are bionatural and biocultural programs which either co-operate or conflict with one another. A person who says the rosary, during which the same prayer is repeated fifty times in a row, infringes the law of phonic monotony and must therefore pay the prescribed emotional fine. Such a devotee of Mary, however, is more than happy to suffer this minor penalty in order to attain other emotional benefits. The same applies to those who shave their heads, grow a pony tail, and repeatedly chant 'Hare krishna . . . ' through the streets (I shall continue to discuss this law in later chapters).

The Emotional Control of Entries through the Anus

As we saw in chapter 5, the anus is programmed to evacuate solid, gaseous, and, exceptionally, liquid waste. However, the penetration of solids, liquids and gases through this channel is wholly prohibited by the genetic plan. The biological 'customs officers' detect the presence or the penetration of any foreign bodies through this orifice, analyse its characteristics, and immediately communicate it to the brain: 'A foreign body of such and such physical characteristics (size, rigidity, and so on), of such and such a chemical composition (e.g. salty water), and of such and such a temperature, has penetrated x milimetres into the rectum.' Once the brain has consulted the relevant program, it notifies the subject about this incident and advises him to impede its presence and gradual penetration by activating an uncomfortable sensation proportional to the damage caused. The neural computer triggers off a minor pain for the penetration of a suppository, and an extremely intense pain for the penetration of a pointed stick (a torture employed in certain inhuman societies). Goya portrayed the latter in one of his *Horrors*.

In some species, such as that of wolves, two males reach a final confrontation during which the leadership of the society (the wolf pack) is decided. The wolf that loses the game adopts the position of a female, and the victor simulates mating. This clearly constitutes a hierarchical rite, or a presidential investiture. In numerous human cultures, a professional or political victory is also referred to as 'giving it to someone up the . . . ', alluding to the taboo word which refers to this noble bodily organ of which the human being is ashamed. The neural computer punishes the male who is made to play the female role (even if only in a metaphorical sense) by activating a feeling of humiliation in him. If a male is raped by another male (a common occurrence in prisons, where a young male may easily represent the female role in a womanless desert), his neural computer will punish him with an uncomfortable feeling for the penetration of a foreign body in a forbidden place, and with a high dose of repulsion, shame and ridicule for having been forced to play the female role. Gastroenterologists currently employ a long tube which is inserted through the rectum in order to explore the colon, take photographs and extract tissue from this area. The patient is first given a sedative in order to withstand the emotional pressures of the brain, which in the eloquent language of feelings clamours: 'Don't let them put that thing into you!'

An Oxford professor and good friend of mine was advised to submit himself to an X-ray exam in order to find out whether he had a congenital malformation in his intestines. 'It's a very simple procedure,' the doctor told him. 'Of course, you will be given an enema.' 'Right', replied the professor, who did not actually understand the meaning of this term. When he arrived at the hospital on the scheduled day, a young attractive nurse asked him to come with her into a private room. 'It must be my lucky day,' thought the professor. 'Please remove your trousers, sir,' said the nurse with a caring smile, 'and your underwear, of course.' The professor did not know what to think, but he soon discovered the meaning of the word 'enema', a definition he would never forget. After receiving this unexpected irrigation, he went to the toilet. 'How do you feel?', asked the nurse. 'Not so well, actually,' answered the afflicted professor. 'Don't worry. It's normal to feel dizzy and nauseous. Are you in pain?', asked the nurse. 'I don't think I could feel any worse,' said the ill-fated professor. Pale, and in a cold sweat, he came out of the toilet. 'Please remove your trousers again, sir,' the nurse commanded. 'What? Again?', asked the stupefied academic. 'I shall have to continue giving you enemas until your intestines are entirely clean. If not, the X-rays will be no good.' After more than a dozen of these operations, the professor went to the X-ray room. He was told to lie on a bed, where he felt as if he had just undergone one of the inhuman tortures devised by the infamous inquisitor Torquemada. 'How do you feel?', asked the doctor. 'I've had better days,' said the professor. The nurse then reappeared with a long, thick tube. 'What's that for?', asked the professor anxiously. 'I'm going to pour a white emulsion into your intestines, so that we can see their configuration on the screen.' After this final, unexpected invasion, the professor implored the doctor: 'Please, hurry up. I can't hold it any longer.' The doctor completely ignored this plea, turned to the nurse, and said, 'More emulsion, please.' The exasperated professor insisted once again, 'I really can't hold it any longer.' The doctor, however, remained indifferent and once again ordered the nurse to pour more emulsion into his intestines. The professor was forced to resist for five more minutes, which seemed to last five centuries. The doctor found no abnormalities in the configuration of his intestinal geography.

I have related this amusing incident because it is of great anthropological interest for our purposes. In this example we find several emotional forces acting against each other. The brain advises the subject to remove immediately the tube that has been inserted through an orifice designed solely to evacuate waste, by activating an extremely disagreeable sensation. When the biological 'customs officers' in the intestines inform the brain about an intrusion of salt water that is flooding the intestines, the neural computer triggers off other emotional mechanisms of punishment and dissuasion: pain, queasiness and dizziness. The subject is thus mercilessly tortured by his brain. The bionatural laws installed in the neural computer activate very powerful emotional mechanisms to let the subject know that this invasion of foreign bodies represents a serious threat to the digestive system and to the whole of the somatic republic. Once again, we marvel at the existence, the functioning, and the aims of such wise laws and precise mechanisms. Nature advises and pressures the subject, but it does not take any steps without his consent.

The genetic plan has also foreseen other needs, and devised other laws and emotional mechanisms. The cultural software of this professor's neural computer contains programs on health and on medical science. These include precepts such as 'doctors can cause you short-term pain in order to improve your health and perhaps save your life'. (It is also true, however, that this program includes the faith in medicine, as well as the doubts that all forms of faith engender.) The case of this professor is therefore interesting for our purposes. He confesses that, had he known the meaning of the word 'enema' and had he been aware of the pain that such a procedure entails, he would have foregone the X-rays altogether. Once he was 'trapped', his neural computer subjected him not only to the emotional punishments prescribed for this sort of invasion, but also to other similarly severe emotional threats of a biosocial character: 'If you give up and tell the nurse that you cannot resist these irrigations, you will be the laughing-stock of the faculty of medicine, and the rumour will undoubtedly spread throughout Oxford.' The fear of these emotional penalties allow this patient to resist the opposed emotional forces which cry out: 'Stop this torture now! Pull that odious tube out immediately!' Once again, the laws of the beehive defeat the laws of the individual in this emotional duel where a person is as much subject and referee as object and target. (On anal sex, see *The Rules of the Game: the Sexes*.)

Emotional Control of Entries through the Mouth

We have already seen how the neural computer is informed by the bionatural and biological 'customs officers' in the mouth about the state of everything that is ingested. However, these agents also inform the brain about the presence of any foreign bodies that penetrate this area. These skilful 'customs officers' detect the presence of a hair that has somehow found its way into the soup and later onto a person's palate. The neural computer finds the following message in one of its bionatural programs: 'a long, thin body of such and such physical and biochemical characteristics must be removed from the mouth; inform the subject about the presence of this foreign body by activating an unpleasant feeling of repulsion at such and such intensity.' Thanks to this ingenious mechanism, the individual, who was enjoying both the soup and the company of a handsome gentleman, discovers that a hair is presently stuck to her palate, and that she ought to remove it if she wants to liberate herself from a feeling of repulsion. If, when she finishes eating, a pip has got caught between two teeth, the neural computer will inform the subject about its presence and about where it is located, advising her to expel it by making her the following emotional offer: 'If you remove this pip from your mouth, I shall cease to disturb you with this minor, though irritating discomfort.'

The neural computer, however, will activate a feeling of suffocation and anxiety if a doctor inserts a thick tube into a patient's mouth, down his larynx, and into his stomach. Practically no one would be able to tolerate such an intrusion without the aid of a sedative. If a fish bone slips through the mouth's 'customs officers' and gets stuck in the larynx, the neural computer will activate an emotional S.O.S. This occurred to one of my children when he was five years old, and it is a frightening incident he is likely to remember for the rest of his life.

In some cultures, babies become accustomed to sucking on their thumb or on a pacifier. The neural computer creates an addiction for a pacifier, and by crying the baby will ask its mother to provide it with this instrument. This constitutes a variation on the *cultura ancilla naturae* theme (of culture as the servant of nature). The pacifier is an artificial nipple that 'deceives' the neural computer (although not entirely), and the latter pays the baby pleasure for sucking on his mother's breast, the source of nourishment, affection and protection. The brain's program may include a specification of the characteristics of a particular pacifier. I shall never forget a sleepless night my wife and I suffered for having misplaced the pacifier our first baby had become used to. We gave him a new one, but he spat it out and began to cry. We tried to reason with him: 'Look at how nice this new one is; the other one was old.' Our baby, however, insisted with even more tears: 'Not this one; I want the other one.' His neural computer rejected a pacifier which was not registered in the relevant program, and hence denied him the pleasure provided by the old one.

A dentist's patient who tolerates injections, drillings and other tortures has no choice but to pay the emotional fines prescribed in the neural computer's software for this forbidden invasion. Human beings, unlike apes, have the capacity to reason, and know that such minor, temporal pains will eventually provide them with greater, more enduring pleasures. A dentist's patient, however, cannot escape his neural computer's emotional punishments. The same applies to medicines with bitter, disagreeable flavours. An Oxford midwife once advised a pregnant Spanish lady to ingest a spoonful of castor oil in order to produce an intestinal revolution that would provoke the baby's birth. This lady told me that she will never forget the sensation of repulsion that this potion made her feel. The neural computer is merciless when it comes to employing its emotional whip. We must once again become aware of and marvel at the workings of the emotional system, which can inform the subject about the presence of a pip that has become stuck between two teeth by activating a small but irritating discomfort, and which if necessary can send the following emergency message: 'A thick tube has invaded your mouth and throat!' Were it not for the emotional system, we would never know that we had a pip stuck between our teeth, nor would we have a reason to remove a tube that had been shoved down our throat.

Emotional Control of Weights

The muscular system is also controlled and protected by the brain's emotional system. The muscles employed to pick up and carry objects are equipped with biological scales that weigh each object requiring a muscular effort. This information is then automatically sent to the brain via the nervous system. The neural computer unconsciously knows the weight of a bag someone is carrying on his shoulder, or of the outfit the Queen of England is wearing when she opens Parliament, or of a pair of earrings hanging from someone's ears, or of the water buckets a Chinese man is carrying, or of the weights a weightlifter is lifting. The subject does not need to weigh an object every time he wishes to carry it, nor does he need to know which weights are too heavy for his muscles. Aided by the relevant laboratories, the brain provides the subject with all of this information in order to protect the health of the muscular system. The neural computer always contrasts the weight of an object being supported by certain muscles of the body, with the bionatural program of tolerated or forbidden weights. If there is an excess of baggage, the neural computer informs the subject that this is the case. The mechanism is comparable to an airport's baggage controls. If a passenger's suitcases do not exceed the allowed limit, the baggage controller will not say a word. However, if the scales indicate that the limit is being exceeded by x kilograms, he will let the passenger know about it, and make him pay for this excess. In a similar manner, the neural computer only informs the subject about an excess of weight, and makes him pay for this excess. The difference is that instead of paying a monetary fine, the individual must pay with uncomfortable sensations: one degree of discomfort for every excess gram of weight. The other difference is that the individual cannot bribe the neural computer. No one can escape the severe emotional control of the brain in the domain of excess baggage, as in every other domain.

The neural computer also takes into account the fatigue gradually accumulated in the relevant muscles, about which it is fully informed at all times. It sometimes happens that after one has already picked up one's suitcases and said goodbye to a tedious 'friend', the latter suddenly starts up a new topic of conversation. A few minutes later, the neural computer sends one an emotional message, which could be translated as follows: 'Put those suitcases down or I shall gradually increase the dose of discomfort you are already beginning to feel.' I remember that during my childhood I had to lug two large cans full of milk from a neighbouring village to my own. Of the four kilometres this journey spanned, the last one was always the hardest. The fatigued muscles in my arms sent me strong complaints via my brain's emotional system. This was due to the emotional and biochemical law of excess weight.

In this domain there are also cultural programs that demand the infraction of this law to different extents and in various ways. Certain professions require people to infringe this law on a daily basis by obliging them to carry excess weight and hence to make an extremely strenuous muscular effort. This is the emotional price that these workers have to pay in order to buy other vital necessities of the human beehive, such as money. Weightlifting also represents a blatant, spectacular challenge to this genetic law. Anyone who dares to challenge it knows that he will have to pay a high emotional price, but also calculates that this will enable him to buy other emotional goods which are worth the struggle: the satisfactions provided by money, fame and victory in this game (which is individual and social). The infraction of this law is also employed as a torture. One of the torments Christ was forced to suffer was an excess of weight: the weight of a heavy cross. According to a Greek myth, Sisyphus was condemned to an eternal punishment which consisted of carrying a very heavy rock from the bottom of a valley to a mountain peak. When he reached the top, the rock would roll back down, and Sisyphus would have to carry it up once again (and so on for all eternity).

Emotional Control of Humidity, Dampness and Dirt

In our modern era we have become accustomed to listening to the weather report the 'weatherman' gives us in the press, on the radio, or on television. This information usually includes the degree of humidity in the air. The genetic plan has installed a biological 'weatherman' which informs us about the degrees of humidity for the different areas of our corporal geography: x degrees of humidity around one's feet, back and other more private crevices. As we have slowly been discovering, nature has wisely designed a series of mechanisms that maintain and defend the somatic republic by establishing a synchronized harmony between the biochemical and the emotional systems. One of these mechanisms measures and regulates, among other things, the humidity of each of the body's external cells. Biological 'weathermen' continuously send the results of their analyses to the neural computer. The brain is thus always informed about the degrees of humidity around the left foot, the chest or any other external organ of the body. In accordance with a genetically installed bionatural program, the neural computer only gives the subject a 'weather report' when there is an excess of humidity, by activating uncomfortable sensations mathematically proportional to the degree of excess humidity. 'The heat in New York is a lot worse than that in Los Angeles because it is very humid,' I have often heard people say. The neural computer penalizes an inhabitant of either of these cities for infringing the law of temperature. However, the New Yorker is further penalized with an uncomfortable sensation of a different nature: the discomfort devised by the brain for an excess of humidity.

We all experience an uncomfortable sensation when our socks are damp and we walk around with our feet wet. The brain warns us of an excess of dampness and punishes us with an emotional penalty proportional to the harm this excess can bring to the somatic republic. If we are surprised by a storm and the rain pours on us, the neural computer will trigger off an emotional mechanism of emergency, since this excess of dampness constitutes a serious threat to the respiratory system and to other systems. 'Poor thing! No wonder my baby was crying! You're all wet. I'm going to change your nappies right now.' A mother who speaks to her child in these terms has discovered the cause of his tearful complaint: his nappies were wet. The baby does not know when, or how, or to what extent a part of his body has an excess of humidity, and why it would be beneficial to remedy this situation. Nature has foreseen it all. The neural computer pressures the baby to cry whenever the law of humidity is infringed. His mother, who is occupied with a million other things, hears her baby's phonic alarm. In this situation various exchanges of information have taken place: (1) the biological 'weathermen' of the baby's gluteus zone have informed his little neural computer about the humidity in the area; (2) the brain has consulted the appropriate humidity levels for the affected zone; (3) the neural computer has detected an excess humidity of 80 degrees; (4) the neural computer has activated an uncomfortable sensation which the baby feels in that area, pressuring him to cry; (5) when the baby cries, he attracts his mother's attention and disturbs her with a monotonous phonic cadence so that she may remedy the situation. Were it not for this complex system of information and emotional pressure devised by the genetic plan, the complex machinery of the baby's (or the adult's) body would not be able to function and maintain itself.

What we call 'dirt' (dust, viscous liquids, mud, and all kinds of particles which stick to the skin) obstructs the millions of exits dispersed throughout the somatic geography, as well as the diverse antennae which detect the humidity as well as the physical and the chemical properties of the bodies that come into contact with the body's cutaneous cells. When I worked for television, I used to feel a great relief when the make-up was removed from my face after several hours on the set. Why? The biological 'customs officers', responsible for ensuring that the millions of exits dispersed around my face remain unclogged so that sweat, dead cells and organic waste may be expelled, informed my brain about the obstruction created by the make-up and about the amount of time elapsed since it had been applied. The neural computer drew my attention to this minor infraction by activating a minor (though in the long run irritating) emotional penalty. A cultural precept obliges anyone who works for film or television to pay a minor emotional fine for infringing the law of the obstruction of cutaneous exits and antennae. Anyone can verify the functioning of this emotional biochemical law by showering after a long journey during which dust and sweat have obstructed these microscopic exits and antennae. A feeling of relief is then experienced because the brain cancels the discomfort which it had activated due to the violation of this law.

Emotional Control of Body Temperature

The human body, like that of any other animal or of any kind of engine, functions at a particular temperature. If the temperature is either excessive or insufficient, the body, like an engine, cannot function properly, and if the infraction is very serious, it may cease to function permanently. A car engine stops if the temperature exceeds a particular limit, and can be reduced to a mass of molten metal if it reaches an extremely high temperature. It maintains a stable temperature due to the functioning of ingenious cooling mechanisms (the circulation of water and of air which cools this water). The human body is also equipped with ingenious cooling mechanisms, such as the mechanism of sweat. When the body is exposed to an excessive temperature, the neural computer (in this case without consulting the subject) activates the mechanism of sweat, eliminating water through a myriad of microscopic holes dispersed throughout the surface of the body. A car engine is equipped with an indicator that keeps the driver informed about the temperature at all times, and with an alarm that goes off if the temperature reaches a particular limit. This system warns the driver of the situation in the middle of the conversation he might be engrossed in with his travel companion.

The human body is also equipped with an equally ingenious temperature indicator, as well as with an alarm for extreme cases. The difference between the mechanisms of the car and those of the human body is that in the case of the latter, these are emotional. The biological thermometers installed throughout the surface of the body inform the neural computer, via the nervous system, about the exact temperature of the objects which are in contact with any of its parts. If the temperature agrees with the bionatural program installed in the neural computer, the latter will not interrupt the subject's thoughts or activities by activating emotional mechanisms to inform him about this. Only when the temperature of an object that comes into contact with a finger or with the entire organism is inferior or superior to the temperature prescribed in the brain's program will the latter inform the subject about the following facts: (1) the part of the body in which the infraction has been committed; (2) whether it constitutes an insufficiency or an excess; and (3) the seriousness of the infraction. By activating uncomfortable sensations which are mathematically proportional to the gravity of the violation, the neural computer lets the individual know about all of this, and pressures him to remedy the situation.

If the air conditioning in a given restaurant clashes with the bionatural program of temperature, the neural computer will disturb us during the meal. 'I was unable to fully enjoy myself at restaurant x,' a friend of mine told me, 'because of the bloody air conditioning. The food was excellent; the wine, splendid; the company, wonderful. But the air conditioning was so high that it practically ruined the evening.' If someone touches an extremely hot surface, or puts his finger into a boiling liquid, the neural computer will unleash such an intense emotional mechanism that the subject will almost automatically withdraw his finger. As soon as we go out into the street, the neural computer immediately lets us know whether or not we should wear a coat. Once again we must become aware of the extraordinary nature of the emotional system, which informs us with instantaneous precision about the temperature that suits the body, by pressuring us with different emotional levers in order to correct all insufficiencies and excesses.

In this as in other domains, culture works as a slave for nature. In fact, human culture could partly be defined as an artificial system which aims to obtain the temperature prescribed by nature for the human body. In this context 'progress' signifies the invention of new products which can help human beings to obey a rigorous law of nature which has not varied in the least since Adam and Eve were created. The neural computers of a 'primitive' and of a 'civilized' man (and even of an ape) are programmed with the same laws and temperature mechanisms: biochemical, emotional laws and mechanisms. The genetic frontier between Man and ape is the fire which the 'primitive' human being invented to protect himself from the cold, the furs he used to keep warm, or the huts he built to shelter his body from the cold as well as from the heat. The 'civilized' human being has invented central heating and air conditioning to abide by the same bionatural laws with even greater humility: 'the greater the cultural progress, the stricter the obedience to natural laws'. When a twentieth-century man drives an air-conditioned automobile, he may feel very civilized and superior to 'primitive' members of his species, to animals and to material objects. Nevertheless, this man is in fact no more than a humble slave of biochemical, emotional laws of nature which he has neither designed nor installed.

If an ape could reason, he would understand and applaud human inventions such as fires, clothing, umbrellas, fans and air conditioning. If, however, he saw human beings placing live coals on their heads, or pouring petrol on their bodies before setting themselves on fire, he would undoubtedly ask himself: 'Why is this supposed descendant of mine doing this to himself?' Once again we find culture, the servant of the human beehive, conflicting with the laws that defend the human individual. The Queen of England must occasionally wear an extremely heavy outfit, as well as a crown, during long and rather dull ceremonies. All of these symbols and rites of the 'tribal totem' are highly beneficial to a territorial human society. The Queen's biothermic agents inform her brain about the temperature, and her neural computer, which is programmed with the same bionatural laws as that of any other member of her kingdom, lets her know about the excess and advises her to take off both the outfit and the crown. The Queen's brain, however, has also been programmed with her society's cultural rules. Hence, while one of her programs (a bionatural one) pressures her to undress, another (a biocultural one) forbids her to take off her crown and her cape, and threatens her with extremely severe emotional fines if she dares to expose herself in public. The bionatural program punishes her with the uncomfortable emotional penalties devised for the infraction of temperature excess (the neural computer makes no distinctions between noble bodies and those of 'commons'). At the same time, the biocultural program threatens her with an emotional message, which could be translated as follows: 'If you dare to remove your crown and your royal cape, and of course if you undress completely, I will torture you with feelings of shame and ridicule of the highest intensity. All your subjects will think you have gone completely mad.' On the following day, such an event would be described on the front page of newspapers all over the world: 'In the middle of the ceremony, and in front of the Prime Minister, the Lords, and the Commons, the

Queen of England suddenly began to undress, and then simply said: "It really is rather hot, isn't it?".'

Many human beings have died in fires, their deaths being due to serious violations of the law of temperature, in order to comply with the rules of the social game (for instance, firemen and policemen). Others have suffered extreme pain in their feet and even lost the use of these limbs, or their lives, as a result of social obligations (for instance, soldiers in the Russian steppes). Pressured by social urges to win the game of climbing the highest mountains in the world, many human beings have suffered horrific emotional tortures for severely infringing the law of temperature. When I was an adolescent, my generational society lobbied me with strong emotional pressures to take extremely cold showers on winter mornings because it was 'the manly thing to do'. The priests of certain oriental religions have to place live coals on their heads and take part in a conversation as if nothing was wrong, in order to reach superior hierarchical positions. During this century numerous human beings, such as certain Buddhist monks, have poured inflammable liquids on their bodies and set fire to themselves as a way of making a social protest. The laws of individual survival are not necessarily the strongest. As we have seen, the laws that defend human societies can pressure the subject with even more powerful emotional mechanisms than those that defend the well-being and the very life of human individuals. This clearly represents a challenge to certain Darwinian claims.

7

Emotional Control of Fatigue and Danger

Emotional Control of Sleep

The human body, like an ape's body or an engine, is a device that needs periods of rest. Unlike a car engine, it cannot fully stop and then start up again, as I discussed in relation to the respiratory system. However, the human body must reduce its activity to a minimum during each day of its life. The subject is completely ignorant about when his body has to rest, or about how and for what reasons it must do so. His neural computer, in accordance with the bionatural program of sleep, will give him the appropriate instructions. In the same way as the mother says to the child, 'It's time for bed,' the neural computer tells the adult, 'You must now get some sleep.' The muscles, the eyes, the legs, the arms, and other parts of the body, including the neural computer's own systems, inform the brain about this state of fatigue: zero degrees, ten degrees, ninety degrees, and so on. In the light of this information, the neural computer activates a particular emotional densitometer: the urge to sleep. As with all other urges, this comprises a precise, unmistakable language. The individual never confuses the urge to urinate with the urge to ejaculate (although both are connected to the same 'escape route'), nor the urge to sleep with the urge to eat. We must become aware of the different colours and shades of the emotional spectrum. It is this qualitative variety of feelings which allows the neural computer to clearly inform the subject about what exactly he ought to do, and where, when, how, and how often he ought to do it.

When the neural computer activates the emotional densitometer of sleep, it instructs the subject as follows: 'Get to bed. Stop talking, reading, and watching television. Interrupt all your activities. Avoid light and noise.' Like all other instructions which the neural computer sends the subject, these imply both a recompense and a threat: 'If you get to bed now, I will make you feel great.' As with all other emotional stipulations, the pleasure offered to the subject for getting to bed is in fact nothing more than the elimination of uncomfortable sensations triggered off by the neural computer, which are proportional to the degrees of fatigue throughout the body.

If the subject disobeys the order to sleep, the neural computer will add strength to the corresponding urges. The law of intensity for this particular emotional mechanism is the following: 'The greater the fatigue, or the more hours elapsed without sleep, the greater the emotional intensity.' It is, like all emotional/biochemical laws, a rigid, mathematically precise, unavoidable law. When we lie down, stretch our legs, close our eyes, and discontinue all bodily activity, we feel a huge relief. This is because the neural computer cancels various discomforts for having obeyed its orders. If we get to bed and the next-door neighbours begin to yell at each other, the neural computer punishes us with a feeling of irritation.

In the end, the biological anaesthetist installed in the brain puts the subject to sleep, without him knowing when or how this has happened. Sleep is indeed a bionatural anaesthesia administered by the brain. The subject must, like a good little boy, lie down and stay still. Without consulting him any further, the brain's anaesthetist then disconnects the subject from the world of images, sounds, tastes and all sensory perceptions, ideas and feelings. When the neural computer puts the individual to sleep, it reduces him to a vegetative machine.

Numerous cultures have compared sleep to death and death to sleep. This popular intuition is an accurate one. Death is indeed an eternal, irreversible nap from which no one ever wakes up (at least not in this world), while a nap is a temporal death from which people wake up (if they wake up). What is the difference between a dead person and one that is merely sleeping? There is no difference between the two in the sense that neither see, hear, think or feel. When a human being sleeps, he does not exist as a being which thinks and feels. It is said that we have no experience of death, but this is not true. We die every day. We know what it is to pass from the world of living – in other words, the world of perceiving, thinking, and feeling

– to the world of death, the world of nothingness (where we do not perceive, nor think, nor feel, and hence we are nothing, as far as we are concerned). If we slept for twenty centuries, during this time we would neither think, nor feel, nor be anything at all. How it is that we walk on and off the stage of thinking and feeling when we wake up and fall asleep is an unfathomable mystery. Only the brain controls the lever which unplugs us from waking experience and connects us again to the sensory, mental and emotional world.

During sleep we occasionally have 'dreams'. One who is taking the eternal, irreversible nap of death 'rests in peace' without ever being interrupted by 'bad dreams' or 'nightmares'. One who is sleeping, however, can feel pleasure and pain, talk, and even solve a complex equation. In other words, he can partly experience the world of perceiving, thinking and feeling. However, it is best to sleep 'like a log' (in other words, to sleep without dreams, to rest without interruptions). To sleep 'like a log' is to temporarily become a log, a material object which can neither perceive, think nor feel. Since during sleep the neural computer is no longer being bombarded by millions of perceptions, it uses the time to order the archives which contain images, sounds, ideas and feelings. The body's muscles and organs repose and regenerate themselves.

Suddenly, the subject is returned to the world of perceptions, ideas and feelings. He has woken up, is resurrected, once again. The neural computer then encourages him to slowly and calmly begin his daily activity. After a rough day of work, we often feel miserable, while the next morning, after a good night's sleep, we feel full of joyful energy. Due to the accumulated fatigue, the neural computer activates these feelings of depression, which it cancels as soon as the fatigue has disappeared. However, when we have slept on a train, or rather when he have attempted to sleep on a train, we still feel exhausted in the morning. The constant movement of the train, as well as the noise, make it impossible for the brain's anaesthetist to do his job properly; hence the many muscles and organs of the body are unable to fully recuperate from the previous day's fatigue. The neural computer lets us know that this is the case by activating a feeling of exhaustion in the morning.

When night falls, the orchestra of the universe (the neighing of horses, the mooing of cows, the singing of birds, and so on) falls silent. This observation can help us discover the laws that govern the animal kingdom. Darwin noticed only one aspect of the laws which govern the behaviour and the relation between the different species: the survival of the fittest, and the evolution from 'inferior' to 'superior' species. However, it is not just that the amoeba evolves into the reptile, and the reptile into the ape, and the ape into Man (this law, in any case, may be nothing but a human prejudice). Such a theory is comparable to speaking of the evolution from clapping to castanets, from the clavichord to the piano, or from the flute to the organ. In reality, each instrument is unique and irreplaceable. To claim that the cello is superior to the violin, to the piano or to the guitar is clearly absurd. In any given orchestra, every instrument has a unique role to play, and all of the instruments complement each other. If the law was as rigid as Darwin supposed, why would the monkey survive, if Man is a superior monkey? Why do amoebas, reptiles and other 'inferior' animals still abound, if the 'superior' ones have arrived on the evolutionary scene? This is not the place to deal with this issue, but I wish to refer to it in relation to the fact that the same programming seems to govern the law of sleep and wakefulness in all species.[1] Some animals, such as bats, are programmed with an inverse law. Their neural computers wake them up at night and put them to sleep during the day. However, even such cases may provide evidence for the law of harmony among all species.[2] These night 'watchmen' fulfil a particular role in the 'neighbourhoods' of the world.

The neural computer is programmed to govern the subject with the emotional law of sleep and wakefulness in accordance with the different phases of his life. The brain unconsciously 'knows' what phase of development a human being is undergoing: two months, two years, forty years, ninety years, and so on. On the basis of this information and of the program of sleep according to age, the neural computer induces the subject to sleep more or fewer hours. A baby's brain forces it to sleep most of the time. As it gets older, the neural computer increases the dose of wakefulness, and when it becomes an elderly man, the brain again increases the urges to sleep.

The neural processor is always fully informed about the state of each organic lab, of each system, and of each part of the body. Following the program of sleep according to the state of the organism, it increases or diminishes the urge to sleep, or interferes with the action of the biological anaesthetist. Anyone can verify the functioning of this law. When we are ill or convalescent, we feel more intense and extensive urges to sleep than when we are healthy. However, if the brain activates an extremely painful toothache, it becomes impossible to fall asleep. A human being who is suffering such unbearable pain would like nothing more than to have some control over his own feelings, to be able to eliminate the toothache, and hence to fall asleep whenever he might wish to do so. However, whether he be a king or a beggar, this poor human being is at the mercy of the toothache and of the urges to sleep. The individual senses his own feelings come and go like clouds that appear and disappear in the sky. Faced with an intense toothache, the brain's anaesthetist cannot do his job. The urges to sleep clash with the pain the whole night through. The subject/object enters and exits the conscious scene during the course of this biological duel between two opposed emotional forces. The toothache attempts to warn the subject about a serious danger, while the urges to sleep try to disconnect him from the world of feelings. In this case we find two independent, opposed bionatural programs struggling against one another, although both defend the somatic republic, and the life of the individual.

Biocultural/Biosocial Programs

Apes do not sleep on beds, and elephants do not swallow sleeping pills. Once again, we find culture working as nature's slave: *cultura ancilla naturae*. Homes, beds, sheets, mattresses or sleeping pills are cultural devices which aid human beings to comply with a biological law to which apes are also subjected: the law of sleep. At the same time, all of these cultural inventions are meant to maximize the pleasure the neural computer grants the subject, who humbly obeys his brain when it orders him to sleep and to facilitate the work of the anaesthetist.

The 'siesta' is a cultural invention of Spanish society which becomes a biocultural precept if and when it is installed in a Spaniard's brain. If such a Spaniard has no choice but to infringe this biocultural imperative, his neural computer will punish him with an uncomfortable sensation that will not allow him to carry out the afternoon's activities in peace. This Spanish cultural precept seems to fit in well with the bionatural program of sleep. After the fatigue that has accumulated during the morning's toils, the neural computer induces both a man and a dog to take an afternoon nap. This gives the brain the opportunity to repose and regenerate itself, and in this way the individual, with a 'clear head', finds himself in an ideal condition to perform the afternoon's tasks. The neural computer cancels both the uncomfortable sensation of fatigue and the urges to sleep, and hence the subject feels 'fit as a fiddle'.

In this domain we also find laws and mechanisms that oppose the law of sleep in order to defend human society. On the eve of important social events, a human being may find it impossible to sleep a wink. The night before a wedding, a close relative's funeral or an exam are often spent wide awake. In such cases, the conflict is between the law of sleep, which supports the individual republic, and the law of wakefulness, which defends the social republic. The biosocial program of the family pressures a bride to stay awake on the eve of an event as important as her own wedding. Tomorrow she will be scrutinized by everyone. As the time of the ceremony gets closer, the neural computer pressures her to stay wide awake. However, the mechanism of sleep, which functions independently, induces her to sleep with the usual daily emotional mechanisms. The bride wishes she could reconcile these two emotional antagonists. She turns in her bed over and over again. 'Come on, I need to get some sleep,' she may say to herself. However, she cannot disconnect herself as if she were a television set or a lamp, unless she resorts to a sleeping pill.

Doctors, priests, firemen and policemen often have to violate the law of sleep and pay the corresponding emotional penalties, in order to fulfil their responsibilities. If a doctor told one of his patients at two o'clock in the morning that he was too sleepy to come to his aid, he would be sanctioned with extremely severe emotional penalties (shame and ridicule). During numerous traditional festivals that take place in Spain, such as Pamplona's 'sanfermines', young people are pressured to sacrifice the pleasure of sleep on the altar of revelry. If any one of them feels too exhausted to go on carousing at four o'clock in the morning, and dares to say that he feels like going to bed, he exposes himself to extremely severe fines of shame and ridicule, to the sarcastic comments of his peers, and perhaps to a dunk in the river (the traditional punishment reserved for those who give up before the night is over). It is not unusual to see young men and women fall fast asleep in bars or in the middle of the street during these festivals. In such cases, the biological anaesthetist – which usually requires his patient to be lying still, with the lights out and in a silent room – can put the person to sleep in spite of the fact that he is standing up inside a noisy bar, simply because he has been awake for so long. All of these possibilities have been foreseen by the wonderfully mysterious world of the neural computer's biochemical, emotional laws.

In certain religious societies, monks must get up at two o'clock in the morning to sing matins in the chapel as a sacrifice to God and the Church. In spite of the intense emotional pressures activated in accordance with the law of sleep, none of these monks would dare stay in bed. The emotional pressures of a social and cultural nature are even more powerful. Nevertheless, one of these monks may suddenly doze off in the middle of the matins. The law of sleep has in this case won a small victory.

Emotional Control of Postures

The subject does not know when he should stand up, sit, or lie down. Thanks to a bionatural program of postures, however, the neural computer 'knows' which posture is most beneficial to the body at any given moment. All the muscles in the body (those in the legs, the arms, the neck, the back, the chest, the stomach and the buttocks) are equipped with biological fatigue meters. The latter measure the degrees of fatigue accumulated in each muscle with mathematical precision, and this information reaches the brain via the nervous system. The neural computer then informs the subject about the degree of fatigue accumulated in particular areas of his corporal geography by activating a feeling of fatigue proportional to such a degree, and in this way advises him to change his posture. This is yet another of the emotional system's ingenious mechanisms.

Suppose we are waiting for a bus. While we wait, our minds occupy themselves with many different thoughts, and preoccupy themselves with all our professional and domestic problems. Time passes, and we are still waiting for the bus. The fatigue meters in the muscles of our legs have informed the brain about the amount of fatigue that has accumulated: one degree, ten, twenty, thirty. The neural computer then distracts us from our occupations and preoccupations by activating a particular uncomfortable sensation, which could be translated as follows: 'I am letting you know that your legs are fatigued with a sensation that corresponds to the amount of fatigue that has accumulated. If you change your posture (if you sit down), I shall cease to disturb you.' The subject immediately understands the brain's unmistakable message: he knows exactly which muscles are fatigued, and what the degree of their fatigue is.

Sometimes we 'feel like' stretching our arms and legs. We feel a great relief when we carry out this operation. The brain has pressured us to stretch our arms, and now immediately rewards us with an emotional recompense, as promised. After sitting for several hours inside an aircraft, we feel relieved as soon as we are finally able to stretch our legs. The brain then cancels the uncomfortable sensation it activated, due to the degree of fatigue accumulated in the legs and the buttocks, because the subject remained in the same position for a very long time. When I have been writing for hours (I always write with a fountain pen), the neural computer often lets me know that a particular area of my index finger is beginning to suffer the effects of the pressure exerted by my pen, and sometimes punishes me with a pain that makes it impossible for me to write in peace.

Even at night, when we sleep, the system of changing postures continues to function. Like a caring mother, the neural computer makes us change our posture almost without waking us up, so that the fatigued muscles may be able to rest. For a few seconds we feel the pleasure with which the neural computer rewards us for changing our posture. After briefly enjoying this moment, we go back to sleep.

The law of postures is partly conditioned by the law of age. During the first few months after birth, the neural computer advises the baby to lie down at all times. Sometimes the baby cries, and its mother, who constantly has to translate her child's tears, quietens it down by turning it over. The neural computer, following the precise instructions of the law of postures installed by the genetic plan at a certain point in the baby's development, will induce it to sit and eventually to stand up. By sending emotional messages, the neural computer pressures the subject to remain lying down, or both to sit and to lie down, or to combine sitting, standing and lying down during the different phases of his life. Were it not for the neural computer's emotional system, the subject would not know what postures to adopt as a baby, a child, an adult, or an elderly person, either during the day or at night, and for this reason the body's muscles would snap, like a rope which had been supporting a weight for too long.

Biocultural Programs

In this domain, we again find culture working as a slave under nature's orders. Chairs, armchairs, rocking chairs and sofas are all inventions that help 'civilized' human beings to obey the emotional law of postures. If a chair is made of stone or wood, the muscles in the gluteal region will send a complaint to the brain, and the latter will in turn inform the subject by triggering off an uncomfortable sensation. The modern human being who sits on a comfortable sofa, where he can adopt different postures, receives a substantial emotional reward from his brain for relieving the muscles in his legs and buttocks. No matter how 'modern' he may feel, a human being cannot alter the rigid emotional laws of the brain. If he wants to 'enjoy himself', he must obey them to the letter.

Although to a great extent it is true that culture helps humans obey the law of postures, it also creates programs that conflict with this law for social reasons. Certain ritual celebrations, which are very beneficial to human society, require the subject to break the law of postures to a greater or lesser degree. Once again we find an emotional duel between laws that aim to defend the individual and laws designed to ensure the well-being of human society. Brezhnev lost his life, according to the press, for infringing this law, for standing for too many hours in Moscow's Red Square as he presided over an interminable military parade. His neural computer undoubtedly pressured him with extremely painful sensations to sit down, but one of its biosocial programs simultaneously pressured him with even more powerful emotional mechanisms to continue standing.

Runners, cyclists and mountain climbers pay a high emotional price for infringing the law of postures – an acute pain in their legs – in order to savour the exquisite taste of victory, an emotional trophy which one of the neural computer's biosocial programs offers them. Xirinacs, a Catalan priest, acquired fame towards the end of Franco's regime for standing outside a Barcelona prison for hours and hours in protest against the treatment of political prisoners. This priest preferred to suffer the emotional consequences of disobeying the bionatural law of postures in order to attain a victory on the social front and to earn a payment of pleasure from his neural computer. The laws which defend the body have powerful emotional mechanisms at their disposal, but the laws which support the human beehive, as we have been seeing, often have even more powerful emotional mechanisms in cases of conflict (especially when the individual in question holds a key position in his society, such as Brezhnev during a tremendously important hierarchical and monarchic rite).

Emotional Control of Danger

In the genetically tended garden of feelings, emotions, and sensations there is a flower which is distinct from all the rest: fear. All human languages have coined one or more words to define this human feeling. We should notice that this emotion, like all others, has been designed and installed in the brain by the genetic plan.

Nowadays, a car can be equipped with an alarm mechanism by means of which, if someone opens a door, a siren begins to sound. Highly efficient electronic alarms can also be installed in homes to alert the inhabitants about fires or trespassers. Nature has installed extremely complex mechanisms of alert within the human brain in order to protect the life of the individual by warning him of imminent dangers or threats. The eyes, the ears and the sense of smell inform the brain at all times about everything that enters the subject's field of perception. If the neural computer, once it has consulted its programs, detects that the individual is in danger, it automatically activates the innate mechanism of alarm (fear), at an intensity proportional to the seriousness of the threat.

Bionatural and Biocultural Evaluation

When a mouse sees a cat, it immediately flees. A mouse's neural computer undoubtedly contains the following instructions: 'If the individual finds itself in the presence of an animal of this particular smell, colour, size and phonic characteristics (those of a cat), the emotion of fear must be immediately activated.' Indeed, even if a mouse has never seen a cat, it panics as soon as it sees, smells or hears a cat in the vicinity. Had nature not equipped mice with this mechanism of alarm, these animals would have no way of defending themselves from feline predators. Whenever my dog ran away from my home in Los Angeles, it was always amusing to see how several cats would immediately climb to the top of the palm trees. It seems evident that the neural computer of a spider, a cat, a mouse, a partridge or any other animal possesses a program of alarm installed by the genetic plan, containing information about the animals that represent a danger to the species in question. The mechanism of alarm is always fear.

Our species is also endowed with similar bionatural programming concerning certain dangerous animals. Any human being who has been confronted by a tiger or a bull has experienced the automatic activation of fear. Man, furthermore, unlike apes, is programmed from his youth with a series of intimidating beings (demons, witches, malevolent spirits) which inhabit an invisible, though real world. Once the neural computer has been programmed with these dangerous creatures, it will activate the mechanism of fear if the brain is informed that one of them is in the area. This is another genetic frontier between human beings and apes.

The Three Phases of Fear

Before fear

Fear is one of the most uncomfortable sensations a human being or a mouse can feel. By activating this emotional lever, the neural computer warns the mouse: 'Look out for the cat! If you find yourself anywhere near this animal, I shall torture you with fear.' This marvellous mechanism thus defends the lives of mice and men. (However, this still leaves another problem unresolved. Why do different species conflict with each other? Why does the cat's neural computer offer it pleasure for catching and killing the mouse, while the mouse's neural computer activates fear in order to save its life? There may be a purpose to the control of the different species by means of depredation, but Man still asks himself: why is the universe founded on murder, on a bloody war between species programmed to enjoy torturing and killing their prey?) When a given human being, such as a soldier, a fireman, a bullfighter, or a racing car driver, is about to confront a highly dangerous situation, his neural computer projects a film on the screen of his imagination in which he is the main character. In this film, he sees himself 'scared to death' before the dangerous situation in which he is about to find himself. As the time of the bullfight, the war or the race approaches, the bullfighter, the soldier, or the racing car driver feels a greater intensity of fear. By activating this emotional mechanism of alarm, the neural computer attempts to dissuade him from risking his life, and encourages him to stay home and avoid these dangers.

'The worst part,' a bullfighter once confessed to me (Pamplona, 1969), 'is when you get to the bullring. You're already in costume. You feel like you're being taken to the scaffold. Then a funeral procession passes by, and you see yourself inside the coffin. You want to calm down and get rid of your anxiety, but there's nothing you can do about it. When you get to the courtyard, everyone stares at you. Then the press arrives. You try to give the impression that everything is fine, and fake a smile. Everyone looks like a ghost to you. In fact, you're not really there with those people. You're like in another world light years away from them. The fear is like a serpent that slowly wraps itself around your body. You can't concentrate on anything. It's so unbearable, you feel like running away to the moon.' The emotional mechanism of fear, as this bullfighter's confession makes evident, is extremely powerful. Once again, we should take notice of the total autonomy with which the brain's emotional laws and mechanisms function: 'You want to calm down and get rid of your anxiety, but there's nothing you can do about it.' However, although this bullfighter confesses that he feels like 'running away to the moon', he does not in fact do such a thing, but confronts his fear and the bull by going out into the ring. Why? Once again, the fierce duel between the emotional mechanisms which defend the life of the individual and those which support human society ends with the victory of the latter.

During the danger

The bullfighter approaches the bull in the ring; the fireman runs through the flames in an attempt to rescue a victim; the soldier aims and fires at the enemy on the battlefield; the racing car driver accelerates around a curve on the track; human beings thus play the most dangerous game, one in which their own lives are at stake. Bullfighters, as well as others who have to risk their lives in order to earn their bread, often say that the worst moments are those which immediately precede going out into the ring. Once the bull is in front of you, they say, there is no time left to worry. By activating the emotional lever of fear, the brain advises and pressures the subject to avoid risking his life. However, once the definitive step has been taken, the brain changes its strategy. When a mouse finds itself cornered by a huge cat, its brain concentrates all its attention on simply saving its life. Running away may not immediately be the best strategy. For a while both of the animals look into each other's eyes and remain frozen, like statues.

When the bullfighter finds himself in front of the bull, his neural computer may pressure him with the mechanism of fear to such an extent that this may force him to forgo the artistry and finish the animal off as quickly as possible. It is extremely rare for a bullfighter to run away from the bull, although it has certainly been known to happen. When the bullfighter avoids putting himself in danger as far as he possibly can, the crowd (which is also a ferocious beast) begins to taunt him mercilessly. His neural computer then activates heavy doses of shame and ridicule. All of the bullfighters I have interviewed during the course of my fieldwork have told me that nothing is more unbearable for them than being humiliated by an angry crowd on a bad afternoon. This illustrates the fighting strength of the mechanism of fear when it conflicts with the emotional mechanism of shame and ridicule. A bullfighter, caught between these two powerful emotional currents, may be swept away by either of them.

Bullfighters also confess that they feel ecstatic whenever they are capable of overcoming their fear, the crowd begins to chant 'Olé', and music is played in their honour. Ortega Cano, one of the most popular bullfighters in Spain today, recently described the experience as follows: 'During moments like those you feel like you're on top of the world. The sheer happiness I feel transports me out of the ring.' The bullfighter's neural computer activates an extremely pleasant emotion when the crowd applauds and cheers. It continues to protect his life by triggering off feelings of fear and advising him to avoid such dangerous risks. However, in accordance with certain biosocial programs, it also rewards the bullfighter with an emotional recompense, which makes him feel like he is 'on top of the world'. Once again, the emotional mechanisms which defend society override those which struggle to protect the life of the individual.

The bullfighter savours the pleasure of being admired by society, and hence continues to risk his life time and again.

After the danger

A person who is dying of thirst derives great pleasure from drinking a glass of water; one who is starving takes delight in satisfying his hunger; one who has abstained from sexual intercourse for days relishes an opportunity to finally indulge his erotic desires. This is a general law of the emotional system which functions with the same rigorous precision as the law of gravity: 'The greater the intensity of the accumulated urges, the greater the emotional recompense provided by the neural computer when the relevant order is obeyed.' As I pointed out earlier, what we take to be pleasure is in fact nothing but the cancellation of unpleasant feelings or sensations. This general law applies to the third phase of fear when the subject escapes the danger: the greater the intensity of the fear accumulated, the greater the emotional recompense provided by the brain. When the brain discovers that the danger is over, it empties the densitometer of fear and the subject feels a pleasure proportional to the intensity of the fear that had accumulated there. During the city of Pamplona's 'San Fermin' festivals, hundreds of young men, as well as some women, run in front of six bulls, which they lead through the streets of the city and into the bullring. After the ordeal, those who participate in this spectacular event can savour a pleasure which cannot be enjoyed by those who chose not to purchase such an expensive emotion. (These runners also receive other emotional rewards: the admiration of their territorial and generational societies for being 'a good citizen of Navarre', and praise in general for their bravery.)

Why do children enjoy riding on roller coasters, in spite of the the intense degree of fear they feel when they plunge down extremely steep falls? Why do people pay to feel fear? If a monkey could reason, he might think this was illogical. I would argue that the child wishes to purchase pleasures that are bought in the brain's market-place by feeling fear and overcoming danger. The hedonist who delights in this genre of pleasure knows that the greater the danger he puts himself in, and the fear he consequently feels, the greater his enjoyment will be.

One of the biological laws we have discovered during our exploration of the emotional continent is the law of the autonomy of the neural computer's programs. The program concerning danger to the individual's life activates fear in the bullfighter, while the program concerning the defence of society simultaneously incites him to risk his life by releasing other feelings (the pleasure of 'feeling like you're on top of the world', the pleasure of being applauded, the threat of shame and ridicule if cowardice is displayed, the pleasure of gaining millions of pesetas, fame and prestige). This precise, inexorable law, like all the other biological laws we have been discovering and exploring, regulates the activation of the different conflicting emotions.

Moreover, this law sometimes regulates the functioning of the same feeling from independent perspectives or departments. It is sometimes said that people have to choose between 'the cold calculations of reason' and 'the passionate impulses of the heart'. This kind of talk vaguely and confusedly hints at the existence of this law. What occurs is not really a choice between 'a cold calculation of reason' and a "passionate impulse of the heart'. The subject is actually caught between two opposed emotional currents, which are generated by different departments. In the case of fear, the neural computer is equipped with two independent departments which evaluate risk: a mental or rational department (what we call 'cold reason') and a sensory department. The situation is comparable to that of a film distributor who makes two different evaluations of a movie's potential success before deciding whether to invest millions in promoting it. One evaluation is based on the statistics derived from an opinion poll, and the other is based on the spontaneous reactions (laughs, applause, silence, yawns, boos) of an audience which views a screening of the film. The neural computer is equipped with two independent departments (a rational and a sensory one) which evaluate the possible risks to the individual entailed by a given course of action, as well as other factors which condition the activation of different feelings.

The neural computer of a person who is about to board an aircraft 'reassures' the traveller and encourages him to do so. In other words, it activates a feeling of calmness which is derived from a rational evaluation: an aircraft is safer than a car, the pilot knows what he is doing, and so on. I shall not consider here the extent to which this rational evaluation is automatic and unconscious (a pure calculation of the neural computer), and the extent to which it is conscious and subjective. What I wish to stress is that this rational evaluation is not entirely 'cold', in the sense that it generates emotional mechanisms of pressure. 'It reassures me to think that it is extremely rare for an aircraft to crash. Hundreds of flights take off every day from all the airports around the world, and one hardly ever hears of any accidents,' a Spanish physician once told me as we boarded an aircraft in Los Angeles. Indeed, this rational evaluation allows the neural computer to 'reassure' the traveller. In other words, the brain administers an emotional 'valium', which is sent by the department of rational evaluation. When the aircraft takes off and the neural computer receives visual and phonic information about the fact that the individual is in the air (a location which this department does not consider to be safe, unlike that of an eagle or a fly), it activates an uncomfortable feeling of fear which is mathematically calculated according to various factors (age, number of times the person has flown, previous experiences, illnesses, or neuro-vegetative disorders). Many people who are capable of confronting other serious risks cannot bring themselves to travel on aeroplanes. Their neural computers trigger off such an intense degree of fear that they simply cannot pluck up the courage to board the aircraft. A distinguished professor and ex-ambassador of the United States confessed to me that if he did not sit in an aisle seat of the aircraft, he would 'feel indisposed'. He explained to me that because he suffered so much anxiety when he was forced to spend weeks inside a submarine during the Second World War, sitting anywhere else terrifies him. This professor does not know why this 'happens' to him. His neural computer, however, is equipped with a program by means of which it inevitably triggers a feeling of panic if he does not sit in a seat out of which he can immediately jump. After each flight, the brain pays every passenger an emotional salary proportional to the fear accumulated.

Chemical, Magical, Religious and
Personal Tranquillizers

Although it may not be true that human beings make choices between 'cold reason' and 'the heart' for the reasons I have suggested, this metaphorical use of coldness is not entirely inaccurate. No matter how many statistical studies demonstrate that travelling on aeroplanes is not particularly dangerous, this hardly reassures certain people, whose neural computers still terrorize them in spite of these rational analyses. In such cases, the emotional dose of calmness has to be increased by other means. Some travellers resort to man-made chemical products which contribute to their feeling of well-being during the flight: alcohol, Valium or other drugs.

The bullfighter, as well as the race car driver, cannot resort to these chemical inventions to confront the invasion of fear, since both of them need their sensory and mental faculties to be in perfect shape. A drunk bullfighter would not be afraid of the bull, but would in fact be exposing himself to a much greater risk. Bullfighters and many other human beings confront the fear of death with magical and religious tranquillizers provided by their society's culture. The bullfighter, particularly on a working day, tries his best to respect the magical code of Spanish society (the avoidance of certain colours, numbers, and 'jinxed' individuals, and the performance of certain prescribed rites). Whatever the actual influence of certain mysterious forces such as destiny or luck may be, the bullfighter who abides by this magical code 'feels more secure'. In other words, he manages to make his neural computer provide him with an emotional tranquillizer which helps him to overcome the fear activated by another department of the brain.

The bullfighter also wears medals which depict Christ, the Virgin and certain saints. Before donning his costume, he builds a miniature altar with religious images and candles to which he fervently prays, and as he waits to go out into the bullring, he makes the sign of the cross with his right hand. A scientist cannot prove whether God or the Virgin are really interested in protecting a bullfighter (animal rights activists would certainly be outraged by such divine assistance). What is beyond scientific doubt, however, is that this bullfighter's neural computer administers more emotional tranquillizers to him for complying with this religious code.

When a group of armed paramilitary policemen burst into the Spanish Parliament during the completely unforeseen *coup d'état*, which took place in February 1981, and began firing their machine-guns into the air, many declared atheists began to pray, due to the sudden intense panic which their neural computers activated in them. This leads one to postulate the existence of the following law: 'The greater the danger and the greater the fear which is consequently activated, the more the neural computer pressures the subject to follow the magical and/or religious code installed in his brain so that it may administer emotional tranquillizers to him.' In a published collection of questionnaires about God answered by numerous distinguished Spaniards, Salvador Dali confessed with admirable sincerity that 'when I sensed the approach of death due to an appendectomy, I first asked for the priest, and only afterwards for the notary'. The book, entitled *One Hundred Spaniards and God*, contains many similar testimonies, such as that of Fernando Diaz-Plaja: 'I, like almost everyone else, have run physical risks in the past, such as a serious operation and the civil war, and, again like almost everyone else, I have felt closer to God when threatened either by microbes or bombs.'

Besides all the chemical, magical and religious tranquillizers, there is a fourth and final category, which one could refer to as personal tranquillizers. A person who is either dying or in danger of losing his life can derive a feeling of calmness from the presence and the physical contact of a loved one or of an anonymous 'good Samaritan'. In 1979, I suffered an extremely serious car accident in the city of Oxford. At that moment I 'felt' the need of my wife, my children, and my loved ones with more intensity than ever before. As I lay on the grass next to the road, surrounded by policemen and onlookers, my neural computer pressured me with the desire for my wife's company. A passing soldier, as compassionate as the Samaritan of Christ's parable, attempted to console me with words charged with affection and goodwill. I shall never forget the relief with which his benevolence provided me. A loved one can undoubtedly be the most effective tranquillizer that can be administered to a dying person.

We ought to marvel at the chemical, magical, religious and social tranquillizers which the subject can find in the pharmacy of his culture, as well as in the biological pharmacy of his brain. However, it must not be forgotten that the prescription must first be presented to the chemist. The same is true of the brain's chemist: the prescription must first be handed over. If the subject wants the brain to administer a magical or religious tranquillizer to him, he must comply with the magical or religious codes that have been registered by his neural computer.

The Sensory Translation of Fear

Like any other feeling, fear is *meta-physical* ('beyond the physical world') and hence neither the eyes nor the ears, nor any other sensory antennae, can perceive it. The genetic plan, however, has designed a simultaneous, automatic and distinct translation of each feeling (often supported by another biocultural translation) into sensory signs (visual, phonic, olfactory and tactile). A visual, phonic, and at times even olfactory grammar of fear has been conceived, installed and maintained by bionature. When the neural computer activates the mechanism of fear, it orders several visual and phonic flags to be raised: pale skin, open mouth and eyes, raised arms, grinding of teeth, and a harsh sound, which every human being's neural computer knows how to translate. Different visual and phonic expressions correspond to different intensities of fear. In Pompeii, the city buried under the ashes of Vesuvius, numerous charred bodies were found which still showed the victims' state of panic.

The brain can even carry out an olfactory translation of fear. In many different languages we find the expression 'to defecate out of fear' (employing the verb prohibited by the aesthetic code). In a radio interview, Félix Rodríguez de la Fuente, the popular host of an extremely successful wildlife programme aired on Spanish television during the 1970s, related how one day he was confronted by the 'king of the jungle'. Although this majestic animal did nothing but look at him for a short while before turning around and leaving, this popular television celebrity confessed that the situation made him feel extremely intense urges to defecate. An olfactory experience of the colourless, odourless and tasteless feeling of fear took place inside the Spanish Parliament on the day of the 'coup' of 1981.

To what extent does the neural computer allow the subject a margin of freedom when it activates the emotional mechanism of fear? As in the case of all other mechanisms of emergency (diarrhoea, vomiting, sneezing, and so on), the neural computer triggers off such a powerful emotional order that before the subject has any time to think about it, he has already gesticulated, or screamed, or even defecated. (We have to take into account the intensity of the fear activated by the brain in accordance with the automatic evaluation of the danger.) My wife and I were recently waiting to buy tickets in a cinema queue. I was engrossed in my own thoughts, when suddenly a human scream made me snap back into reality. Just as my wife was about to hand the ticket clerk a five-thousand peseta note, someone slapped her hand, took the money, and sprinted off. The attention of all of those who were waiting in the queue immediately turned towards my wife because the phonic alarm of fear was immediately translated by their brains. We should note how a series of actions and reactions were automatically set off. My wife's neural computer orders her to sound the alarm of fear. Before she has any time to think about it, her throat and mouth have emitted this sound. The neural computer of everyone in the vicinity immediately perceives this sound and, in accordance with its program on alarm mechanisms, interrupts their mental/emotional activity and compels them to observe what is happening. My wife's neural computer translates something which only she has felt, an invisible fear, into the phonic world. The neural computer of everyone around her perceives this phonic signal, immediately translates it, and, following a specific program installed in the brain, makes them occupy and preoccupy themselves with the person who has sounded the alarm of fear. The interrelation between the emotional, the chemical, the physical and the social world is undoubtedly one of nature's most amazing feats. The emotional system itself is perhaps nature's greatest masterpiece, although it has thus far been generally neglected and ignored.

Part III
Emotional Control of Society

8

Emotional Laws of Laughter and Language

Laughter as a Biosocial Mechanism of Warning and Punishment

In our excursion through sentiment we encounter a singular feeling: the urge to laugh. The brain pressures us to perform two acts simultaneously: a visual one, consisting of very specific facial gestures, and a phonic one, consisting of the production of certain sounds with the phonic instruments (guttural cords, tongue, teeth, lips). We have been able to discern the rationale behind the feelings analysed so far: if the neural computer fails to inform and pressure the individual with the emotional mechanism of hunger (when, how much, and in what manner he should eat), his body and life would waste away. But why the devil should the neural computer suggest and provoke the production of the gestures and sounds of laughter? 'Well, laughing is healthy, pleasurable. It relaxes your nerves. It's an escape valve.' We must recall, however, that each time we obey the emotional demands of the neural computer, we 'relax': eating, copulating, urinating, drinking. Considering the way in which nature seems to work, what can account for these urges to laugh? Why do we receive such a pleasurable salary when the gestures and sounds of laughter are produced? This scientific conundrum must be resolved.

If we notice, we will observe that the task advised by the neural computer is to translate an interior feeling into an exterior display: to send a visual and phonic message. What is this message? To whom is it directed? And with what purpose? Unlike the desire for food or the urge to excrete, it does not appear that the organism should require this drive to laugh and to make these sounds and gestures in order for the body to function or maintain itself in good shape. One suspects that here the neural computer offers the individual an emotional salary for a task useful and indispensable for his society. This is the law in our working hypothesis: 'The neural computer is bionaturally programmed to trigger off the emotional mechanism of laughter – urges to laugh – each time it receives information through its sensory channels of the infraction of a social norm, whether this norm belongs to a bionatural or a biocultural code, with the object of drawing attention to, judging, and penalizing the infraction.' As we will see, this law is as rigid, automatic and inexorable as any physical, chemical or biological law. Laughter is not a joke of nature, but a biochemical and emotional mechanism indispensable for the maintenance of the rules of the social game.

Let us begin with an example. In the 1970s an African man approached the priest at a Catholic mass wearing a brassière on his head, the straps tied at his chin. None of his fellow Africans felt the slightest urge to laugh at the sight of this bra-hat. The European clergyman, on the other hand, was unable to resist going into hysterics. In this African community, brassières did not exist, nor were the cultural rules regulating the use of this article of clothing generally known (who can use it where, how, and when). In this society the young girls received holy communion bare breasted, in the same way that European girls walk around bare faced (unlike Muslim girls, who must hide their countenances behind veils). The African who purchased the brassière in a market where 'white' goods were sold, by tying it around his head proclaimed to the four winds a visual message which, translated into words, would yield something like the following: 'As you can see, I can afford the luxury of buying a "white" adornment. Admire my economic superiority, my high grade of civilization, my cutting-edge fashion consciousness. Writhe with jealousy. One-nil.'

The neural computer of the European priest, by contrast, was programmed with a radically divergent dress code, including the following norm: 'Brassières may not be worn except as female underwear.' A woman wearing one on her head would also have provoked laughter. The priest's neural computer received data about the bra-wearing African from its photographic information system; discovering this social infraction, automatically released strong urges to laugh, despite the state of pious concentration required during the distribution of the Body of Christ. Simultaneously, a different set of cultural codes installed in the brain of this priest pressured him to resist 'cracking up' (a prohibition on laughter during the celebration of a sacred rite of this nature). In this case, the urges to laugh were stronger. He was able to withstand his desire for some time, but when the moment arrived to give this African man holy communion, he was unable to contain himself and had to retire to the sacristy to laugh heartily for a few minutes. As happens with all desires that are resisted for a certain time, once the individual finally gives in (begins to urinate, to ejaculate, to scratch, etc.) the neural computer forces him to continue until the emotional densitometer returns to zero degrees.

In this case we were dealing with the infraction of a biocultural code. In other cases it may be a bionatural code. A nose of gigantic dimensions – 'Once there was a man to a nose attached', in Quevedo's version – may provoke laughter. Here we are dealing with the infraction of a bionatural law ('the size and design of a nose must follow a certain blueprint'). The mechanism of laughter functions with the same rigidity and precision whether it reacts to a bionatural or to a biocultural code.

These are the elements or steps required for the activation of the emotional mechanism of laughter:

1. The human brain. The brain of no other animal is capable of acquiring the program of laughter. Here we find a further genetic frontier between man and ape: *homo risibilis*.
2. One (or many) bionatural or biocultural codes of social rules must have been installed in the neural computer.
3. A law from one of these codes must have been broken.
4. The brain must have received the information regarding this infraction through its sensorial channels.
5. At this point the neural computer automatically activates the urges to laugh.
6. The neural computer simultaneously consults other programs, which may pressure the individual with opposing emotional mechanisms to resist the desire to laugh.
7. The individual approves of these urges, or perhaps they are too strong for him to keep them in line (they 'split his sides' or 'crack him up').

8.   The individual laughs: the neural computer sends orders to the appropriate facial muscles to raise the flag of hilarity, and to the phonic instruments to play the melody of laughter.

The human being finds himself subjected to the rigours of this law as he is bound by the laws of digestion, circulation, growth and death, having had no part to play in its conception, design, installation or functioning.

When the traffic policeman blows his whistle or switches on his siren, he means to alert all drivers and pedestrians to a certain fact: someone has committed the infraction of a norm of the traffic code. This is one of the functions of laughter: to elicit others' attention and make them aware that someone is breaking a social norm (for example, a bearded woman breast-feeding a child in public). The motorized traffic policeman has at his disposal visual and phonic systems that attract attention (brightly coloured intermittent lights and deafening sirens). The brain's policeman also elicits the attention of others with visual and phonic signals (a deaf man has no difficulties identifying a laughing man).

Secondly, a traffic policeman can judge and condemn the violator of a norm of the traffic code, making him pay a fine proportional to the seriousness of the infraction (from a minor economic sanction to a prison sentence). He who laughs at someone, for having committed an infraction, is judging and punishing him with a most severe fine: ridicule. Every member of society is programmed to be a judge, policeman and torturer of all other members of his society, whether he is aware of it or not, whether he likes it or not. Without this truly ingenious system, the diverse social codes could not be maintained, in the same way that all manner of agents, policemen, judges and punishments are necessary to maintain the social order. In reality, the judicial system and police forces are yet new variations of *cultura ancilla naturae*, 'culture as a servant of nature'. Infractions are expected by the genetic code, but the infraction does not eliminate the rule, as we saw earlier, while a system of reporting, judging and punishment exists.

Undoubtedly, laughing is one of the most pleasurable feelings. But nature is a calculating economist and gives away nothing for free. It pays a high gratification for laughing, because the laugher plays simultaneously the roles of the policeman who reports and draws attention to the transgression, the arbiter who judges/condemns, and the torturer who inflicts the painful lashings of laughter on the poor victim. Nature, having come to realize the importance of these indispensable social tasks, has stipulated an emotional salary appropriate to the job. The brain's biological cashier does not hand out its emotional pay-cheques according to a regular weekly or monthly rhythm. It pays by the job: this much for eating or drinking here and now, that much for laughing at the man over there.

In relation to the functioning of this emotional mechanism, we also come across a law of intensity and its corresponding densitometer: 'The neural computer triggers off a certain intensity of urges to laugh – and a correspondingly intense pleasure once they have been satisfied – proportional to the degree of the infraction and the importance of the law, as automatically calculated according to the code installed in the software.'

Factories of Artificial Laughter

Human beings have become aware that laughing is extremely enjoyable, and that it requires little effort: no more than moving a few facial, mouth and throat muscles. With minimum exertion, a great compensation is obtained. But a person cannot laugh whenever he pleases. Let us suppose that a traffic policeman is paid only by commission – if no one breaks the law, he makes no money. For this agent, every single infraction is a blessing. If the neural computer detects no infractions, the urges to laugh are not activated, and thus not a penny of pleasure is doled out. The neural computer is prepared to have the individual feign laughter, to laugh externally even without an internal feeling. Not only is deception possible with words (the use of sounds which do not correspond to the ideas or interior feelings of the individual). In a similar way, untruthful translations of the feelings of laughter into exterior signals is also possible.

Sometimes a whole group may burst into hilarity. One of those present may not know what the others find funny, but still laugh to avoid appearing ridiculous or ignorant. It may be that his neural computer lacks the relevant rules of play, and therefore fails to detect the transgression. In this case the individual in question pretends to have understood the infraction to avoid being punished by laughter himself, for failing to be in tune with the latest trends, etc. (i.e. for committing an infraction of certain social norms). He laughs mechanically to avoid having others laugh at him wholeheartedly. It may also happen that his neural computer functions at a somewhat slower pace than those of the group in question. If, after the laughter of his companions has died down, he suddenly lets out a loud guffaw, he will be the object of ridicule. To avoid this fine he imitates the spontaneous outburst of the others, since his neural computer has not yet detected the infraction of any norm. But in such cases we may notice that the neural computer does not reward him who follows the motions of laughter mechanically, lacking true urges to laugh. Any reader may verify the workings of this law. It does not suffice to produce the gestures and sounds of laughter to obtain the corresponding reward from the emotional bank. From this new perspective we can observe the precision and rigidity of this, as of all other laws of the emotional system. The neural computer pays a particular pleasure only after having activated specific urges which have been fulfilled, following pre-established norms and not according to individual whim.

Without an infraction, there is no fine; without a fine, there is no commission. This is the emotional law of laughter. The human being, who has devoted himself for centuries to the science of 'having a good time', that is, of maximizing the quantity and quality of pleasures obtainable from the neural computer, has invented artificial or prefabricated laughter. Situations can be created in which people commit infractions that are false but which may 'fool' a neural computer that is successfully misled by its sensorial information. Clowns, comedians or political cartoonists are manufacturers of artificial laughter. Notice that the clown puts on an 'abnormal' nose and 'abnormal' feet, and breaks all the norms of dressing, walking, reasoning, and of various other codes. Society allows the creation of these fictitious infractions. No rule is actually broken and the audiences enjoy themselves. Here, however, it may happen that an infraction in the long run may become the rule, and thus no longer funny at all. In English the past form of the verbs 'to blow' and 'to brake' may have once been 'blowed' and 'braked', following the regular verb patterns – saying 'blew' or 'broke' would have been ridiculous deviations. But if an infraction ceases to be an infraction and becomes a rule (a fascinating process which I shall later turn to), the punishment disappears. From that moment on, a person who utters the words 'He blowed up the balloon' or 'I braked it' becomes the object of mockery.

Children who for the first time observe a man with 'ridiculous' feet, nose and attire will find him riotously funny. Their neural computer detects these novel infractions and rewards the child who laughs. But there comes a moment when the neural computer 'knows' that for a clown the big red nose, oversized shoes, make-up and silly outfit are something normal and even prescribed (in the same way that the irregular 'broke' or 'blew' are now rigorously prescribed forms). These 'normal' clowns no longer provoke any laughter by their mere appearance. They must invent new unexpected tricks and pranks which will be detected and identified by neural computers as infractions of social norms. Every orator, every politician, every preacher attempts to recreate scenes in which actors infringe social norms of all types. If he manages to make the audience laugh, he will have gone a long distance in winning them over to his side. The spectator, having enjoyed himself, feels much more disposed to listen to whatever the orator or politician in question has to say.

To Laugh and to be Laughed at

It is one thing to punish and another to be punished; it is one thing to torture, and another to be tortured; it is one thing to laugh, and another to be the object of mockery. If laughter is one of the most pleasurable of activities, its victim or target feels one of the most painful sensations provided for by the genetic plan. 'No one laughs at me!' 'I will tolerate anything but to be ridiculed!' We hear such commentaries all the time. The neural computer warns and threatens every human being – men from every latitude, historical period, culture, race or class – with the cruel whip of ridicule. Every day, when he gets up and prepares to enter the public stage of the great world theatre, he feels the following warnings and threats: 'Observe all the rules of the game, in dressing, in talking, in walking; ignore none of the prescriptions of the ethical, aesthetic, economic or political codes . . . or else you will appear ridiculous, you will be mocked, and I will punish you cruelly with the emotional whips reserved for such buffoons.' (My own translation from the emotional to the verbal language.)

We thus encounter the following law: 'To the pleasure obtained by him who laughs corresponds a disagreeable sensation of the same intensity by the violator of the social norm.' Laughter is a two-faced coin: the agreeable face of its producer and the disagreeable face of its target. Man has neither the liberty to prevent his neural computer from activating in him the desire to laugh nor the ability to check its application of painful ridicule. Both processes function with an absolute independence from the individual's consciousness and choice. I once visited an auditorium in Santa Monica, California, to listen to Beethoven's Fifth Symphony with my three sons. A very dignified lady glided gracefully across the stage to the microphone in order to give a short introductory speech. Having hardly spoken the words 'Ladies and gentlemen . . . ', she slipped and collapsed awkwardly on the floor, limbs flying everywhere. We were all unable to prevent our neural computers from triggering off strong urges to laugh (as well as feelings of compassion). Titters, giggles and outright cackles half-muffled with hands or handkerchiefs could be heard. Some had to run outside to explode with laughter in the lobby. Without a doubt this woman's neural computer punished her for finding herself in such a ridiculous position. The neural computer, like any machine, works without emotion and punishes mercilessly.

If we were not constantly threatened by the lashings of ridicule, we would go out into the street naked or dressed as we wished, and would fail to respect the millions of other social rules to which we are subject (a monkey need not shave, clothe himself with countless rags and ornaments, or put on make-up). Laughter is a biosocial mechanism of censorship which protects the whole corpus of the social rules of play, from the most important to the most trivial. A lecturing professor's open trouser zipper is sufficient cause to drive a classful of students into fits of amusement and to subject the lecturer to waves of embarrassment when he finally discovers the reason for the snickers and giggles spreading throughout the room. A woman once let an audible 'toot' escape from her 'rear end' while standing in a bus. She deliberately let her handbag fall to the floor and said, 'Oh, I've dropped my fart.' The whole of the bus blew up in hysterics; the woman fainted. I was told this anecdote by some Estellicas (inhabitants of Estella, Spain) as a true story. *Si non è vero, è ben trovato.* The whole process is automatic: first the spontaneous laughter provoked in these passengers, strangers to each other, each in the world of his or her own worries; and secondly the emotional torture to which this unfortunate damsel, against whom none present had any complaint, was subjected.

The human being fears no policeman, judge or torturer as much as the policeman/judge/torturer of ridicule installed in his own mind and in those of 'others'. Someone who commits a traffic violation may quite easily avoid being caught 'red handed' by the relatively few police officers who patrol the streets. But Nature, in her incomparably astute plans and provisions (which outdo the KGB and the CIA by millions of light years), has designed a system whereby each human being is programmed as the policeman/judge/torturer of every other human being in relation to a vast set of social norms. And his neural computer will continue to punish the slightest of infractions with the emotional mechanism of laughter, even if he is completely unaware, as an individual, of this state of events. The human being knows from the emotional directives laid out by his neural computer that if he goes out on the street and commits certain infractions, he will not be able to escape detection, judgement and punishment by anyone who happens to be walking by.

A Universal and Cultural Language

We must distinguish between the hardware and the software of laughter. The hardware is common to all members of the species, a rigorous genetic monopoly of the human family. This hardware is composed of physical, biochemical, sensorial, mental and emotional elements. Among the physico-biochemical elements we find the visual and phonic instruments that produce laughter, as well as the nervous system that transmits messages from the brain to these instruments, and of course the biochemical component which the brain itself constitutes. Furthermore, there exists a bionatural program – bionatural software – of emotional punishments corresponding to codes common to the whole of the human family. An adult male with a squeaky high-pitched voice is detected by the neural computer of every human being as an infraction of the code regulating the proper voice-pitch of the adult male, and this infraction is punished by the genetic fine of ridicule. Laughter is thus a universal language, a genetic or ecumenical Esperanto that was not destroyed by the Tower of Babel.

On the other hand, each human society – territorial, religious, generational, etc. – is characterized by its own codes, by its own rules of play. An Englishman who speaks not a word of Chinese is present at an assembly of Chinese people conversing in their language. Suddenly, they all break out into laughter. This Englishman knows that these people have switched from one phonetic code – that of their own society, Chinese – to another phonetic language common to both the Chinese and the English: the language of laughter. Nevertheless, the Englishman cannot participate in the amusement of this Chinese gathering. Within the system of laughter there is a common bionatural program and various biocultural ones. Only when a neural computer has acquired a certain cultural code will it be able to identify an infraction and punish it with the whip of laughter.

The Game of Ridicule

From the species of Confucius, Einstein and Beethoven, of Marx and Christ, certain individuals emerge here and there, in remote and modern times, who create new rules of play. If these new codes are confronted by old, established and sacred norms of a particular society, an a-normal or extra-ordinary individual of this type will have to face the exacting tribunal of ridicule. Don Salvador de Madariaga told me how in the 1930s he witnessed a relevant scene from the world's stage. An unknown doctor, at an international medical symposium in London, presented a new theory which challenged many of the 'untouchable' rules and dogmas of the 'sacred church' of medicine of that period and latitude. Some of those present began to giggle timidly and soon laughter began to spread throughout the auditorium. Eventually the audience came to resemble a circus crowd rather than an assembly of respected medical minds. When the shower of snickers and chuckles had finally died down, the poor doctor meekly resumed the exposition in his rudimentary English. This time they roared with it. The audience would quieten down. The doctor, sweating profusely, would utter a new sentence with a weak and trembling voice. 'Hah, hah, hah!' was the spontaneous, immediate, and explosive reply from the crowd, now truly enjoying the show. The doctor, crushed, humiliated, pierced through and through by the cruel spikes of ridicule, picked up his papers with shaking hands and stepped down from the podium. He left without having been able to expound his theories, gasping for air, a contorted expression on his face. He who dares to challenge the rules of the social game – in whatever arena – is denounced and punished by the lashings of ridicule. This poor doctor was forced to give up. He had lost the game.

Nature has designed the human being like a bee within its hive. It allows for any human bee to confront and reject the rules of the game of his particular hive, but he will have to pay the emotional fine of humiliation. Nevertheless, nature has also designed the individual as a potential reformer of the rules of the beehive. An individual can in part create his own hive ('Marxists', 'Christians', 'Freudians', 'Buddhists', 'Mohammedans') with the rules of the game drawn up by himself. This doctor, fiercely attacked by the members of his own society with the emotional weapon of ridicule, lost the first battle. But he stubbornly persisted in his crusade to convince his colleagues that his theories were not as risible as they believed. Twenty-four years later, in another international symposium at the same forum in London, the president of the congress stood and addressed the assembly: 'Twenty-four years ago, Doctor Trueta presented us with theories that seemed to us absurd and ridiculous. We laughed in his face. Today, we know that it was he who was in the right, and now both doctors and patients are indebted to him. Millions of limbs and lives have been saved in the war thanks to his innovative ideas and techniques. I believe that in the name of justice we must stand and offer him our sincerest apologies for our ignorance and stupidity with our applause.' The entire assembly gave him a thunderous standing ovation, every man present feeling a lump in his throat, while tears welled up in Doctor Trueta's eyes.

The genetic plan has not foreseen that within the beehive there can emerge a Doctor Trueta, a Buddha, a Marx, hippies, Jesuits, feminists, or the 'Flat Earth Society'. Laughter is a tribunal of justice which no one can escape. But the exceptional individual may continue the game. We are in the presence of two players foreseen in our species by the genetic plan: Doctor Trueta versus the medical establishment (his own society), the individual versus his beehive. The individual initiates the game by trying to prove with his words and/or actions that a certain accepted rule or code is incorrect, absurd, and/or immoral. The brains programmed with this code attack the challenge with the darts of laughter. The individual loses the first round. Doctor Trueta, or the individual trying to reform society, finds himself the overwhelmed victim of this first attack, like a boxer floored by a well-aimed punch. He hears two diametrically opposed emotional speeches, which translated into verbal language would sound something like this: 'You're being ridiculous. Everyone sees you as a lunatic. They think you are mad as a hatter. Stick to the beaten path and everything will be much easier.' 'Stick to your guns. All pioneers and wise men have had to drink the bitter cup of ridicule to the last drop. Pay no attention to your tormentors. One day they will all know and recognize that you were right, and will applaud your wisdom, your valour, your integrity.'

If the individual has the tenacity and courage to continue in this brutal contest – a single bee versus the whole hive – he may eventually emerge victorious. New rules eventually displace the old. Infractions become rules and perhaps in the future begin to be questioned, attacked and replaced again. Sometimes the creative and pioneering individual who confronted certain rules – in the scientific, political, ethical or religious field – has been ridiculed in life and even excommunicated, poisoned, exiled, stoned or crucified. Nevertheless, if his code was the true or most just one, it will eventually attract followers until it becomes 'normal' and ordinary. Galileo Galilei had to swear that the Earth did not move. Now we scoff at those who mocked Galileo. Christ was ridiculed to the point of being clothed as a mock king, complete with a crown of thorns and a red tunic, while being saluted, between guffaws, 'Hail, King of the Jews!' The new ethical code preached by Christ, dictating forgiveness for enemies and understanding for the prostitute or the thief, was rejected by his contemporaries, who executed him. However, twenty centuries later millions of human beings call themselves Christian.

If the individual who attacks the current rules of the game – of whatever type of society – fails to attract a few followers who may initiate a social 'snowball', his vision may be lost. He will have remained a loser, and his new theories and his new code will die with him. Sometimes what occurs is that a scientific or ethical pioneer manages to form a small marginal community which is ridiculed and perhaps persecuted by the society at large. Christ was followed by a few contemporaries of humble origin, twelve, one of whom betrayed him for a few coins, ten who disappeared from the scene when he was arrested and executed, and one who risked his life bravely by accompanying him during the agony and death at the cross. However, after his death and partly as a result of it, these few Christians challenged the two societies in the area: the Jewish one and the Roman one. In both societies these Christians were the 'butt' of every joke: 'Have you heard about these guys who say if you get slapped on one cheek you should offer the other to be slapped as well? Ha, ha, ha. They're stark raving mad!' At this point the game is played between a small marginal minority and two huge, powerful, respected and respectable societies. Ridicule is one of the most powerful weapons. At first such a tiny rebellious community appears to have little chance of winning, but Nature has foreseen that such a group may continue the game and become a majority that may impose its own rules. After twenty centuries the Jewish society has maintained its religious/cultural code, while the Roman one with its old empire – today, Europe – despite having once dominated the Jews, despite having unleashed a merciless persecution against that 'group of dangerous madmen', converted to Christianity. The popular saying 'he who laughs last, laughs loudest' contains a profound and accurate intuition. It points to the fact that the game of ridicule involves many different rounds, and that the last battle or war may be won after defeat at the first and even many successive battles.

Different societies – political parties, religious sects, scientific or pseudoscientific schools, etc. – make use of the powerful mechanism of ridicule in their competition for followers, for votes, for converts. The weapon of ridicule can be extremely powerful if it is used judiciously at the appropriate moment. Every politician attempts to ridicule his adversaries during the election campaign as effectively as possible. 'Mr. So-and-so – a rival in the election race – has described you as a wolf in sheep's clothing,' a journalist taunted Churchill at a press conference. 'Poor devil,' replied Churchill, calmly puffing his famous cigar, 'He is a sheep in sheep's clothing.' The next day, the whole of the United Kingdom laughed in unison at the unfortunate politician whom Sir Winston 'crushed like a cockroach' with this ridiculing stomp.

We must also be aware, furthermore, that every human society, even an 'anarchic' hippy or punk one, whatever its claims and proclamations about the abolition of order, limitless freedom and the like, is subject to the same strict rules of ridicule. The punk must punctiliously observe the rules of the punk game: dying his hair in bright primary colours, cutting and sculpting it according to very precise canons, wearing the punk uniform, no less strict than that of Capuchin friars (indeed currently punks follow their dress code more closely than do these medieval friars, who in most places no longer tonsure their hair, sport beards, or even wear their habit in public). The punk must also respect a 'hardware code' – a punk is recognizable by the clanking of his metal studs and chains as a cow is by its bell; a musical code, a linguistic code, and others. A punk dressed in a suit among punks is as ridiculous as a yuppie dressed as a punk among yuppies. The neural computer of the punk warns and threatens him continuously (translating from the emotional to verbal language): 'Watch it! Respect all of the rules of the punk life-style or prepare to suffer the poisoned darts of ridicule.'

The game of laughter is played, therefore, along two fronts: the punk within his own punk society, and the punk versus the 'establishment'. So, first of all, the individual, as the member of any of his multiple beehives, is constantly subject to these warnings and threats from his neural computer: 'Careful! Dress, talk, act, eat, and do everything respecting this society's rules of the game, unless you want to appear ridiculous.' It is possible, as we have seen, for the individual to rebel against his own society and dare to be ridiculous. On the other hand, the punk laughs at the clothes of the upper classes, their 'prison', their manners, their life-style, while the upper classes find the chains, studs, brightly-coloured 'mohawk' haircuts, and life-style of punks laughable.

Biocultural Brakes on Laughter

We also find in human societies cultural programs which condemn to a greater or lesser degree the practice of injuring people with the whips of laughter in public. These programs may enter the brain and become biocultural programs which are maintained by their own emotional mechanisms. The religious program of Christianity, the program of 'good manners', and the program of hierarchy, among others, advise the individual not to laugh at anyone in public. In fact, it is quite unusual to 'laugh in someone's face'. Every human being fears that others may laugh at him behind his back, rather than in his face. Someone who laughs blatantly at another who trips over, who stutters, who walks with an unusual gait, or who suffers from some physical abnormality would be censured by shame and would appear ridiculous from the code of 'civilized' manners, of Christianity, of adult behaviour, and others. The human being is subject to such a variety of diverse and conflicting codes installed in his computer, which threaten him with punishment for every error, that he may appear ridiculous for not laughing when he should or for laughing at the wrong time. The code of hierarchy also directs the code of laughter, as it does so many others.

On one hand we come across the following law: 'he who laughs is to the victim of laughter as the winner is to the loser'. As we have seen, a game of several, sometimes multi-secular, rounds is possible in this case, until 'he who laughs last' wins the game. In this case, hierarchy is the effect or product of the very game of laughter. On another level, within established hierarchies the subordinate must never laugh at his superiors, unless he has decided to renounce his position in the company or relevant society. A person in a superior position may play more or less cruel jokes at the expense of his subordinates, who must tolerate these pranks if they wish to maintain their livelihood. Subordinates must also, if they are ambitious and have any intention of rising up the ladder of flattery, chuckle at the witticisms of the well-placed executive, the company director, or the minister, even if they find these lacking in any humour whatsoever (using the aforementioned artificial and false laughter).

Seriously and in Jest

'Have you said, Mr Tamames, that one can no longer find Reds even in China?', a Spanish economist and politician was asked in a television programme in October 1987. 'Well, yes, I said that ironically. Obviously, it's a joke' (quoted from memory). In human society – in all of its varieties – a certain program, certain rules of play, certain times and places have been created where the joke, the jest, the parody or sarcasm directed even at those in power, is allowed and where no one should take offence. In human society there are hunting grounds where the season for false laughter may be officially opened. Laughter permitted as a joke is not serious, and therefore does not function as a social punishment. Laughter is a powerful mechanism of control when it is meant in earnest. The court jester was authorized to laugh at the monarch and at the courtesans. At carnivals, it was and still is allowed to ridicule the municipal or national authorities. Political cartoonists in the most respected newspapers fulfil *servatis servandis* the role of court jester: they are authorized to laugh at political figures in a joking context. It is not serious ridicule.

Nevertheless, even the jokes of the buffoon, of carnival revellers, and of political cartoonists may carry out a more serious censuring function than it might seem. Authorized ridicule, as 'pretend' criticism, as 'purely innocent' joking, may actually turn into a fierce and biting social critique, and even into a check-mate that has left more than one politician out of the game. It is hardly coincidental that dictators ban court jesters, political cartoonists, and television programmes containing political satire. Even in democratic nations, many comedians have suffered fierce persecutions and attacks of every type for ridiculing certain politicians 'in jest'. In Great Britain it was rumoured in the press that a certain prime minister had ordered the immediate dismissal of the head of the BBC after a comedian's jokes about his 'romantic companion'. It is curious also that Franco did not authorize, during the forty years of his stay in power, the showing of Charlie Chaplin's *The Great Dictator*, a humorous film, a film of jesting ridicule.

The rules of the humorous game allow anyone to 'fool around' with or 'play a prank' on another and require that the victim of the joke not take it seriously, because 'it's only a joke'. If the latter in fact does exhibit anger, he only makes himself appear more ridiculous. Frequently, under the pretext of 'playing a harmless prank with no desire to offend', more than one innocent victim has had his soul skinned alive. The human being fears ridicule over everything. No one finds being laughed at amusing, even if assured that it is all in jest. How astute is Nature to incite every human being to enjoy laughing at his neighbour, at his friend, and at his enemy, at everyone, seriously or in jest, while it threatens all and sundry with the punishment of ridicule. Nature kills two birds with one stone. Firstly, every human being has his eyes peeled for the infractions of others. If he catches somebody out, his neural computer will reward him immediately with the pleasure of jeering at the deviant (even if it has to be 'behind his back': 'When I get home and tell my wife, we're going to have a riot!'). Secondly, every human being knows that he is constantly being spied on by others at every moment and in every place, and that all are waiting for the first opportunity to enjoy a laugh at his expense. The urge to laugh, the pleasure of laughing, and the fear of appearing ridiculous together comprise one of the most efficient emotional mechanisms that could be conceived for preserving the established rules of the game and human society itself.

Abnormal Laughter

In chapter 3 I alluded to a young man who used to walk through the streets of Pamplona, at the time when I studied in this city, surprising passers-by with his sudden and resounding outbursts of laughter. The whole of the city came to know the reason for this bizarre behaviour. The abnormal cackles produced by this poor man were the chronic side-effect of the meningitis he had suffered as a small boy. His emotional system of laughter was damaged, and his neural computer continually triggered off urges to laugh. Breakdowns and faults in the emotional system may occur as they do in the digestive system or in the carburettor of a car. Sometimes a person feels continuous urges to urinate or defecate. He visits the toilet again, but does not manage to get rid of the torturous desires. Notice how here we are dealing with *a-nomalies* (from the Greek *alfa*, without, and *nomos*, law), with ab-normal sensations; that is, with infractions to a law which do not invalidate the law, but rather suppose, presuppose and ratify the law. We could not know that it is ab-normal that someone should laugh 'without rhyme or reason', cackling away all over the city, if we did not suppose a law exists: 'A human being laughs when there exists a reason for him to laugh.' These anomalies of the emotional/biochemical system may occur, but rather than invalidating any law, from a new perspective they underline and emphasize the laws that direct the emotional system. The individual does not laugh haphazardly, randomly or at whim. He is subject to strict laws of the emotional system of laughter and to the observation of others, as he is subject to the strict laws of the urges to eliminate liquid, solid and gaseous wastes. The neural computer has the last word.

Biosocial Timer of Laughter

If an infant, as it emerged from its mother's womb, rather than cry let out a few loud chuckles, the global village would be more shaken by the news than by the landing of Rust's aeroplane in Red Square:
'BRITISH NEWBORN LAUGHS AT BIRTH.'

A-nomalies, events which transgress norms or laws, sell. Everywhere we come across the same strategy of Nature as installed in the neural computer: pleasure awarded for detecting and condemning the a-nomaly, with the object of discovering and upholding the law (or eventually to replace one law with another, as we have seen).

Within the meticulous program of the emotional system and of the biosocial systems, the genetic plan has foreseen certain biological timers which initiate processes at predetermined times. Nowadays we can purchase electronic ovens with timers that allow a household cook to leave the house with the chicken roasting at a certain temperature. There is no need to rush back home from the shops to prevent the fowl from turning into a blackened, cindered nightmare, as the oven switches itself off.

We find in our exploration of the geography of the brain certain mechanisms which activate feelings automatically, following precise and rigid laws. Within this meticulous programming are included a number of biological timers or clocks installed in the brain which trigger off the commencement of certain emotional systems. It is normal that a baby should give soft kicks in the mother's womb during the last months of pregnancy. The neural computer does not yet activate in the foetus the desires to cry or to laugh. When the brain receives information about a particular stage in the child's development, it nudges him with the emotional prod of the urges to stand and make his first steps. For the work done, the child will be paid an emotional salary that stems from the applause and admiration of the audience present (mummy, daddy, brothers, sisters and neighbours). Gradually, the neural computer initiates him in the process of learning and practice of laughter.

With my own babies I have carried out the following experiment repeatedly. Certain ab-normal gestures produced by daddy's face already provoke laughter in the child of a few months. The neural computer begins to detect infractions to the 'normal' repertoire of facial expressions and triggers off the urges to laugh. As the neural computer begins to assimilate new sets of rules, the range of laughter-provoking stimuli expands. At 18 months, if I wear a feminine article of clothing such as a brassière, my child laughs immediately. His neural computer has grasped the cultural norm regulating the correct placement of certain articles of clothing, has detected an infraction, and has activated the urges to laugh. The more codes assimilated by the neural computer, the more infractions will be detected and the more laughter will be provoked. Laughter, like speech or crying, is a language and a code which begins to be used when the neural computer gives it the green light, in accordance with an innate biological timer. From that moment on, the neural computer develops this language by a gradual and accumulative process.

The Music of Language: an Innate and Universal Language

'Words . . . came to be made use of by men . . . not by any natural conexion that there is between particular articulate sounds and certain ideas, for then there would be but one language amongst all men; but by a voluntary imposition.'[1] (Locke forgot to add 'and particular feelings'.) Locke's argument seemed impeccable. However, in our sherlockholmian exploration of the neural computer we have become accustomed to doubt what had appeared most obvious. Nature, like the cunning thief, seems to delight in leaving false clues in our path as if to mislead us into adopting erroneous theories, which nevertheless seem 'as plain as the nose on one's face' (though at the same time this encourages us to scrutinize the most commonplace beliefs and never trust completely what seems most self-evident).

In Locke's argument, there is an explicit premise: 'If there were a natural connection between particular articulate sounds and certain ideas, there would be no more than a single language for all men.' This premise appears logical and indisputable. Locke does not continue by arguing, 'As we find no such connection anywhere' (second premise), 'there is no single language for all men' (conclusion). This second premise and the conclusion seem so evident that they are left implicit in Locke's assertion. Witness the huge diversity of human languages: Chinese, Russian, Japanese, Quechua, English, and a whole slew of tongues unintelligible to each other. However, our consciousnesses (but not our neural computers), dazzled and confused within this infinite linguistic hall of mirrors, have failed to notice a single language common to all men. I admit Locke's first premise but reject the second, and therefore abandon his conclusion. I would argue for a natural connection (which we will call bionatural for previously given reasons) between certain articulate sounds and certain ideas (and certain feelings, we will add), and, therefore, following Locke's first premise, I conclude: 'there is a single common language for all men'. How is this possible?

We can find, within English or German, or any human language, a double language: the verbal and the musical, the words and the music.. The music of language, the musical language, is innate, bionatural, universal (across history and geography). The text of language, the verbal language, is cultural, variable, unintelligible in relation to that of others. Even through time the same language changes and transforms itself until becoming unintelligible with earlier versions (Latin becomes French and Spanish; the Spanish of the fourteenth century seems a foreign tongue to present-day Spaniards; Spanish developed along divergent paths to become Mexican, Argentinian, Cuban . . .). Reducing a song to its lyrics, ignoring the music altogether, would be confusing a part for the whole, and seeing only one of the two sides of the same coin. 'C'est le ton qui fait la chanson' (it is the tone which makes the song), according to a French saying. Though we should not go to the opposite extreme and devalue the words, a song without music would be inconceivable. In fact, both languages, the music and the words, are important, irreducible, each carrying its own mental and emotional messages.

Something similar occurs with any human language, *servatis servandis*. In the speech of an American or a German, the music is as important as the words. Both linguistic codes – the musical and the verbal – carry their own unique and irreducible mental and emotional messages. This is the law I believe I have found: 'The neural computer of every human being contains a pre-installed bionatural program designed to decipher and reproduce the musical language common to the whole human species, which accompanies the verbal aspect of all variations of human speech.' By musical language or music of language we understand the melody, the rhythm, the tone, the pitch and the volume, as in a song. Without stopping here to examine in full this little-known side of the language coin, I would like to point out a few of the most salient aspects. The bionatural software for the musical language installed in the neural computer includes:

(1) *The species which emits the sounds.* The neural computer of a blind American, upon hearing a Chinese person talking, a donkey braying, and a cow mooing can translate the music of these languages by deciphering a crucial social concept: the species of the animal which produced it. Although the blind person cannot translate the verbal sounds – the words – into concepts and feelings, not having assimilated the relevant software, he can, however, detect the music proper to human speech and common to all men, included in Chinese and in any human language. We can discover here a general plan, a design of musical codes for the different species: a musical language common to the members of each species and different from every other. The neural computer of each species can decipher the music which corresponds to its kind.

(2) *The age of the speaker.* The neural computer of a blind American can identify the different tones of voice of a baby, of a child of two, five or ten years, of an adolescent, of an adult, or of an elderly person, even if they speak nothing but Chinese.

Furthermore, this program has been installed in the brain in such a manner that this wondrous machine, upon hearing any human being in whatever language, can immediately translate the tone – a sound – into a concept: 'This Chinese individual is a child of about two years of age.'

(3) *The sex of the speaker.* The neural computer of every human being is programmed with the capability to translate the voice-pitch of the speaker of whatever language into the following concept: the speaker is male or female. The neural computer of a blind American immediately detects the sex of a Russian speaker upon hearing a few words. (This law is analysed in detail in my book *The Rules of the Game: the Sexes.*) This, like other genetic laws, can give rise to a-nomalies due to a congenital defect, an illness, or other causes. Once again we can verify how the infraction, far from disproving the law, presupposes and ratifies it. The neural computer immediately detects the infraction – for example, a

high-pitched voice in a male adult – and punishes it with the emotional fines of laughter and embarrassment. One day I phoned a distinguished professor and writer whom I only knew through his writings. When I heard 'Hello,' I asked 'Are you Mrs So-and-so?' 'No. I am Mr So-and-so,' he retorted angrily. My neural computer had given me a precise report of the sex, which corresponded to the genuinely feminine voice heard. Detecting the infraction of this biosocial law, it immediately activated two emotional mechanisms: I felt embarrassed and I felt the urge to laugh. My children found this incident hilarious.

(4) *The individuality of the speaker.* Visual, phonic, olfactory and other types of signals of identity with corresponding connections to the mental and emotional systems allow certain key structural positions of the beehive to be recognized: the species, the sex and the age. In these cases, the individual is perceived by the neural computer as a flea or as a monkey, as a male or as a female; in other words, as a de-individualized individual, or as the cell of a particular beehive (see chapter 4). But, on another level, the individual has been endowed with signals of identity which are specific and unique to him: fingerprint patterns, facial and bodily contours, and countless others which may escape our consciousness but not our neural computer. Among these individual patterns created by the department of genetic design of biosocial laws, we find in the music of all languages a voice-pitch specific and unique to each person, unmistakable from others. The neural computer does not contain pre-existing software with individual tones of voice – not even that of the mother, if our research is correct – but it will create a file of voices.

The neural computer keeps a record analogous to a telephone directory: a detailed list of the tones of voice of the spouse, of each child, of persons with whom one has professional, commercial or other relations. No sooner has the neural computer heard a single word, 'hello', it is able to extract from the musical language the voice-pitch of the individual speaking. Someone could object, 'How can you speak of a universal language when in this case we are dealing with something individual, the antithesis of the universal?' The universal language consists of genetic programming common to every neural computer, including the ability to recognize the voice of any individual, regardless of language. Today, the neural computers of many Japanese, Russian or European people can identify the voice of Clinton or John Paul II, though they may not be able to translate their verbal messages due to a lack of the relevant software.

(5) *The mood of the speaker.* The universal symphony includes various melodies attuned or harmonized with a whole range of different emotional states. The neural computer contains a pre-installed table of correspondences between these diverse melodies and particular feelings – to speak of a *tabula rasa*, a blank slate, is a striking if classical error. Consequently, every neural processor listening to human speech, even if the conceptual and emotional content of the verbal sounds cannot be decoded, immediately detects the 'mood' of the speaker by translating the melody of different emotional states.

Additionally, the neural computer of each of us, though we be unaware of it, gives orders to the orchestra of our guttural cords, teeth, tongue and lips to play the tune corresponding to our mood, the sum of feelings active at the time we speak. When we ask the neural computer to send a specific set of verbal messages, it carries out our petition, but simultaneously sends complementary phonetic messages: musical signals that correspond to our current feelings and which the brains of the speakers with which we converse will immediately translate.

Genetically Specified Melody of Anger

'Darling! I've told you a thousand times that nothing irritates me more than finding no loo paper in the toilet!' My neighbour, shouting at his wife in this way, called her 'darling', but this word was no demonstration of fondness or affection. 'Darling', in English, is a sound which, as far as the dictionary definition goes, must be translated in relation to a concept and a feeling of intimate love. However, if the volume is increased and the word is spat out in someone's face, the music of the language implies concepts and feelings of anger and aggression. The melody of anger is characterized by a loud volume (different intensities corresponding to different intensities of anger) and by a fast rhythm. Every neural computer can immediately decipher the emotional content of this melody, though it may not know the verbal symbols.

Genetically Specified Melody of Love

Sometimes the words and the music of language pedal in synchrony on a harmonious tandem, supporting and reinforcing each other mutually, as occurs also in song. 'Darling', 'Baby', 'My love', 'honey' are words of love which may be accompanied by a sweet, soft music, with a slow rhythm and a low volume. When a husband shouts 'Darliiing!!' at his wife, the words tell her that he feels love for her at this moment, but the music warns her that he would gladly slap her. Words and music may send the same message across two channels, but also diametrically opposed ones.

'Please, go ahead, you repulsive overweight cow,' a student from Pamplona, Spain, spoke in a warm and friendly tone to a Bulgarian woman ignorant of Spanish. This Bulgarian woman's neural computer could decode the friendly melody, which in this case had little to do with the text of the phrase.

Genetically Specified Melody of Sadness, Depression, and Happiness

'As soon as you speak two words over the phone, I can already tell if you are happy or sad,' said a wife to her husband. Indeed, within the neural computer of every human being are recorded two clearly distinguished melodies and rhythms: those of sadness, and those of happiness, each with a plethora of quantitative and qualitative nuances. In 1979 I interviewed Catalonian poet Salvador Espriu in his house in Barcelona on the Paseo de Gracia. 'Is something wrong?', he asked me. One of my children had just been operated on in a Barcelona hospital, and, though I struggled to prevent my anxiety from interfering, my neural computer ordered my guttural orchestra to interpret the melody of worry. My conversation with Salvador Espriu was limited to academic matters far removed from the apprehensiveness caused by my son's operation, but the brain of this eminent poet and thinker recognized the melodic message emitted by mine. When Ronald Reagan gave his first press conference in November of 1986, after the eruption of the 'Irangate scandal', his verbal message was an ode to joy, to his characteristic optimism, to peaceful tranquillity, but his musical message revealed deep misgivings, anxiety and guilt.

One day my daughter Elena, then seven years old, interpreted the *Happy Farmer*, the well-known piece by Schumann, at the violin while I accompanied her at the piano. I suddenly had the idea of playing this same tune in a minor key. 'Daddy,' Elena said, 'that's not the *Happy Farmer*; that's the *Sad Farmer*.' This anecdote opened up a new horizon in my search for the harmony between the phonic and emotional systems. Major keys are undoubtedly a phonic translation of the feelings of happiness, in opposition to minor keys, the sounds of sadness. One only need change a song from a major to a minor key to transform Schumann's *Happy Farmer*, as Elena said, into a *Worried Farmer*. Yet again we come across a new variation on the theme *cultura ancilla naturae*. Bach, Mozart or Joaquín Rodrigo compose original works with a strong individual stamp, but within certain phonic-emotional laws. If Mozart wishes to express feelings of deep dejection, he must resort to a minor key. The phonic-emotional laws that regulate musical compositions are rooted in the phonic-emotional laws conceived and installed in the brain of any Einstein or Bach. Imagine a person who must buy a newspaper, give a parliamentary speech, and take a taxi, on the day a loved one has died. The verbal messages directed to the paper vendor, the MPs, and the taxi driver will be completely different from each other, but all of them will be accompanied by the genetic melody of sadness.

(f) *The state of the organic orchestra of the individual.* Apart from the difference between the sounds of a trumpet and a guitar, there exists a phonic abyss between a Stradivarius and a cheap violin, between a hand-made Ramirez and a mass-produced guitar. When speaking, the human being emits a series of melodies which, among other things, reveal the different qualities of his organic orchestra. An orator may 'captivate' (interesting metaphor) his audience not only with the verbal content of his speech, but by the very quality of his voice. 'It's worth going to listen to So-and-so merely to hear his voice. What a voice! Marvellous!' Comments of this type are often heard.

An instrument may also be damaged or out of tune, and the human vocal instruments are no exception. When he speaks a person emits sounds which betray the state, from perfectly tuned and preserved to seriously out of tune and damaged, of his organic orchestra: natural or false teeth (or a total lack of these tools used for eating and talking); tongue in a perfect state or else partly or totally missing, or perhaps swollen; well-preserved guttural cords or else inflamed, damaged, or perhaps recently operated on due to cancer. The neural computer of every human being includes within its phonic-emotional software a biological tuning fork. Each time it receives phonic messages from a speaker, the brain can use this tool to detect the various qualities of the organic orchestra and of its various instruments, as well as its disadjustments and dissonances. The neural computer of a blind American can immediately detect the serious cold suffered by a Japanese speaker.

The Music of each Language or Dialect

Not only does an innate and universal Esperanto exist, a common musical language and associated program in the neural computer of every human being; in addition, each language is characterized by its verbal content but also by its own music. German can be distinguished from Italian by its music as distinctly as by its words. Within a single language, what we call different 'accents' are similarly a melody and rhythm specific to certain groups in relation to racial criteria (the American English spoken by blacks versus that spoken by whites); in relation to territorial criteria (the Spanish spoken by Mexicans, Argentinians, Cubans and Spaniards; or the English of Australians, North Americans and the inhabitants of various areas of Britain); or in relation to class criteria. The musical characters of 'upper' and 'working' class English in Britain are two melodic and rhythmic worlds. It is often amusing to observe impoverished members of the upper classes attempting to compensate for their economic inferiority by emphasizing their accent over that of the *nouveaux riches*. The latter struggle in vain to master the interpretation of a musical composition which requires years of training from the earliest years, when the neural computer records such sounds with the greatest accuracy.

Finally, in this extremely brief note on a world in serious need of exploration (the innate and cultural grammar of the music of languages), we would like to point out that within each language there exists also a correspondence between certain concepts and emotions. In other words, in the same way that the sound 'wicked' in English corresponds to a precise concept (verbal code), the musical sound (melody and rhythm) with which it is pronounced can imply different concepts and feelings. When an English youth sees something he likes, he might exclaim 'Wiiickeeed!', respecting both a rule of the verbal code (use of a specific word in a specific context) and of the musical code (music specific to this situation). 'Rain? Sure it's rained. But RAIN? Nah, it hasn't RAINED', it was once explained to me. Everyone present immediately understood the speaker's meaning. The text is almost identical in each phrase, but the accompanying music implied the following: 'We might say that it has rained if we understand by rain a slight drizzle. But if we refer to a serious rainstorm, then no, it hasn't rained.' Dictionaries only explain the conceptual meaning of words, that is, of the sounds. But it leaves aside altogether the meaning of the music, of the diverse melodies and rhythms which, as we are beginning to discover, are sounds no less important or less pregnant with ideas and feelings.

9

Emotional Laws of Crying, of Shame and of Smiling

Phonic and Visual Systems of Crying

Crying is a phonic and visual system of communication bionaturally installed in the neural computer of every human being. Like laughter and speech, it is a phonic system of communication exclusive to the human species, a genetic frontier between man and ape: *Homo lugens* (the crying animal). No monkey or any other animal is equipped with orchestral instruments to play the melody of weeping, nor are non-human brains prepared to decipher its mental or emotional meaning.

As a phonic system, crying can be distinguished from laughter and from speech (musical and verbal language), and there is no possible confusion between these four phonic systems. Due to the wondrous programming of the phonic/mental/emotional systems, each of these can be distinguished by its unmistakable musical score, both melody and rhythm. Simultaneously, as occurs with laughter, crying is a visual system. Ideas and sentiments, metaphysical products invisible and inaccessible to the sensorial antennae of the brain, as we have seen, are communicated from brain to brain by means of a double translation, both phonic and visual. The visual language of crying is also unique. It is characterized by unmistakable signals produced by the facial muscles – eyebrows, forehead, lips – and by tears, drops of a clear liquid and singular chemical composition which come out of the eyes. One of the functions of the eyes is to see, but another is to release tears.

Again and again we discover the great economy of Nature, which makes use of the same bodily organs for many radically divergent tasks.

The neural computer of a deaf person can detect and decipher the visual signs of a weeping person, and that of a blind person can detect and decipher the phonic signs of crying. Here we can observe the interest of Nature in having brains send each other the mental and emotional messages of lamentation: it has created two separate languages, one phonic and one visual, for them to do so. If a neural computer cannot use one of the two due to a malfunction in either the visual or the auditory antennae, it can always rely on the other. The neural computer connected to cameras and microphones in perfect shape receives a double sensorial translation of the mental and emotional messages which the other brain wishes to send. Finding such an interest and foresight in the natural plan, we scientifically suspect that these messages must be of the greatest importance.

The first language

When a baby is born, its neural computer receives precise information about this transcendental event in a human being's life. Immediately, following a bionatural program, it activates the urge to cry in the newborn. The infant, perfectly equipped with the appropriate instruments, delivers its first speech and interprets its first role as an actor on the great world stage: it cries. Crying is the first and only system of communication with which nature endows a baby to communicate with adults. Nature has meticulously installed the entire complex system of weeping so that as soon as the baby is born, it can bawl to perfection. Here we can observe the fallacy of the *tabula rasa*, the blank slate.

Crying, like laughter, smiling, shame and other languages, is installed in the neural computer and initiated by different biological timers, but without the intervention of culture or any previous training. The neural computer contains the complete program necessary to translate the mental/emotional messages of this system into its sensory signs, as well as to translate these sensory signs into mental/emotional messages.

A mental and emotional code

The neural computer of the baby, each time it learns from the digestive system that, 'The milk has been processed and amount X of new milk is required', activates the emotional mechanism of crying: the baby feels the urge to cry. In this phase of its life, the urges are completely impossible to repress, and the neural computer forces the baby to emit the visual and phonic signs of weeping. The same occurs each time that the brain receives news of any bodily necessity (infraction of the appropriate temperature; the need to change posture in the cot; an excess of humidity when the nappy is wet; a stomach ache, etc.).

The neural computer of the family dog receives this same phonic information through its highly sensitive organic microphones, but lacking the appropriate software it is unable to translate these sounds into concepts: 'What's wrong with this kid?' Nor can it translate them into feelings – the dog feels nothing. On the other hand, the neural computer of the mother, who is at that moment occupied in other activities with her husband in bed – let us suppose! – immediately translates this phonic message into a mental message ('Something is wrong with my baby: he's either too hot or too cold, hungry, uncomfortable in his cot, or in pain') and an emotional one: the mother feels compassion for her baby. 'Of course. Poor baby. It's feeding time.'

As the mother breast-feeds and talks to it the neural computer of the baby begins to create a data file of information about its mother: her voice-pitch, the soft touch of her nipples and breasts, the melody in her speech (melody of affection). The infant suckles on her breast and goes back to sleep. The mother knows that she has 'hit the nail on the head'. On other occasions, she turns him over in his cot and gives him his sucker, but he keeps on crying. She changes his nappy, but the bawling continues unabated. The mother then knows that something is wrong with her child. Crying is the only system of communication between the baby and his mother (or other adult).

Levers of negotiation

Sometimes two participants may play a game to the death, with different weapons. An eagle may enter into mortal combat with a snake. The object of the game is to kill and devour the adversary. The eagle's weapons are its ability to fly, its powerful talons, and its sharp beak. Those of the snake are the organic cord that is its own body, the technique of wrapping this coil around its prey in order to crush and suffocate the victim, and the poisonous needles in its mouth. Crying is one of the weapons which nature has placed at a baby's disposal in order for it to negotiate with an adult, or for a female to win the game against a male.

I will now analyse a match which took place between a two-year-old boy and his parents at three o'clock in the morning. The boy wanted to sleep in his parents' room, where he felt safer. The parents had decided that under no circumstance were they to set such a bad precedent. The arsenal of a two-year-old child consists of crying. That of his adult parents includes their power of reason, of argument, of flattery, of blackmail, and of course, of a much greater physical strength.

The game begins. The child begins to cry at three a.m. The parents are awoken. Every manner of curse materializes in their minds, against the child, against this confounded life, and against the selfish partner that seems to be feigning sleep. The infant continues to scream. The monotony of crying is programmed within an adult's neural computer to activate the feelings of irritation and anger. 'The baby is crying,' mumbles the mother. 'I can hear it,' answers the father, a reply which translated fully results in 'Why haven't you got up yet – you're the mother aren't you?' The mother does get up, and goes to the baby's room: 'What's wrong? What do you want?' 'I wanna sleep with mummy and daddy.' 'You're not coming into mummy and daddy's room.'

The infant counter-attacks by crying. The mother resorts to her rational weapons. 'Look, darling. This is your room. It's much nicer than mummy and daddy's room. Anyway, you have all your favourite dolls and toys here.' The boy insists: 'I wanna sleep with mummy and daddy.' 'Sweetie, listen: you know that you're always a good boy and that's why your mummy and daddy love you so much. But if you're bad, then you know that daddy will get very angry and the bogeyman will come.' The mother has blackmailed the child with ethical threats, with the appearance of a sinister character, with the withdrawal of paternal and maternal love, and with the threat of paternal authority. The child has put in his dummy as a sign of truce, and, with a great sigh, has stopped weeping. The mother gives him a kiss as a reward. The child has lost the first battle. Mummy returns to bed.

Five minutes later, the child, unconsciously knowing that the adversary will weaken with a renewed attack after an apparent truce, begins to cry again. 'I'll go,' the father says this time, 'I'll show that little runt.' 'What do you want?', the father asks with the voice of a raging monster. The child perceives that the game has acquired new levels of aggression and toughness. 'I wanna sleep with mummy and daddy.' The father offers him an alternative, 'Do you want me to tell you the story of Snow White?' The child replaces his sucker, accepting this new countermove. Daddy, mentally cursing Snow White, the dwarves, and all of their mothers, begins the story with drooping eyes: 'Once upon a time . . . '. He finishes a rather abbreviated version of the story, gives him a kiss, and returns to bed. The infant has lost the second battle.

After five minutes, the boy returns to the charge with the same weapon: crying. 'Let him cry if he wants,' suggests the father, 'He's as stubborn as the rest of his family. Let him cry. Pay no attention.' The child plays the melody of lamentation ceaselessly. This melody unleashes high emotional doses of irritation within his parents' neural computers. After ten minutes that seem ten centuries, the father finally gets up. 'You're a stubborn mule. Listen. I don't want to redden your little butt, but if you continue to cry, you'll be asking for a good spanking. You understand?' The infant can see that the game has reached its climax. He brings out his last-ditch resource: the *tutti* of crying. The father now fears the neighbours will be awoken. He takes the boy and smacks his behind four times, calling him 'every name in the book'. The child suffers his torment silently, without so much as a squeak. He no longer needs to cry. He has won the game. Confronted with the arsenal of the parents, which appears formidable and invincible, the baby's weapon of crying may appear to be a joke. Nevertheless, the infant may win the game.

Tears, the flag of love

The Christian Gospels report that when the people saw Christ weeping, upon hearing of the death of his friend Lazarus, they said 'See how he loved him!' One way of discovering and measuring the love of one person for another is to analyse the emotional/biochemical reaction of crying automatically produced in the brain upon learning about the death of a certain person.

'I thought I had completely forgotten Mary. We were engaged years ago. She married another man and had children. I also married another woman and have had children. When I heard about her sudden death, though, I felt a terrible ripping sensation inside me. I cried like a baby. Then I realized that deep down I continued to love her.' I heard this story from one of those fellow passengers sometimes met on an aeroplane who pours out his life to you as if he were a close friend (intimate ephemeral friendships between people who will never meet again).

Let us analyse this automatic, spontaneous reaction, partly emotional, partly biochemical, which surprises the person who experiences it. The brain progressively creates what we might call the 'mental village': a set of persons who enter the brain, each with particular sensorial, mental and emotional characteristics. The brain had recorded information about each time that this gentleman spoke with this young lady, each time that they caressed each other, each time that they argued, each time that they shared a table or a bed. When the neural computer receives news about the death of a person, it automatically consults the relevant *curriculum vitae* as registered in the cerebral archives. Then the brain, following the laws of the crying program, automatically triggers off the urges to cry: 80 degrees of intensity for 80 degrees of accumulated love. Perhaps it simultaneously releases the urge to cry with an intensity X and a sensation of relief with a different intensity according to accumulated hate. Sometimes the brain has stored so many degrees of love and so many of hate in different archives. Once again we can observe how the individual has no say in the release of the urge to cry, to laugh, to eat or to urinate. The brain is the only director of the emotional orchestra, following a bionatural and biocultural score. Does a biocultural score of crying also exist?

Biocultural score of crying

Crying, as we have seen, is regulated by software installed in the neural computer according to innate laws. In no culture does the baby talk or laugh as he is born. In every culture the baby 'speaks' the same language of crying, another of the genetic esperantos. In no culture is the husband permitted to resort to sobbing to negotiate with his wife. However, certain rules of the cultural game also exist which partly govern the use or abuse of crying. In some societies it is allowed – perhaps recommended and even prescribed – that certain women may interpret the role of paid mourners in the great world theatre, at the funeral of certain persons or personages. They are mercenaries. They do not cry from feeling sadness for the deceased, but to make a few pounds. Can the individual therefore cry whenever he wants, ignoring the instructions of his neural computer?

The genetic program has foreseen that people may laugh falsely, as we have seen. In this case the neural computer pays out no emotional salary whatsoever. The same occurs with tears. The individual may cry deceitfully, as he may speak or laugh deceitfully. If he cries without having felt any urges to do so, the neural computer will grant him no emotional compensation. In every culture it is recognized that crying, when a loved one has died, is very cathartic. Here, the law regulating all urges functions according to the same three stages: (1) the brain triggers off the urges to empty a reserve: of urine, of semen, of tears; (2) the individual obeys the orders: the relevant deposit is evacuated; (3) he receives the promised emotional salary (in reality, as we noted, the neural computer simply stops prodding him with the uncomfortable feelings of desire). In the case of tears, one cannot fake their production, in the same way that one cannot urinate with an empty bladder. One can feign sadness for the deceased by emitting the melody of crying, but will fail to release a single drop from the eyes. Mercenaries often use certain chemical products to provoke a heavy flow of tears.

We must notice that these mercenaries of lamentation are women and not men. A group of men crying loudly at a funeral would be a comic spectacle. Again we come across a variation on the theme *cultura ancilla naturae*, culture working at the orders of nature. Though fictional weeping may be permitted by some cultures in certain cases – the case of paid mourners at funerals or of actors in theatre, film and television – 'crocodile tears' are always prohibited. Sometimes parents reproach their young children for resorting to tearful 'shows', when they resort to cheating during the game: crying without the urge to do so, deceitful crying, 'stringing them along' with fake tears. A married couple once fought a verbal skirmish in my presence. The husband: 'I'm not impressed by your crocodile tears. My wife's tears once reached my soul, but now I know it's all a hoax.' The wife: 'How can you say that? You know I could never deceive you.'

The community of tears

A community is a group of socialized or de-individualized individuals with something in common (comm-unity: one for all). Sometimes a society is unified by the common lamentation of all its members over the death of a person that 'lived' in their brains with a high degree of admiration and affection. The members of a family comm-unicate and comm-une with strong emotional bonds when they cry over the death of the father, the mother, or perhaps a child/sibling. A territorial society may also feel especially united at the death of a loved totem (see my book *The Rules of the Game: the Tribes*), or of a loved totemic figure. 'De Gaulle est mort; la France est veuve' (De Gaulle is dead; France has been widowed). With this declaration, Pompidou announced the death of De Gaulle to the French. It was a romantic and almost poetic phrase, but also scientifically well-aimed. The French, divided by their economic, ideological and political disputes, united to lament the death of a great Frenchman, loved and respected at that time by all *les enfants de la patrie*. The death of Churchill perhaps unleashed a similar wave of tears in the brains of the British. In Spain, the death of Franco failed to produce a comparable explosion of sadness and tears. On the other hand, the death of TV personality Felix Rodriguez de la Fuente deeply moved the entire nation.

Biosocial Laws of Shame

In the biological republic of emotions, one feeling is distinct from all others: the feeling of shame.

Emotional and visual mechanism of prevention and censure

The neural computer, with the release of the urges to eat, informs us about when we need to eat and simultaneously pressures us to perform this crucial duty so that the human organism may receive indispensable vital energies. With the emotional offer of the pleasure of laughing, it invites and incites us to interpret the roles of judge, police officer and torturer of those who flout the rules of the social game. There is no feeling which has not been meticulously designed by Nature to inform and pressure the individual in relation to some important task which he must carry out, whether for his body or for his beehive. For what reason then should have Nature – in her foresighted hi-tech biochemical and emotional plans – installed the feeling of shame within the neural computer?

Let us begin to delve into the laws and mechanisms which regulate the function and functioning of this emotion with an example. An upper-class Mexican woman attended a social gathering with her husband, both dressed in formal attire. Everybody except for them, however, arrived at the occasion in ripped jeans, T-shirts, and such informal wear. 'My God, how embarrassing! I turned as red as a tomato. I mean, my face was just burning. I wanted to die. I've never been so mortified in the whole of my life,' I was told by this woman (Los Angeles, 1984). Let us analyse this case. (1) We can observe that we are dealing with an extremely uncomfortable sensation, with an emotional punishment ('I wanted to die'); (2) It is not set off when the human body suffers a dangerous bodily invasion, as in the case of the pain released by the neural computer when a knife pierces the leg; (3) the invisible interior feeling is simultaneously translated into visible external signs ('I turned red as a tomato').

We discover the following biosocial law: 'The neural computer, when it discovers through its sensorial antennae that an infraction of certain social codes has been committed, automatically activates the feeling of shame with an intensity proportional to the infraction committed, and at the same time raises the exterior flag of a "blush" through the pumping of a specific quantity of blood to the face.' We have seen that the brain translates the interior feeling of laughter to the exterior by means of visual and phonic signs. The sensorial translation designed for shame is like the early films of Charles Chaplin, a purely visual and silent message. But Chaplin was right to stress the eloquence of silent film, in some ways more eloquent than 'talkies', as, in the former, no sound distracts the viewer.

That upper-class lady's tomato-red face was an eloquent silent movie scene, prepared within the incredible world of the neural computer's biosocial laws. All of those guests in 'grunge' and 'hippy' uniforms, on seeing that blushed countenance, knew that this poor young lady was experiencing the interior torture rack of humiliation. As with the process of activation of the emotional mechanism of laughter, these are the previous stages: (1) a biosocial code (bionatural or biocultural) must be installed in the neural computer; (2) a norm from this code must be transgressed; (3) the neural computer must receive precise information about this infraction from its sensory spies; (4) the neural computer, upon obtaining knowledge of this deviant act, simultaneously activates two automatic processes without needing to consult the individual: it subjects the deviant to the emotional punishment of shame and paints his face red by ordering the appropriate biological departments to pump a precise quantity of blood into the face.

Bionatural and biocultural programs of shame

Shame itself, as a feeling, and its visual ambassador, the blush, is not something Chinese (geopolitical), Christian (theopolitical), Marxist or fascist (ideopolitical), or middle class (econopolitical): it is something human, unique to the society of the *anthropos* (anthropolitical). Shame is another of the genetic frontiers separating man from ape: *Homo verecundiae*, 'the ashamed animal'.

The program of shame includes a biosocial timer. If the biological timer of crying is activated at birth, that of shame begins to function in a later stage of human development. A baby does not blush, nor does it feel shame. Embarrassment, like laughter, functions when a norm from either a bionatural or a biocultural code has been transgressed. The neural computer is programmed with the code of normal speech. It identifies stuttering as an infraction of this bionatural code. He who stutters is threatened by his neural computer: 'If you stutter in public, I will punish you with a high degree of shame and give you a bright red face' (linguistic translation from the emotional language). In the case of the Mexican woman, her neural computer had acquired the cultural code of the society of her time, becoming biocultural and thus functioning from that moment on with the censuring mechanism of shame.

Social function of shame

We discover that shame seems to ride on the same tracks as laughter, and that it appears to have the same function assigned to it: warning and threatening the human being before he makes his entry onto the great stage of life: 'Careful! Take good care in your dress, in your hairstyle, in your whole appearance. Watch your every gesture, your words, your actions. If you break any social norm currently in force, I will punish you with shame and ridicule' (translation from the emotional language of the neural computer).

There exists no judicial or police system with a more forceful preventive weapon than the threat of shame and ridicule. Furthermore, if the prescribed social norms are indeed broken, the neural computer punishes mercilessly, as it had warned, with the individual an absolutely helpless victim of the most painful emotional fines of shame and ridicule.

At this point, the following questions suggest themselves: Has nature placed two saddles on the same donkey? Is not laughter a sufficient mechanism of prevention and censure? What additional function does the mechanism of shame fulfil? Are there cases where shame is activated, but not laughter (or vice versa)? Are both always activated inseparably from each other? These are not easy questions to answer rigorously. We notice that when the neural computer triggers off the urge to defecate, it simultaneously activates the desire to urinate. On the other hand, the urge to urinate is not necessarily accompanied by the desire to defecate. Similarly, it seems that when the neural computer sets the mechanism of ridicule in motion, it also activates the mechanism of shame. But when it activates the mechanism of shame, it does not always set off ridicule. A husband, caught in the act of slapping his wife, is punished by his neural computer with shame, but not with ridicule. A husband observed while receiving a severe beating from his wife would be penalized by ridicule as well as by shame.

The neural computer knows when it must trigger off the emotional mechanism of shame and/or of ridicule. We, as individuals, do not. Nevertheless, we have the ability to discover these emotional and biological laws, and I believe I have discovered in this study at least the ABCs of this alphabet and language. In any case, both laughter and shame are biosocial mechanisms of prevention and censure. The neural computer warns and threatens the individual with two emotional rifles, which injure in different ways. These two mechanisms of censure are dissimilar and complementary. Nature, which has allowed human beings a margin of individual election it has not granted the bee or the monkey, has provided mechanisms of censure such as shame and laughter which it has not installed in the neural computer of any animal except for the human being.

The shameless person

It is often said of certain people that they 'have no shame'. Is it possible for a human being to lose his shame in the same way he may lose his sight or his hearing? Any 'normal' law-abiding citizen finds the occupations of begging or prostitution shameful. Have the beggar or the prostitute lost their shame? A Spanish congressman once decided to 'let his hair down' at a Parisian brothel. He bumped into a lass from his own native village. Both suffered the lashings of shame at such an unexpected and unfortunate encounter. 'I'd be too ashamed to deliver crates of beer back home in Madrid, as I'm forced to do here in Los Angeles,' a Spanish man from an aristocratic family confessed to me. In both of these examples we can see that sometimes the human being flees from his own society, from the society where he is known, to ply certain trades or carry out certain tasks which are regarded as shameful. In these cases we cannot speak of someone who 'loses' his shame, since the person has gone to where he is a stranger precisely to avoid having to pay this severe emotional fine.

What happens to the human being is that frequently, he is submitted to two opposing emotional currents. One of these may be shame, but it need not necessarily be the strongest. In Luis Buñuel's film *Belle de Jour*, an upper-class Parisian woman has married an aristocrat. He's handsome, rich, gentlemanly, intelligent, and affable. They love each other dearly, but they are unable to express their affection in the erotic domain. Having been raped as a young adolescent, her neural computer, every time she tries to make love, triggers off such an intense emotional mechanism of repulsion that she is unable to overcome it. Each time her husband approaches her with this intention, despite his extreme tenderness, she cannot help rejecting him in the end. He is extremely understanding and does not force her, hoping that some day she will overcome her trauma. She suffers tremendously and, despite all of her best intentions and efforts, the problem continues day after day. In the end she takes a drastic decision: she goes to a brothel to cross this sexual frontier by force. In this way she hopes to finally be able to offer herself to her husband completely. One of the first clients is an intimate friend of her husband. Her neural computer, as it had warned her, crushes her with the terrible club of shame. This woman has not 'lost' her shame; she is not 'shameless'. Pressured by the emotional lever of her phobia towards the sexual act, and by the emotional lever of shame in the opposite direction, she decides to go to a brothel ready to pay the emotional fine of shame for presenting a stranger with her 'shameful parts', and especially the possible emotional torture awaiting her if she should meet anyone she knows.

Is it possible, however, for a prostitute to lose her shame in the long run? Can a human being, having flouted the emotional mechanism of shame a certain number of times, end up 'having no shame'? To a limited extent, the neural computer may create an anti-shame or shame-proof program. The prostitute must undergo great shame with her first client, but not with client number five thousand two hundred and two. Her neural computer has created an emotional program which permits the prostitute to strip naked and offer her 'shameful parts' to her clients without feeling any embarrassment. Nevertheless, this prostitute continues to be subject to the program of shame outside of the restricted context of the brothel. When she attends a fancy dinner and is asked 'So, what do you do?', she would never reply, with a proud grin, 'I'm a prostitute,' as one might say 'I'm a senior executive.' Nor will the host introduce her to the other guests with these words: 'Distinguished friends: I have the honour of introducing you to the well-known prostitute Miss So-and-so, one of the most famous, desired, and popular daughters of joy in this city. She has embraced ministers, judges, respected academics, in short, the very cream of society.' The threat of shame and ridicule would not allow this host to pronounce such a speech. All of the social – and thus biosocial – codes installed in the brain are protected and defended by the emotional threats and fines of shame and ridicule.

However, sometimes, indeed quite often, the human being is subjected to opposing emotional pressures, threats, and extortions, shame being among them. 'One of the worst moments for a bullfighter is when, on a bad afternoon, the whole plaza begins to shout

and chant "Sinvergüenza! Sinvergüenza!" ("Shameless! Shameless!").
It's terrible. It really entails drinking the cup of humiliation to the
dregs. I'd rather be gored!' (from my fieldwork on the symbolism of
the bull, Pamplona, 1969). The Spanish epithet 'sinverguenza' is a
verbal dart tipped with venom, thrown by the spectators/judges/tor-
turers at the bullfighter. The neural computer of the matador translates these sounds, with the supreme skill of the brain's simultaneous
translator, into the mental and emotional code. He resists this emotional storm, heavy with thunder, lightning and hailstones, as best
he can, pressured by another emotional storm of fear provoked
by the less than friendly bull before him. Spanish culture has coined
the phrase 'vergüenza torera' (bullfighter's shame) to emphasize an
intense feeling of embarrassment.

Indeed, it is otherwise unusual to attend a public spectacle in
Spain, or in any modern nation, where the whole roused mass lashes
a victim in public with the whips of shame and ridicule. I myself
have witnessed in the Bullring of Pamplona – perhaps the most
prone to this type of mockery and censure – how the audience
sang an improvised ditty by the name of 'the jumpy dwarf' for the
'vertically challenged' matador; on other occasions the whole plaza
became an impromptu choir dedicating a well-known chant, 'We all
want more,' to the mortified bullfighter.

Homo rationalis → *Homo verecundiae* → *Homo occultationis* (the rational animal → the shameful animal → the concealing animal)

The Book of Genesis tells of how when Adam and Eve ate the
forbidden fruit 'the eyes of them both were opened, and they
knew that they were naked; and they sewed fig leaves together, and
made themselves aprons'. In this biblical narration, a relationship is
established between reason, shame and the action of concealment.
There exists, in fact, a genetic kinship between the *Homo rationalis*
– Man's ability to see himself reflected in the mirror of reason; the
Homo verecundiae – the feeling of shame activated when the mirror
of reason reveals his nakedness and his *partes pudendae*, his 'private'
parts; and the *Homo occultationis* – the only animal determined
to hide the parts of his body of which he feels ashamed.

Reason–shame–concealment is a triple genetic frontier which separates humans from apes. No monkey can see itself reflected in the mirror of reason, discover its private parts and feel ashamed: 'My God! Don't let anyone know I'm such a repugnant animal! May no one discover my subjection to the humiliating vileness of having to evacuate such disgusting liquids and solids! How shameful!' For a monkey, its face is as honourable as its anus, its hand as its penis. Only Man discovers his reality and feels shame before some of the parts or aspects of his own self.

From here emerges a further emotional mechanism: the desire to hide the parts of the body – or of the 'soul' – which provoke shame in humans. Fig leaves, clothing, make-up, cosmetic surgery, and so many other human inventions are rooted in the same triple-layered ground: *Homo rationalis* → *Homo verecundiae* → *Homo occultationis*. Without the feeling of shame, humans would never have occupied themselves with covering the parts of their bodies that embarrass them; they would never have invented such and so many ingenious devices with the purpose of covering parts of the body or aspects of their behaviour which they are ashamed to show in public.

Agents of the *homo occultationis*

(a) *Dirty words and euphemisms.* In all human cultures, the words that define the parts or products of the body catalogued as the somatic geography of shame are banned by the emotional inquisition of this emotion. A professor may not make the following announcements before his students: 'Next Thursday there will be no class. I am going to have a fistule surgically removed from my arse.' The word 'head' is in all cultures a proper and respectable word, which may be used in private or in public without the neural computer triggering off the emotional mechanism of shame or of ridicule. Man is proud of being a rational animal. In his game as a human versus the ape, he feels victorious: Man 1; Monkey 0. He wins the game of beings. The rational being is superior to the non-rational being (the brute).

But he discovers, on the other hand, that like the monkey he is a factory of faecal products. Blast! The neural computer threatens him with the emotional fine of shame if he dares perform certain vital functions in public (evacuating gases, urinating or defecating), show those shameful parts publicly, or even pronounce the words which refer to them. Subsequently, Man realizes that he has no option but to make use of these terms in particular circumstances: to point out to a doctor where it hurts or to explain where he was wounded at a judicial court. These terms have been registered in the brain together with the emotional threat of shame. The patient who told his doctor, 'It hurts when I sh——', would be flagellated by the whip of shame. Man has resolved this dilemma with the invention of a new development in the art of concealment: the creation of euphemisms. Anus, rectum, phallus and copulate have all been excavated from the same euphemistic mine of language. With the passing of time, euphemisms, by their association with these shameful parts or actions, may progressively become contaminated until being converted or rather perverted into words censured by shame.

(b) *Cosmetic surgery and artificial organs.* The neural computer pays a high dosage of satisfaction to the young woman who plays with a great advantage in the game of legs, of hands, of faces, of hair, and of the general design of the body every time she goes out on the street; the blind and fierce game of the woman's magical mirror ('Who is the most beautiful of them all?'). But her neural computer will punish her mercilessly with the emotional lashings of shame for having a huge and somewhat deformed nose. An eighteen-year-old girl with a large nose is subject to the same emotional law of shame in a 'primitive' society as in the computerized Europe of the twentieth century. The laws of corporal design of the woman, and of the shame which punishes corporal ab-normalities, has not varied in the slightest. Once again we surprise culture and civilization working to the orders of genetically specified laws of nature: *cultura ancilla naturae.* Modern plastic surgery allows a person to remove 'the fly from the soup', reducing the size of an attractive young girl's nose and correcting her deformities. There is nothing more modern than a plastic surgery operation. But, if we notice, we can interpret this development as scientific progress working as a humble servant at the orders of the biosocial, atavistic and immutable laws of shame and of the nose-design of the female (or of the male) in the human species.

A woman would suffer the painful lashings of shame applied by her neural computer if she showed her single breast in public (the other having been removed due to a cancerous infection). Modern plastic surgery may endow her with a breast which fulfils no function for her somatic republic, but which nevertheless fulfils a very important role in the social republic. This attractive young girl may then display her breasts on a Spanish beach without paying the emotional fine of shame. Plastic or wooden legs and false teeth can be used to walk or to eat, but also serve to conceal and to free the wearer from mortifying shame.

The secret agents of the *Homo occultationis*, like all spies, may be detected. Artificial hair, the wig or toupee, has no other function but to hide a polished bald pate. The man who covers his baldness tries to avoid the emotional censures and fines of shame and ridicule, and at the same time fears that people will notice his toupee, will laugh sotto voce or perhaps will begin to attack him with unkind jokes. The emotional threats of shame and laughter lead certain hairless gentlemen to wear artificial hair and others to display their baldness in all its glory and splendour. The individual, once again subjected to two opposing emotional currents, takes the road he believes will allow him to walk with the least danger of feeling 'bullfighter's shame' or 'looking like a fool'.

(c) *Clothing and make-up*. In every human society there exists a precise cultural code of concealment (which parts must be covered where, how, by whom and when). The fines foreseen for the infractions are shame and ridicule and, perhaps, additional penalties such as economic sanctions, jail or perhaps the death sentence. The most common rule in most cultures is the obligation to cover the anal and genital areas. On the other hand, in a nudist camp, a girl who wore a bra would be breaking a rule and would be sanctioned by shame and ridicule. A woman who displayed her face in a Muslim society, where it is forbidden to show this part of the body, would be mortified by shame. The cultural code of dress and of the bodily parts which must be concealed in public varies, but once this code is installed in the brain and becomes biocultural/biological, it functions with the same rigour and the same emotional censures of shame and ridicule.

Modern Man may naively suppose that he has advanced greatly in the ascendant climb of progress, of liberty, of individual election. He is subject to the same biosocial and emotional laws of shame and ridicule as were Adam and Eve, who 'felt ashamed' and resorted to fig leaves. Cosmetics, creams and powders stem from the same branch of Man, the *Homo occultationis*. The lady who attempts to disguise the wrinkles of her face or the paleness of her countenance follows the instructions and threats of her neural computer, which warns her, upon seeing herself in the mirror, with the language of emotions: 'If you appear at the party with those wrinkles and that pallid colour, I will redden you with shame.'

Biosocial Laws of Smiling

In Latin, *sub-ridere* (to smile), from which the verb *sou-rire* in French or *son-reir* in Spanish are derived, implies that smiling is a lesser laugh, a prelude to laughter or a laugh reduced to its most subtle expression. A smile may, indeed, sometimes be a laugh barely begun or incomplete, but in this case it is accompanied by the sounds of the language of laughter also emitted at a minimal volume. Such is the case of someone who, without opening his mouth, produces some of the sounds of the language of laughter while drawing his lips into a slight smile, when he reacts to a joke that he has not found very funny. But, except in these cases, the language of smiling is one as different from that of laughter as the latter is from the language of crying.

Flag of affection and of submission

Smiling, as shame, is a mute and purely visual language. It is another of the languages of the *tabula scripta*, another of the universal, genetic and innate languages installed in the neural computer. And it is a language proper and exclusive to the species of the *Homo subridens*, the 'smiling animal'. Here we come across another genetic frontier separating humans from apes. The signs of smiling have not varied since Adam and Eve, and may be deciphered by the neural computer of a Chinese or a Yanomamo person. The Tower of Babel did not manage to pulverize the universal language of smiling. The instruments of smiling are always the same: the face, the lips and the teeth. To these precise, unique and unmistakable visual signals the same feeling, genetically installed in the software of the neural computer, always corresponds. He who laughs enjoys it, while he who is laughed at suffers. The smile, unlike laughter, is not a mechanism of censure. Laughter, as we saw, wounds the object of social censure. The neural computer is genetically programmed with the program of the smile in the following stages:

(1) The brain receives information about a certain person through its sensorial agents.

(2) The neural computer offers the individual a report based on its programs and on the curriculum vitae stored therein.

(3) If the neural computer automatically concludes that the person in question is a pleasant one, it activates a feeling of affection towards that person and the urge to smile; that is, the urge to translate this feeling to the exterior by producing the signals of the mute language of smiling. We may notice that when we decide that 'he really strikes my fancy' or 'I can't help it, but So-and-so gets on my nerves', we imply that it is not us who decide or choose these feelings of aversion or attraction towards others. This intuition is scientifically correct. It is, in fact, the neural computer that examines all people, following unconscious laws, and which triggers off feelings of affection or repugnance towards each person who enters the brain's sensorial field of action. As we have seen, the neural computer examines oxygen, haddock, beer, the poison of a mosquito sting, in short, any objects or foods which penetrate into the human organism, advising that we welcome them, with the activation of pleasant mechanisms, or advising that we reject them as inopportune guests or dangerous enemies. This mental processor also minutely examines each person that makes contact with us.

(4) The individual, obeying the emotional instructions of his neural computer, smiles. With his smile he communicates a visual message which, translated to the verbal language, would result in the following: 'I like you. I find your presence and your personality quite pleasant.'

(5) The neural computer of the recipient of this visual message of smiling immediately translates it to the mental and emotional language, activating a feeling of affect and the desire to translate this feeling back into the visual language of the smile.

Biosocial timer: the second language of the human species

Within the genetic plan for the different human systems of communication, a precise law installed in the brain regulates the order of each system's appearance, thanks to activations by automatic biosocial timers. Crying is the first language that the neural computer activates in the infant at birth. Smiling is the second system of communication. A few weeks after birth, when the child still has no teeth, it premieres in the great world theatre with its first smile. It is the first time that the baby tells his mother, with the infinite power of this mute language, 'Mummy, I love you.'

Smiling as a reward and as a negotiating weapon

'When you have a baby, you become a true slave. You breast-feed him, you bathe him, you change his nappies . . . You don't live except for him. You think you've finished with the whole thing and suddenly off you go again. But! When he smiles with that little mouth, totally devoid of teeth, it drives you crazy, of course. Is there enough gold in the world to pay for the toothless grin of a baby?' I have recollected abundant testimonies of this type from mothers. The smile is a pleasant gift, and therefore at the opposite extreme from laughter. We delight in being smiled at, and we are hurt by laughter. For this reason the human being makes use of smiling as a powerful weapon when bargaining is to be done. In the prelude to every negotiation, he who is trying to obtain some favour or sell some mule will attempt to win over his interlocutor by the use and perhaps abuse of the powerful mute language of the smile. There are people who speak well, who sing well or who write well. There are also persons who smile well: persons with an extraordinary ability to 'charm' people with their smiles. These people are classified as 'charming'.

There are snakes with the ability to bewitch birds with their gaze, immobilizing them until they are devoured. A 'goddess' may spellbind a man with her stare and with her 'irresistible' body. The smile is one of the most powerful and irresistible mechanisms that a human can use to 'win someone over', to 'have someone eating out of his hand', to charm another human being.

False smiles

A baby is incapable of feigning his feelings or of sending a visual message of affection when he feels aversion towards a person. On the other hand, an adult may disguise his feelings of hate and repugnance towards a person by raising the flag of smiling over his face. Human beings may lie with their smiles, and with more difficulty with their tears, intentionally translating their feelings into false phonic and visual signals. Frequently, many men and women lie or exaggerate when they smile to seduce or manipulate someone. Perhaps people may lie as often or even more often with the language of smiling than with that of words. However, though the genetic code permits humans to smile without having been previously advised to do so by the neural computer with the appropriate emotional activation, smiling well without these urges and fooling other neural computers is not as easy as it may seem. Carter, the American ex-President, was continually made the target of jokes due to his artificial and mechanical smile. The neural computer is perfectly equipped to distinguish a genuine from a false smile.

When a photographer prepares to take a group picture, he always asks the subjects to smile. Diplomats, those in the business of public relations, politicians and all those who enter into the public spotlight, are advised to smile. All of this proves the importance and the power of this 'silent film' language. But perhaps it is more difficult to lie with smiles than with words. The neural computer, with the sagacity of Sherlock Holmes, detects the hypocrisy hidden behind the smile of a 'fox'. Perhaps there may be human beings who reach great heights in the art or artifice of faking a smile. But undoubtedly, those who reach others very deeply are those who smile genuinely, translating to the exterior a profound and true affection. The smile of Christ, who loved prostitutes, thieves, lepers, ill people and outlaws alike, without a doubt must have possessed an irresistible magnetism for all those who enjoyed his presence. Who has not been surprised by the genuine smile of Mahatma Gandhi, a stark contrast with the mechanical smiles of toothpaste advertisements? I came across a priceless quote from Tolstoy in a book by Gironella: 'Trust in men according to their smile.' St Augustine wrote that 'the eyes are the windows to the soul'. This is no preposterous metaphor, since, in fact, the eyes not only receive information, but constitute in themselves a source of information. The eyes translate into the sensorial world the mood of the person, in other words, the feelings which have been activated by the neural computer. The smile is another of the 'windows to the soul'. Tell me how you smile and I will tell you who you are.

Hierarchy, equality and the smile

Whoever must interpret the role of a beggar, in whatever context, whoever must ask for some favour, cannot or should not refrain from having his smile always at hand. On the other hand, a person in a position of superiority, with the power to grant favours, can enjoy the privilege of denying his inferiors the slightest twitch upon his lips. This is the hierarchical law genetically installed in the neural computer: 'he who smiles is related to him who remains serious as an inferior person is to a superior person' (within a specific hierarchical scale). A serious countenance was a sign of authority among the Aztecs as it is among the Mexicans of the present day.

10

Emotional Laws of Anger and Revenge

We know that if we place a container full of water on a hot range, the temperature of this liquid will begin to increase until, at a certain level, it will begin to boil and evaporate. This is a physiochemical law. In all of the languages that I know, the metaphor of becoming hotter and cooler is used in relation to a specific feeling within the family of pleasant and unpleasant sentiments: ire, anger, wrath, infuriation, indignation (in all languages we find an abundance of terms that label this emotion). In English, for instance, we speak of a hot temper, of boiling or burning with anger, and of cooling down.

In the same way that we know when, how and why water heats up, boils and evaporates, we can discover the laws and mechanisms that activate different intensities of the feeling of anger. Both the physiochemical laws which regulate the temperature changes of water, and the biological laws which activate the emotional mechanism of anger, are laws which function with absolute independence from the individual's consciousness and free will. A person does not fly into a rage when he decides to do so, in the same way that he does not feel a toothache at will ('And now I shall suffer an intense toothache, which I will offer to the blessed souls of the departed'); only when the neural computer automatically activates any of these feelings does the subject experience them. The program of anger is bionatural, and therefore innate and common to all the members of the human species. As we shall see, however, there also exist biocultural programs which partly regulate the functioning of this feeling.

Biosocial Laws which Activate the Feeling of Anger

A toothache is an unpleasant sensation contained within the genetic plan, which the neural computer triggers off when it receives information about a growing cavity. Anger or rage is a feeling installed by the genetic engineers within the neural computer which should be activated whenever the individual is attacked by another member of his beehive (human, territorial, religious, economic, ideological or other beehives) as an individual ('You, so-and-so, are a cretin and a shameless lout') or as a member of his beehive ('The British are a band of mental midgets'). The design of the human being, a meticulous, rigorous and far-sighted plan, includes a biological ministry of individual defence within human brains. By activating a toothache, the neural computer informs the individual about a malfunction in one of the working tools of the digestive system and advises him not to use it (if he bites down with this tooth, the neural computer will make him writhe with agony). Without this ingenious system of pain distributed across the various organs, the individual would not know when he should not bite with a particular tooth, or walk on a damaged foot. The pain of bodily parts forms part of the defence system of injured, malfunctioning or diseased organs.

By means of the no less ingenious activation of anger, the neural computer automatically informs the individual about an aggression being suffered as an individual or as a member of his beehive, and triggers off a specific set of urges: the urges to take revenge or to defend himself with an intensity mathematically calibrated by the neural computer, following a precise program – 'an eye for an eye, a tooth for a tooth'. Without this feeling, we could be insulted continuously and yet feel no desire to attack our adversary, and thus to defend ourselves. If we interviewed a rose and asked, 'Why are you so beautiful and yet so aggressive? Why do you have such sharp thorns?', the rose could reply, 'What can I say? That is how I was made. I'm just following orders.' Nature has endowed roses and carnivorous plants with certain defence and aggressive mechanisms; she has endowed the bull with horns, the eagle with talons, the scorpion and the tse-tse fly with poison. We might notice that she has given the rose only physical mechanisms of aggression: thorns. On the other hand, she has equipped the eagle with both physical mechanisms of aggression – talons and beak – and psychological or emotional mechanisms of aggression: the urges to capture, to attack and to kill the members of certain species. The neural computer activates this emotional mechanism of aggression in the eagle, without which the physical instruments would be of no use whatsoever. The eagle's brain 'tells' it in the emotional language, 'If you attack and kill a rabbit, I will pay you this emotional salary (that is, I will free you from these annoying urges).' The eagle does not eat an animal which it has not trapped and killed with its own beak and claws. Such is the system of emotional and physical aggression installed in the eagle's brain by the genetic plan.

In the system of defence and aggression installed in the human brain and body, there exist also mechanisms of physical defence – the hands, the feet, the fingernails, the teeth; and psychological or emotional ones – anger and the urges to return the ball of aggression. The human neural computer is meticulously programmed to detect any aggression – phonic, visual or physical – through its sensorial agents. Once the brain has detected a particular aggression, it automatically triggers off the emotional mechanism of anger in mathematical proportion to the degree of the attack.

Phonic Aggression and Phonic Translation of Anger

As we saw in our discussion of the musical language of speech, shouting is a musical language of aggression. Each time that someone shouts at us, the neural computer immediately activates the emotional mechanism of anger and pressures us to hurl the same verbal stones back at the screamer: 'Don't even think about shouting at your father that way! If you raise your voice at me again, you're going to get it!' A father could be heard yelling these words at his son during a calm Madrid night. The law of hierarchy, on the other hand, advises the subordinate to refrain from shouting: 'The boss has the last word and the privilege of shouting at his subordinate.'

Another type of phonic aggression the neural computer immediately detects springs from the linguistic reserve of insults. Every language contains a more or less extensive family of aggressive words taken from the fecal and genital area of signification. Sir Edward Evans-Pritchard once remarked to me in Oxford, in the presence of his dog Barco, 'Have you ever noticed that we never quarrel with our dogs? We don't quarrel with them because dogs don't speak. On the other hand, we quarrel with our wives, children, colleagues or friends, because once in a while a tactless, inopportune or offensive word is spoken. Words poison love, friendship, human relations.' An interesting observation. Two dogs, by barking at each other, send emotional messages of anger translated into the phonic language. In our species, one of the phonic vehicles of anger is the insult.

In Le Puy (France, 1964) I visited a Spaniard who had been arrested for having knifed a Frenchman: 'He started to taunt me when I was calmly having a drink. I began to get pissed off when he began to ask me if we ate beetroot in Spain. Then my blood began to boil when they all began to laugh in my face and ask me why I had come to France if I was so happy in Spain. I finally flew off my handle when he said Spain was a pile of sh——. I brought out my jack-knife and killed him dead.' In this case, the neural computer of the Spaniard, programmed with pride in its own territorial beehive, deciphers the attacks of the members of a rival territorial beehive, which it receives in two phonic languages: the verbal (insults made by the Frenchmen) and that of laughter (a universal language). The neural computer deciphers the emotional charge of aggression carried by each sound in both languages (words or laughter). The brain of this Spaniard increases the densitometer of anger and advises him to counter-attack with the same verbal weapons. When a Frenchman uses a very violent sound in reference to his country ('Spain is a pile of sh——'), the neural computer recommends that he kill the speaker. The Spaniard follows the instructions of his neural computer and 'kills him dead'.

In Los Angeles, a friend of mine was strolling down Hollywood Way around half past midnight on a Saturday. An old man in pyjamas yelled at him from a balcony, 'Sons of B——! I can't sleep with all that racket you're making.' He then shot at my friend with his gun, injuring his arm. Among the sounds which the neural computer translates into an emotional wave of anger of greater or lesser intensity, are those which interrupt our sleep, our activities, our inspiration, our leisure time. From my house in Los Angeles I heard a neighbour shout one afternoon: 'That damn alarm! Turn it off A--hole!' Another answered, 'Shut up, you S.O.B. How about turning yourself off?!'. Ambulance sirens, police helicopters, anti-theft alarms that go off accidentally, a baby crying desperately at two a.m., a couple quarrelling boisterously, car horns honking at every street crossing, children fighting and screaming, all of these comprise a continuous phonic invasion and aggression of the life of the inhabitant of Los Angeles or London, which the neural computer automatically and inevitably translates into an attack of anger of a greater or lesser voltage. The bionatural language of enragement is located within the higher volume levels of the musical language: shouting. Among the bionatural phonic aggressions are shouting, laughter, crying and bothersome or interrupting noises. The insults of each language constitute a biocultural language of anger.

Visual Aggression and Visual Translation of Anger

A visual grammar of anger is genetically installed within the neural computer. The eyes, the eyebrows and the lips, among others, have been designed by the genetic engineers to translate, with visual signs, the invisible feeling of ire to the exterior. The neural computer of a baby is already equipped to detect the visual messages of anger. When someone insults, shouts and gives someone a 'dirty look', he is sending a message of anger across three channels: two phonic and one visual.

Each territorial society tends to create its own visual grammar of anger and aggression. In Italy, it is possible to assault another with a sound – *cornuto* – or else with a gesture – raising the index and little finger, and withdrawing the rest; in several cultures children stick out their tongue, women shake their buttocks, and men make some gesture that represents their phallus. The neural computer which has assimilated this biocultural grammar of anger can translate these visual messages and similarly give orders to the appropriate muscles so that they translate the interior ire into this mute and eloquent language.

Physical Aggression and Physical Translation of Anger

The neural computer is programmed to detect the phonic and visual languages of aggression and to unleash automatically the mechanism of ire and the urge to 'pay the aggressor back in his own coin'. The most powerful or eloquent language of anger is made up of kicks, punches, scratches and bites. If someone stomps on our foot or slaps our face resoundingly, the neural computer automatically triggers off the mechanism of ire and the desire to return the stomp or to 'break his face'. We can all verify the automatic, rigorous and inevitable functioning of this mechanism. We place a lighted match near a container with alcohol: a flame is immediately produced. We slap a gentleman on the face: his neural computer immediately lights a burning indignation within him. We must contemplate from this new perspective that it is a biological machine, a biochemical computer programmed with rigorous laws and mechanisms, which drives the functioning of a feeling as personal and subjective as is the anger we feel at a particular moment.

Cultura Ancilla Naturae: Culture as a Servant of Nature

A tiger must make do with transmitting its infuriation to another tiger by using the instruments which Nature has placed at its disposal: gestures made with the eyes and snout, and attacks with its claws. A tiger cannot additionally shoot a gun, let alone bomb a group of tigers from a rival tribe with a Hiroshima-type projectile dropped from a plane. The human being is not the animal best armed by Nature, but thanks to the territorial beehives which he inhabits and thanks to his ability to discover certain physical and chemical laws, he has been able to create and accumulate the most varied and powerful arsenal of weapons for killing (particularly his own kind) of any animal species. The 'savage' and the 'civilized' individual are ruled by the same emotional and biosocial laws of anger and aggressivity. The difference lies in that the 'civilized' person has at his disposal, due to the works and grace of his own society and culture, an arsenal of instruments of attack infinitely superior to those of the 'savage' to vent his ire and his desire for vengeance, particularly the ire of the *homo tribalis* (see *The Rules of the Game: the Tribes*). Once again we find culture and 'civilization' working as the humble servant of the most atavistic biosocial mechanisms imaginable. In the development of these feelings of anger and aggression, installed in the brain of the *homo iratus*, we have not progressed a single millimetre from Cain to Hiroshima.

Biocultural Programs of 'Self-control'

A monkey is not born into a society full of guns, tanks, bombs and missiles, but neither can it understand the Christian message of 'forgive your enemies; bless him who curses you; turn the other cheek to the one who slaps your face'. On the one hand, culture places at the disposal of the human being a whole repertoire of insults, gestures, weapons, and even elaborate rites for the celebration of victory over 'the enemies' (other human beings) at war. On the other hand, he also finds social and cultural programs which, once installed in the brain, function as true emotional brakes on the urges to attack and take revenge. No spider among spiders could one fine day embark upon a campaign for peace along the following lines: 'Fellow spiders: what ill have our sisters the flies ever done to us? Why must we entrap them in our sinister webs, assassinate them, and eat them? Why don't we become vegetarians?'

In the human species, certain individuals like Christ appear preaching messages of peace, of forgiveness, of turning the other cheek to the aggressor. The neural computer of any human being may receive this program and assimilate it to a greater or a lesser degree. It is possible to practise forgiveness as one may play the violin, and the neural computer may create an anti-violence program of very diverse characteristics. Mahatma Gandhi and Adolf Hitler are two clear examples of opposite poles in this domain. Not even Mahatma Gandhi could prevent his neural computer from setting off feelings of ire and desires for vengeance when the English insulted Indians or when someone in South Africa forcefully removed him from his first-class train seat for being 'coloured' and threw him from the train onto the ground. But an opposing program, from the same neural computer, may counsel him, 'Calm down; forgive him; bless him; love him.'

Yehudi Menuhin or Andrés Segovia, after many years of practice ('five minutes of inspiration and ninety-five of perspiration', as the latter used to say), install within their brains incredibly elaborate programs which allow them to manipulate their instruments with an unparalleled dominion. The brain of Mahatma Gandhi, after many years of training and putting into practice the Christian ideal of forgiving and turning the other cheek to the person who slapped the first, acquired an enviable program of 'self-control'. The genetic program of laws regulating the activation of anger, and of the urge to give the person who struck Mahatma Gandhi 'a good thrashing', does not disappear. Otherwise there would be no need for 'self-control', in other words, for struggling tenaciously against the emotional attacks of ire. In the same way, Gandhi confessed that despite many years of practising celibacy he felt daily, and especially in the company of young, beautiful and sweet women, intense urges to foresake his purity.

We must take notice of the functioning of the biological laws which regulate the emotional system. A bionatural program such as a man's desire to deposit the male seed in the place foreseen and prescribed by the genetic plan, or else the desire to attack an aggressor, never changes, nor can it change. The testicles of every male – whether St John of the Cross or Mahatma Gandhi – following biosocial instructions and independent and rigid laws, will continue to produce millions of sperms and store them in the testicular refrigerator (the scrotum is located outside of the body so that it remains at a lower temperature, and thus carries out the function of a refrigerator). Once this refrigerated tank is full, the neural computer will inform the male that he must carry out a specific duty useful for the beehive, pressuring him with the strong emotional lever of erotic desire. The bionatural programs make concessions to no one.

However, the human being finds in his society cultural programs which an ape does not find in his, and furthermore, the neural computer of the former is prepared to assimilate these programs, which become biocultural. A monkey does not come across another monkey in his group that advises celibacy, in order to enjoy the love of God, to better serve the brothers of his species and group, or to distance himself from 'base desires'. In all human societies a partly religious, partly ethical, partly aesthetic or 'civilized' code has been developed which advises 'self-control', restraint from anger, knowledge of how to hold one's tongue in time. Thus, in the Book of Proverbs, we read: 'He that is slow to anger is better than the mighty; and he that ruleth his spirit, than he that taketh a city.'[1] Lao-tzu, the founder of Taoism in the sixth century BC, expressed this same concept and propounded this same ideal: 'He who conquers others is strong; he who conquers himself is powerful.'

The human being thus finds himself subject to two opposing programs: that of anger and that of 'self-control'. The neural computer may acquire a program of greater or lesser 'self-control' from infancy, even reaching the Himalayas climbed by one such as Mahatma Gandhi. The programs of reproduction and of defence, with all of their related physical, chemical and emotional mechanisms, are already installed in the brain. On the other hand, the program of playing the violin, of celibacy or of 'self-control' must be installed in the brain after many hours, days and years of 'perspiration', of cumulative repetitive exercise. The musical Himalaya reached by Andrés Segovia or the ethical Himalaya reached by Mahatma Gandhi is not climbed in one day.

Hierarchical Laws of Anger

'The day I win the lottery, the first thing I'll do is go to my boss's office and get a load off my chest. Too many years I've had to put up with his petty whims, his bellowing, his insults, his cruel jokes. At last I'll be able to tell him what I really think of him. By God, he's going to get it. What a relief! It will be the greatest pleasure of my life.' As the words of this 'employee' (Pamplona, 1978) illustrate, he who is placed in an inferior position within the hierarchical scale of any society (and a communist or egalitarian society is no exception to this rule), must master the emotional pressures to shout at the boss when the latter shouts at him, or to counter-attack with insulting phrases when he receives poisoned verbal arrows. The neural computer pushes him to reciprocate the blows from the innate program of anger, while the department of hierarchy pushes him to suffer silently all of the insults and shouts with no less vigorous emotional exhortations. The brain's department of defence, after a stormy session with the boss in which the employee has had to put up with visual, phonic and emotional thunderstorms without uttering a word, offers him a documentary in the brain's projection room where the employee can be seen to 'tell it like it is' to his boss. The neural computer pays him a small emotional pittance for insulting his boss in this projection room, but does not free him from the desire for vengeance demanded by the program, unless he truly 'gives him a piece of his mind' face to face. As we have already been able to verify for each case, every neural program is regulated by its own autonomous, rigid and inflexible laws: either the individual follows the neural computer's instructions exactly or otherwise it will continue to pester him with the relevant unpleasant emotional mechanism. And so this poor employee day-dreams of removing a heavy emotional weight off his back 'the day he wins the lottery': the urge to equal the score with his boss, an eye for an eye, a yell for a yell, an insult for an insult.

The Japanese – if my information is correct – have invented an ingenious system in this domain. Certain factories include a room where the supervisors and heads of the company are represented in the form of life-sized plastic dolls, painted with very realistic features and colour tones. Any employee may go to this hall when he feels the need, and can scream at, insult and kick his boss. The Japanese have decided that excessive hatred accumulated by an employee towards his boss decreases his productivity. Therefore, this type of emotional sauna will allow him to free himself from some of this weight, and in this way he will be able to concentrate more easily on soldering the delicate components with which he works. If the neural computer pays out a small pleasure for insulting the boss in the hall of the imagination, the reward is greater for insulting the plastic boss which appears to the brain as more realistic through its sensorial agents; but it does not pay the true pleasure reserved for the Japanese employee who goes to his boss's office to call him names and to 'clear his conscience'.

In Rome, on the last day of the year, one is allowed to break plates by throwing them out of the window. Once a year, society may declare open season on certain normally prohibited actions: it is possible to deceive (1st of April in Britain or the US, 28 December in Spain), sex or hierarchical roles may be inverted (carnivals or Mardi Gras), or anger may be vented by throwing plates. Here again we may observe how the exception confirms and reaffirms the rule.

If the hierarchical law we have just explored exclusively affects the subordinate, another hierarchical law applies to the superior. In a press conference given when he was President of the United States, Ronald Reagan shouted 'Shut up!' at a somewhat intrusive journalist, an exclamation that resounded through microphones across the whole of the global village, from Washington to Tokyo, London to

Sydney. If this 'shut up' had been proffered by a senator, it would not have been notorious, falling short of the rank of an international scandal. Here we come across the following hierarchical law, which this time applies to those in a superior position – who are also merely 'following orders' within the complex machinery of the beehive: 'The higher the position on the hierarchical ladder, the greater will be the infraction of the code of self-control (control of anger).'

Religious Brakes on, and Accelerators of, Anger

Unlike the elephant, the human being has a neural computer programmed with a religious program since childhood. Frequently this religious program includes forgiveness and mastery of anger; therefore, the religion installed within the brain functions as biological and emotional reins on the 'wild horse' of this 'passion', which may occasionally try to bolt away. Thus, every Christian carries within his mental village the figure of Christ, who preached with his example and with his words that we bless those who curse us, turn the other cheek to those who slap our face, and forgive our enemies. Of course this mental character is held to a greater or lesser degree, with vast differences between the ex-seminarist Stalin and St Francis of Assisi.

'I never understood the meaning of forgiving one's enemies until my daughter Mary was raped and killed. If your 20-year-old daughter is murdered, you feel the most intense desires to see those miserable worms receive their just reward. You want to see those heartless assassins hung in the public square. Then you feel also the infinite beauty of Christianity, of forgiving your enemies. I ask God every minute that he help me forgive my daughter's murderers.' An intimate friend and colleague of mine, professor and dean of the UCLA (University of California in Los Angeles), opened up his soul and revealed to me the fierce battle fought between the urges to kill and the urges to forgive. A group of drug addicts kidnapped and killed his daughter and tossed the corpse into the Pacific; she was an intelligent, sweet, kind-hearted young woman, loved by all and in the flower of her youth (Los Angeles, 1984).

Once again we can verify that each program is watertight, independent and automatically autonomous. The urges to kill are included within the neural computer: upon it 'knowing' that a loved daughter in the flower of her youth has been murdered, the biosocial ministry of defence unleashes the emotional mechanism of ire with intense desires to kill. At the same time, this pious professor of Irish descent had been programmed by his parents, by his own wife, and by this very daughter with the Christian precept and ideal of forgiveness. Mary herself had written a beautiful and poetic prayer about forgiveness which her father, weeping uncontrollably, read in the days following this cruel tragedy.

Nevertheless, Christ himself, on certain occasions, acted under the influence of rage, calling the Pharisees 'whited sepulchres' or 'generation of vipers' and overturning, whip in hand, the tables of the merchants in the temple. On occasion, religion may act as an accelerator of anger, of 'holy wrath'. Yahve appears in the Old Testament as a wrathful God that punishes the tribes which are enemies of his 'chosen people' mercilessly. Rabbi Kahane, member of the Knesset (Israeli Parliament), invoked the wrath of Yahve against the 'evil Arabs', while the Ayatollah Khomeini invoked a 'holy war' against Iraq and the divine wrath against the Great Satan – the United States; and decapitated or hanged Iranian adolescents 'in the name of God'. Neither Mahatma Gandhi nor the Ayatollah Khomeini may fit within the society of apes. The monkey is governed from its neural computer by bionatural programs of anger, but the hardware of its neural computer is incompatible with the biocultural programs of education, civilization, Christian forgiveness or 'holy wars'.

Vengeance: 'A Dish that is Eaten Cold'

The feeling of indignation is regulated, as all feelings, by an emotional densitometer. This densitometer is characterized by the time required for it to return to zero. When a husband has tangled himself up in a quarrel with his wife, and his anger has reached very high levels, even after they have made up and his wife tries to calm him with soft caresses he may reject these conciliatory gestures: 'Leave me alone. I'll get over it.' Although an electric range may be turned off, the water that was boiling on it requires some time to stop bubbling and cool down. A scientifically parallel process occurs with the emotional mechanism of anger. Although the fight or the cause of anger may be over, the densitometer of anger takes some time in returning to zero degrees (on the other hand, the incredibly intense urges to ejaculate return to zero degrees during the seconds that this load is ejected).

From a new perspective we surprise the emotional mechanisms working by their own little selves with a cadence, rhythm, quality, quantity, beginning, and end that follow laws completely independent from the conscience or free election of the subject. An individual is a spectator who must content himself with watching how clouds appear, disappear, take on a thousand different forms or cloud the sky over completely. Similarly, the subject is a spectator who watches how the 'emotional clouds of his celestial soul' appear, disappear, and take on diverse colours and intensities. There is nothing as objective and unconscious as the government of feelings, trusted completely to a biological machine, an automatic computer programmed by Nature and by culture. Freud here aimed off the mark.

The Spanish say that 'vengeance is a dish that is eaten cold' (La venganza es un plato que se toma frío), suggesting that revenge is plotted quietly, coldly, unemotionally. Can we attach any scientific validity to this popular expression? When a naive husband with blind faith in the 'unquestionable' fidelity of his wife returned unexpectedly at 2 a.m. and surprised his 'best friend' tangled with her in their bed, his neural computer triggered off anger with the densitometer of urges to kill both at one hundred degrees. In all courts, such a crime would be mitigated by the presence of 'passions which may blind reason'. If this husband did not kill the couple at that moment, the 'volcano' of anger that would have exploded in those circumstances would have stopped hurling lava after a while. But the desire for revenge may last for months and even years. The 'law of the cuckold' (see my book *The Rules of the Game: the Sexes*) continues to replay a documentary for the hapless husband in the brain's projection hall, in which he continues to see his wife embracing his best friend in his own bed. Every time the neural computer shows him this documentary – as he shaves, while he drives, or during his struggles to fall asleep – the emotional lava of ire flows again from the volcano. Finally, this husband, pursued by the urge to reclaim his crushed male pride, which year after year continues to pester him with the same tune, 'Kill that man who made a cuckold of you and I will leave you alone,' takes a decision: 'All right. That's enough. I'll kill him once and for all.' Such a case is described as a premeditated crime, committed 'in cold blood'. But we are not dealing with 'cold' blood, nor is vengeance a dish eaten 'cold'. What happens is that the desires of vengeance may continue tormenting an individual day after day, year after year, until finally the individual prefers obeying these emotional orders and releasing himself from their ceaseless torture. The law of urges – of all urges – as we can see, is that they are tenacious and persistent, and never refrain from pestering the individual while he fails to obey their orders to the last comma.

Society as a Community of Indignation
(*e pluribus una indignatio*)

Anger, when it is unleashed in the members of a human beehive (particularly the territorial one), is a feeling which unites with very powerful bonds, creates a community, and makes it function as a single team that seeks vengeance against the team-beehive that attacked it. The Jewish Holocaust, as the climax of a long chain of persecutions across twenty centuries, is one of the mechanisms that unchained the Jewish rage, conserved the mental and emotional identity of this society, and pressured Jews to build the State of Israel in 1948. Each time that the members of a foreign and rival beehive attack the common symbols – for example, the flag – or the territory itself, the 'tribal' ire is automatically set off in the neural computers of all those who have been programmed with these symbols and with the love for and feeling of belonging to this territory. (I apply the adjective 'tribal' here to every territorial society with militarily defended borders; see my book *The Rules of the Game: the Tribes*.)

11

Emotional Laws of the Ethical System

Homo ethicus: the Ethical Animal

'Marineland' is a Los Angeles aquarium which includes 'Dolphin Theatres', where these aquatic mammals 'perform'. But a dolphin is not born with a program installed in its brain which would allow it to interpret the role of the actor who raises waves of admiration among the spectators at these theatres. The neural computer of the dolphin has been installed with software which includes the programs of its digestive system (what it must eat, how, when and how much) and of its reproductive system (its neural computer, by means of emotional releases, will inform it about what animals to attract, with which it should mate, by the use of which channels, when, how often and in what way). The hardware of its brain also allows the dolphin to acquire the software which its trainer teaches it.

Within the neural computer of human beings, there is no pre-installed ethical program, as there is no pre-installed program of the English language. Up to this point, the computer of the dolphin and that of its future trainer are equal in terms of these *tabulae rasae*, blank slates (the ethical slate, and the slate of human language). The trainer will never be able to make the dolphin understand the meaning of right and wrong (the mental key to the ethical system), or to have it function with the sensation of guilt or of satisfaction at feeling like the 'good guy' in the film (the emotional mechanisms of the system). The hardware of the neural computer of a human being is perfectly equipped to unconsciously assimilate the ethical system he will find in his society from youngest infancy, as it is fully prepared to assimilate the language of the society in which he is born. The human being is as much a rational animal, *Homo rationalis*, as an ethical animal, *Homo ethicus*. No animal except for him is able to understand the mental and emotional meaning of good and evil, though Darwin, with the insistence of a fervent believer in the dogma of evolution, was determined to prove that animals function with an ethical system. It seems scientifically indisputable that ethics is an impassable genetic frontier between our species and apes.[1]

Ethicopolis: the Ethical Society

The beehive, as such, produces wax, honey and a social system with very precise rules. Within this system, the bee works like a piece of clockwork. Neither the beehive, nor the anthole, nor the band of monkeys provides the bee, ant or monkey with an ethical system. On the other hand, every human society – especially the geopolis or territorial society – is an ethicopolis, an ethical or moral society. Inevitably, a human being is born into a society which provides him with a linguistic system and an ethical system. The neural computer of the child unconsciously assimilates the rules of the linguistic game and of the ethical game. In so far as the ethical system of his beehive is installed in his neural computer, it becomes a bioethical program, which from that moment functions with its own laws and biological mechanisms. Within the hardware of every human's neural computer is installed a particular feeling unique in its nature: the feeling of guilt. This is the emotional mechanism peculiar to the ethical system. Similarly to the feeling of shame or of laughter, the feeling of guilt is innate and genetically specified. However, the neural computer will activate this emotional mechanism in relation to the current ethical code of the individual's territorial society in so far as it has been installed in its software.

A 'primitive' society or a 'civilized' one is an ethicopolis, an ethical society regulated by moral rules: this action is good, and that is a bad action. If a Nuer – a member of a 'primitive' Sudanese society studied by Evans-Pritchard – lets an organic gas 'escape' in public accompanied by the sounds of a trumpet fanfare, he will be lashed by the emotional fines of shame and ridicule, as would any Harvard professor who accidentally committed the same breach during a lecture on the 'evolution of Man'. Both individuals, the 'primitive' and the 'civilized', unlike apes are governed by the extremely severe taboo that strictly forbids the firing of organic shots in public, under the terrible emotional fines of shame and laughter. Malinowski, well-known within the world of anthropology as a pioneer of fieldwork, narrated a myth of the Trobriand Islanders – a Pacific society – on incest.[2] Two siblings once met on a beach. They began to run, to swim and to play around until between game and game they began to kiss playfully and finally gave each other the erotic embrace forbidden by incest. Both felt so tormented by the guilt-feelings that they decided to commit suicide. In this case these 'savage' youths were programmed with a very strict rule ('sex between siblings is a bad action'). The neural computer has codified this ethical norm, and on obtaining information about the infraction released upon these youngsters the terrible blow of guilt with a very high voltage. If the Harvard professor had 'fallen' into the temptation of making love with his daughter – a run-of-the-mill infraction in this 'advanced' society – he would have been brought before the same emotional tribunal of guilt as the 'savage' siblings from the Trobriand myth.

In Milwaukee (US), I met a man of over forty years who was accused by his own daughters (aged nine and ten) of having fallen into the pit of incest (1986). His lawyer recommended that he deny the crime. This man, ignoring his lawyer's counsel, declared himself guilty. 'Why did you declare yourself guilty, you fool?', his lawyer demanded. 'Because when the moment of truth came I felt so tormented by the weight of guilt that my lips, themselves, without my being able to stop them, confessed: guilty.' Although we speak of a free, permissive, civilized, evolved society, both the 'savage' Trobriand society and the modern society of the United States are ruled by the taboo of organic gases and by the taboo of incest with the same biosocial and emotional mechanisms in the brain. In all territorial societies, an ethical code directs all the other social systems: economic, family, political, religious. The specific rules vary, but not the codes themselves. There are human societies in which atheism is preached (though no monkey can preach atheism, itself a religious program), but no human society, the 'most primitive' or 'the most evolved', preaches the elimination of all morals. Every human society is an ethical society that instils its moral precepts into its members, programming this system into the cerebral location allocated by the genetic plan. Even the most radical anarchists preach anarchy as a rigorous ethical system in which the political and economic systems and their agents are condemned as 'the bad guys'.

Ethical System and Political System

The whole political system is regulated by the ethical and bio-ethical system. Every territorial society condemns 'treason against the fatherland' as the most ignoble ethical action and 'giving up one's life for the fatherland' as the most noble action imaginable. Certain ethical systems, such as the Marxist one, preach internationalism, the ideal of 'working-men of all countries, unite', the destruction of all frontiers that separate man from man. There is a game – in the scientific sense I have given this term – between diverse ethical systems, and man is forced to take sides with one or another ethical team. Already in 'savage' societies there exist prophets, visionaries, 'witches' who preach opposing ethical sermons from various pulpits.

As I have already treated this topic extensively in my book *The Rules of the Game: the Tribes*, here I will merely show the tip of the iceberg of tribal ethics. The same international Marxism led by the cry 'the working-men have no country' succumbed to the tribal ethics of the territorial teams (Chinese Marxism versus Russian Marxism). In fact, under the cosmetic universality of the comrades of the whole world, the territorial frontiers were reinforced, and tribal sentiments were intensified to unsuspected extremes. The greatest crime in the Soviet Union was to be accused of anti-Soviet activities. The tribal ethic, the loyalty before everything else to China, to Russia, to Nuerland, to Aztec society, to Iran or to Euskadi (the Basque Country) continues to be in full force in the twentieth century. There exists an ethic opposed to 'nationalisms', held by Christians, by Marxists, by Esperanto-speakers, by 'civilized' men and women who declare themselves 'citizens of the world'. But even the man who occupies and preoccupies himself most over the universal, ecumenical, anti-nationalist morality, though he may carry this ethical program in his brain, also carries the ethical program of his tribe. When least expected, the most fervent 'citizen of the world' will 'put his foot in it' with some word or action in the most rancid tribal taste. Treachery against the homeland and *dulce est pro patria mori* – 'it is sweet to die for the homeland' – are concepts registered in every human neural computer like indestructible bioethical bastions.

In the bellicose and imperial game, all territorial societies have attempted to win with weapons and to convince with a morality presented as the only and true one. During the Cold War, the Soviets, in their imperial game with the Americans, attempted to persuade minor or minimal tribes – militarily handicapped ones – that the ethic of equality preached by them was the only true one, while the evil American capitalists and imperialists were the 'bad guys' in the film. The Americans preached the opposite ethic: the 'bad guys' were the Soviets, who crushed the liberty of their own citizens and subjected them to the most vile slavery.[3]

Within each society, an ethical code regulates the political system. Nixon had to leave the White House by the back door for having broken an ethical norm of the current rules of the ethical/political game.

Economic and Ethical Systems

Marxism is not only an economic system, but above all an ethical system (incidentally, it is not even very economical from the standpoint of 'business is business').[4] In fact, in the nations where Marxism was adopted, the economies have become very stagnant, and these states became very retarded in the economic race of nations. We need only to compare the booming economy of capitalist China (Hong Kong and Taiwan) with that of the communist side. Supposing that the ethic of communist countries was superior to that of capitalist ones (better distribution of goods, elimination of the exploitation of man by man, and other Marxist moral fairy-tales), we still find quite a contrast between the bicycles of the Chinese and the automobiles of the Taiwanese, let alone those of the Japanese. The communist half of Germany had to ask the capitalist half for loans. Which energy is more powerful, the ethical one or the economic one? Who wins the struggle, money or morals? The facts demonstrate that the ethical system may hold back the economic system.

Today, Deng Tsiao-Ping[5] and Boris Yeltsin preach the ethics of capitalism with unusual fervour: let's forget the ethical 'non-sense' and the anachronistic moral fairy-tales; we need to improve the economic situation. Socialists and communists themselves have taken notice of the fact that ethics may slow down the economy. The latter is regulated by its own laws. Its key terms are gaining, growing, increasing production and exporting. Its commandments are encapsulated in the laconic tautology, 'business is business'.

The Spanish writer Benito Pérez Galdós said that sometimes morality is a purely economic question. He refers to more than one woman who, purely out of economic necessity, perhaps to pay for medicines for her son and even for her own husband, has been forced to sell her own body. An incisive observation. The neural computer of such a woman has pressured her with strong emotional levers to obtain money in any way possible, even though the same neural processor pressures her in the opposite direction with threats of guilt (and shame). The economy – tied to other factors (such as, in the present case, the love towards an ill child or husband) – may be the motor of morality, but morality itself may be on many occasions a motor of the economy or an obstacle to its progress. 'If I could be a scoundrel, I'd be a multi-millionaire. I'd bribe everyone like so many representatives do; but I would never sleep that night, nor could I live at peace with myself,' a commercial representative once confessed to me (Los Angeles, 1984). From the economic 'business is business' point of view, the minister who bribes, the minister who is a merchant or even a huckster in the secret market of political influence, selling licences and permits as if he were selling watermelons, is a good businessman. On the other hand, from the ethical standpoint, he is committing reprehensible actions classified as 'corruption' – a suggestive metaphor.

On 18 November 1987, all of Spain and even the whole global village hung in a state of suspense over the resolution of the kid-napping of a five-year-old girl, Melodie, for whom the perpetrators demanded 1,500 million pesetas. A human being may, for economic motives, kidnap a five-year-old girl, subjecting her, her parents and her family to a Dantean inferno. It is good business, from purely economic premises. However, the ethical system disapproves of and condemns this action as something sordid, something utterly despicable. These two powerful forces – the economic and the ethical – are cause and effect. Both systems are installed in the brain and pressure the individual with strong emotional levers. But why should some human beings prefer to undergo economic rather than ethical straits, while Melodie's kidnappers ravage the most elementary ethics to obtain a good few millions? Each neural computer is programmed in very different ways, from the individual's infancy (particularly with the ethical behaviour of the parents), though the subject's own decisions may also play a part.

The Ethical System and Other Systems

The ethical system governs all the social systems to a greater or lesser extent, and even the somatic ones. The 'glutton' *cuius deus venter est* (whose god is the belly), he who does not eat to live, but lives to eat, commits an action reprehensible by the ethical system. He who rapes, he who 'cheats on' his wife, he who breaks the law of incest is condemned by the ethical system in all cultures, with some modifications. Sometimes an ethical infraction of the sexual system may seriously affect the political system. Gary Hart, candidate to the Presidency of the United States, had to abandon this political marathon after being surprised leaving the house of an attractive young woman, Donna Rice, on a particular weekend (and this happened in 'the land of the free'). In Britain, John Major's government has also suffered from the exposure of such 'scandals' by the tabloid press in recent years.

Legal, Ethical and Religious Systems

The legal, ethical and religious systems are sets of rules with rewards and punishments which, once stored in the brain, function with the emotional mechanisms we are in the process of discovering. These three systems, though related and often closely intertwined, are by nature different. The legal system is the system of laws of a territorial society – national, municipal, provincial – approved by the relevant (or even irrelevant) authorities and codified in some book. It is the written law. If a traffic policeman 'catches' a driver speeding and gives him a heavy fine, the neural computer of this driver will bother him with an emotional activation of anger for having been fined, but will not torment him with any guilt. On the other hand, if a senator strongly programmed with the ethic of matrimonial fidelity sleeps with some lawyer, his neural computer will trigger off feelings of guilt in mathematical proportion to the registered program. In this case, the senator has commited no legal infraction, and his territorial society will give him no tug on the ear, but on the other hand, the bioethical judge in his brain will condemn him without reprieve to the emotional punishment of guilt.

The ethical system is in turn different from the religious system; every religious system is ethical, but not every ethical system is religious.

Biosocial Timer of Ethics

Neither a foetus nor a newborn has a brain equipped to decipher and record an ethical system. Gradually, as the neural computer of the child acquires the linguistic system, it will begin to decode and register the first ethical rules, learned from his mother: 'A good boy doesn't do that'; 'You're a bad boy, if you behave this way.' Little by little, the neural computer will begin to 'write down rules on the ethical slate' prepared by the genetic plan, and the feeling of guilt will begin to function. By means of conscious and especially unconscious recordings, the neural processor will daily work on the installation of a bioethical system of increasing complexity and power.

Emotional Densitometer of Bioethics

As with all emotional mechanisms, the mechanism of guilt is governed and regulated by an emotional densitometer: 'The neural computer automatically activates the feeling of guilt, upon receiving (unconscious) information of an ethical infraction, to a degree calculated in relation to the quality/quantity of the recording of the relevant rule, to the importance of the rule, and to the seriousness of the infraction committed.' If St John of the Cross, when he came across a shapely Castilian lass, had given in to the 'temptations of the flesh' (bionatural program of his reproductive system), his neural computer would have set off a dose of culpability much greater than that of Don Juan, who – let us suppose – had joined a monastic order, taken the vow of celibacy and tripped over the same stone. The neural computer of Don Juan would have recorded a very tenuous and recent program of celibacy in comparison with that of St John, who would have possessed a program of celibacy of many years, with millions of emotional 'antibodies' produced (quality/quantity of the recording of the rule). The neural processor also sets off a greater emotional intensity of guilt for having committed a moral infraction of incest than of adultery (importance of the ethical rule broken). It activates an emotional dose of guilt greater in the thief if he robs someone of a billion dollars than if he steals a thousand (quantity of the infraction committed).

Biosocial Law of Remorse

Re-morse is a very interesting metaphor which originates in the Latin verb *re-mordere*, to bite again and again, and which is applied precisely to the feeling of guilt. It presupposes that within a human being some kind of fierce dog bites the offender with its razor-sharp canine teeth, without the latter being able to do anything to drive it away. This biting and 're-biting' dog is a scientifically accurate image. Indeed, we are dealing with an emotional mechanism that is unchained like a dog that was tied up and tortures the offender of a serious ethical infraction, defenceless before the repeated and savage bites of the emotional canine of guilt. Whoever conceived and installed the ingenious judicial and police system of ethics in the neural computer does not seem to have asked its user, the human being. He restricted himself to placing and chaining up this emotional watchdog in the neural processor. Like the dog that guards the entrance of familiar territory entrusted to him from intruders, twenty-four hours a day, the emotional watchdog of morality does not sleep, and watches for the entrance of any ethical intruder. If the individual commits a serious infraction, the neural computer unleashes this dog, which will bite the perpetrator of the infraction again and again without mercy. The metaphor of 're-morse' contains the scientific intuition of the independence and the automatic, objective functioning of this feeling.

An uncle of mine killed a small girl with his car a few years ago in Pamplona. My uncle, a model citizen and scrupulous driver, was driving at the prescribed speed and obeying the traffic code closely, as he always did. A five-year-old girl saw her mother on the opposite side of the road and ran towards her, throwing herself literally before the wheels of the car – it was impossible to brake in time. She died on the spot. When my uncle arrived home he could only repeat a single phrase over and over to his wife: 'I have killed her. I have killed her.' My aunt could not understand what had happened. My uncle is the most peaceful, good-natured and humanitarian man imaginable, incapable of killing a mosquito. From then on, the judge/policeman/torturer of his brain's bioethical system has not stopped tormenting him with the emotional torture of guilt: 'You killed that innocent girl.'

Let us analyse this case. (1) My uncle's neural computer has been programmed with the following ethical rule: 'Killing an innocent person, especially in the flower of youth, is an extremely serious moral infraction punishable by a fine of guilt of a very high volt-age.' (2) The sensorial agents of my uncle's brain inform him of this accidental homicide. (3) The neural computer, following the unconscious and automatic instructions of the bioethical program, releases feelings of guilt of the specified intensity. My uncle is subjected to the torture of this horrible sensation, like an intense headache, which he can do nothing to prevent. My uncle consults the department of reason, which revises and scrutinizes everything. Reason removes an emotional weight from him: you are completely innocent. But we can once again verify the independence of the various separate and uncommunicated departments of the brain, of the diverse, completely independent programs. 'I know I am innocent,' my uncle affirms, 'but I feel guilty. I cannot help it.' The neural computer follows the unconscious instructions of its sensorial agents, which report that my uncle killed the girl. A person who kills intentionally must receive an even greater emotional punishment, since the sensorial department and the rational one both inform the bioethical department that the moral infraction is inexcusable.

Pascal made that well-known declaration that 'le coeur a ses raisons que la raison ne connaît pas'[6] (the heart has its reasons, which reason does not understand). This French thinker guessed or glimpsed that there sometimes exists an absolute separation between the 'cold' arguments of reason and the arguments of the emotions (as in this case). In fact, we are dealing with two types of emotion: those which proceed from the analysis of the rational department and those which proceed from the sensorial department. The emotions of the sensorial department are in principle the more powerful ones. Let us recall the thoughts of St John of the Cross: 'lovesickness cannot be cured without the presence and the figure'. Reason assures St John of the Cross that God is everywhere and that He lives always with him; this information is translated into very pleasant sensations. But St John of the Cross understands that the physical presence of the loved one – God or whoever, the sensorial information – is translated into highly superior emotions. This is the law of the brain.

One of the implications of the 're-morse' metaphor is the duration: the dog bites, 're-bites', and bites again. My uncle confesses that twenty-five years after the accident he still suffers the emotional gnashings of this fierce dog. How long does the feeling of guilt or remorse last? As we have seen, in the majority of cases measuring the duration of an activated feeling is a simple operation: until the urges have been granted exactly what they asked for. The urges to eat, to drink, to urinate, to defecate or to copulate do not cease until the individual eats, drinks, urinates, defecates or copulates until the last foreseen or prescribed unit. Period. However, the duration of the feeling of guilt seems to be a different story. The neural computer warned the individual that if he committed such a crime, he would be subjected to this emotional torture. The crime has been committed and the emotional rock of guilt has been placed on the psychological shoulders of the criminal. Until when?

The first thing that must be asserted is that the duration of guilt, like the whole automatic process of all and each of the emotional mechanisms, functions automatically and with a complete independence from the individual's free will. The criminal would be ecstatic if he could avoid the bites of the emotional watchdog which continues snapping at him months and years after the crime. What wouldn't he give to disconnect himself from this emotional torment, as he disconnects the television set by simply pressing a button or as he turns off the motor of his car with half a turn of a key? Nature has not endowed the individual with this key or switch to turn off a toothache or the pain caused by the guilt reserved for the criminal. We can state the following law: 'The greater the ethical infraction, the greater the duration of the feeling of guilt.' Minor ethical transgressions lead to emotional fines of guilt of a lesser degree, which last as little as frost on a sunny day.

The Urges to Confess, to Pay, to be Forgiven

A spectacle as fascinating as a view of Niagara Falls – such is, in truth, the discovery of the dazzling world of the brain's bioethical engineering: the bioethical tribunal by which the individual is judged according to a series of biocoded laws, and eventually condemned and imprisoned in a cell where a bioethical torturer will be charged with whipping and tormenting him with the emotional instruments ordered by the judge, in the measure and for the duration prescribed by 'his honour'. The criminal, before being judged, condemned and jailed by the exterior courts, will be judged, condemned and tortured by the bioethical tribunal of justice in the brain. This prior trial will proceed without delays, without the individual being able to hide his crime, and with no possibility of him bribing the judge or torturer: 'Please, that's enough! Leave me alone at least tonight! I can't take it any more! Have some mercy!' The neural computer is a machine 'without a heart' and without feelings. This is why it is said that God always forgives, Man sometimes forgives, but Nature never forgives. The exterior tribunals, the judges, the jails, the police, the torturers, the electric chair are once again variations of the theme *cultura ancilla naturae*: culture which, as a humble servant, works at the orders of her mistress, Nature.

The person who commits a crime or a serious ethical transgression is subjected to two opposing emotional currents: from one direction, one emotional current pushes him to hide his crime (biological ministry of individual defence). But from the contrary direction, the bioethical judge, by means of the emotional lever of guilt, pushes him to confess his crime to his society (biosocial ministry of the defence of society). This bioethical judge speaks to him in the emotional language (if we translated from the emotional to the verbal language): 'You have killed an innocent person. You have committed an extremely serious action. Now I am forced to torture you day and night with this terrible rock I have placed on your shoulders. As you can see, I do not allow you to eat peacefully, relax with a good film, or enjoy your love-making. Your life is a torment. If you confess your crime, you will feel a great relief: I will remove this great load from you. You will be judged and condemned by others. The punishments will be severe. But is not this torture infinitely worse than all of those?' Which of these two emotional currents is the stronger? Everything depends on the quality and quantity of the bioethical program. The criminal born and raised in an orphanage or in a family where the father was a drunk, a thief and a murderer who daily beat his mother, a prostitute, has received a very tenuous bioethical program. After his first crime he feels very weak urges to confess it, as compared with much more powerful urges to hide the deed.

Unamuno, the great Spanish thinker, declared that 'confession is very useful because it allows one to sin again more comfortably'. Unamuno, with his characteristic sarcasm, meant that the confession of the Catholic Church is usually a hypocritical and useless act: the sinner does not go to confession to stop sinning, but rather to free himself from the weight of guilt and thus sin more at peace with himself. Whatever the more or less sincere or hypocritical attitude of the sinner about to confess, what seems scientifically correct is that, upon confessing the sins committed, the neural computer cancels the feelings of guilt (the urges to confess). Here we discover the workings of this astute emotional mechanism, which pushes the individual to confess his ethical shortcomings. Nature, like the FBI, offers a considerable emotional sum to the person who unmasks the deviant (in this case the deviant himself is the one who will obtain this emotional reward for denouncing himself). Psychoanalysis runs on similar tracks: the freedom from guilt obtained by confessing it. In the same way that the neural computer offers a savoury reward to the individual for emptying the tank of urine or of sperm, it offers the sinner/criminal/deviant an emotional recompense for emptying his tank of guilt: exposing it to his society. (The confession to the psychoanalyst or to the priest may be partly or wholly a 'cure that is worse than the illness', for reasons we cannot here even begin to discuss.)

Scruples: an Emotional and Biosocial Malfunction

St Ignatius of Loyola tells of how, after several days of retreat and meditation in Manresa, in the strictest solitude, he was besieged by the most absurd scruples. He felt guilty, for example, if he stepped on two straws forming the shape of the cross. *Scrupulus*, in Latin, refers to the little stone that slips into our shoe and prevents us from walking comfortably. It is not an excruciating torture, but a continuous annoyance that finally makes us 'go mad'. The *scrupulus*, the little stone which has slipped into the bioethical shoe, prevents us from walking comfortably along the paths of thought and feeling. St Ignatius consults the rational department of his neural computer.

The report submitted by this department calms him down: 'accidentally stepping on two crossed straws is a completely innocuous action'. But the rational department is an uncommunicated, independent and isolated department, as any department of the brain. St Ignatius cannot suppress the feelings of guilt provoked by these scruples, released by his bioethical system according to sensorial information. How has such a scruple slipped into the bioethical system? It is not easy to find the causes of mechanical or emotional malfunctions. However, in the light of the way in which the neural computer acts according to the quantity/quality of the recording of a particular program ('the greater the intensity of the recording, the greater the emotional fine for the infraction detected by the sensorial agents'), we can understand that the obsession and concentration of St Ignatius on Christ's cross may have led his neural computer to detect and thus to punish the slightest and most insignificant profanation of any sensorial form of this symbol.

'I'm disconsolate,' my friend Andrés Segovia told me in a Los Angeles hotel room (1982). 'What's wrong?' 'You want to know what's wrong? Listen . . . listen to this.' He then played a few lines from Bach's *Chaconne*. To me it seemed that Bach would have delighted in the way his music sounded from the guitar of this great maestro. 'But, can't you hear how it wavers and becomes out of tune? The guitar which, like a woman, is all sensibility, has been affected by the change in climate and altitude.' The neural computer of Andrés Segovia perceived an 'imperceptible' musical infraction when he played the guitar which my own brain, owner of musical programs which allow me to play toccatas and fugues by the great Johann Sebastian Bach, was unable to detect. I cite this example to understand how the neural computer detects infractions and activates the corresponding emotional fines in accordance with the quantity and the quality of the program recorded. The bioethical program of Hitler was, without a doubt, very different from that of Mahatma Gandhi, or that of Herod from Christ's.

Scruples may also proceed from other sources. Benito Pérez Galdós, in his famous novel *Fortunata and Jacinta*, describes the case of a curious character – Ido del Sagrario – who, after making himself 'drunk with meat'[7] – in Galdos's words – imagines that his wife is cheating on him with a marquis. This poor man is literally poor and lives in a working-class quarter of Madrid, never having known the meaning of a good sirloin steak except by hearsay. His wife was never beautiful, even as an eighteen-year old. One good day he is invited by someone to a large succulent hunk of red meat. He becomes 'drunk with meat' – an incisive and sharp expression from this profound thinker – and this state of drunkenness affects the emotional system of his erotic program and transforms his wife into a goddess of beauty who sleeps with a marquis. When he 'sobers up', the sexual scruple vanishes. An anomaly or malfunction of an emotional system may thus intervene or interfere in another.

Bioethical Energy

Feelings are powerful forces which frequently oppose each other and push the individual in contrary directions, like the law of gravity that attracts the bird or plane towards the ground, the headwind that pushes both flyers backwards, and the motor energy of the dove or of the wings and rotor blades of the plane which push it forward, flying and fighting against opposing forces. If oxygen is one of the energies which allow a human being – and a monkey – to live and feel, ethics, once installed in the brain and transformed into bioethics, is one of the energies which, with its powerful emotional mechanisms, pushes the human to take certain actions or to avoid performing certain others. We have already seen how the ethical forces sometimes struggle against particular economic, political or other forces. Here I want to draw attention to the functioning of bioethics as energy that moves and pressures the human being.

Judas is an interesting case in this regard. The *Homo oeconomicus* must have pressured him from his brain with these types of arguments: 'Judas: this is the chance you've been waiting for. Thirty silver coins! You'll be rich. Come on, this is the chance of a lifetime. Here everyone sells what he can.' The *Homo ethicus* must have counter-attacked: 'But how can you commit such an abominable act? I will torture you with the terrible whip of guilt. I'll make you wish you hadn't.' The *Homo oeconomicus* won the first match, but the *Homo ethicus* won the game. Judas may have acquired an economic program superior to the ethical one. Judas, the subject of consciousness, capable of taking his own decisions, also intervened. But the game between the *Homo oeconomicus* and the *Homo ethicus* did not end when Judas had bought economic shares by selling his ethical shares. The representative of the bioeconomic program spoke to him (translating the emotional into the verbal language): 'Congratulations, Judas. You're rich. Look at the thirty silver coins. Count them, caress them, enjoy them.' The representative of the bioethical program did not stay silent: 'Judas, you miserable wretch. You are despicable. You have sold Christ, the most innocent man, who did nothing but good wherever he went, who treated you with so much affection. Recall with what kindness and love he asked you 'With a kiss you betray the son of Man?' Judas, condemned and tortured by the courts and the horrible prison of the bioethical system, decided to return the thirty silver coins: 'I have given you an innocent man. Here are your thirty coins.' When these men refused to accept the coins, Judas hanged himself. Such is the power of the bioethical judge and torturer installed in the brain.

We can notice that it is not an exterior judge – another man – who condemns Judas. It is the bioethical judge who condemns him and it is the bioethical torturer who subjects him to an emotional torment he cannot escape day or night. The rules of the game may be broken, but not without incurring the automatic, unappealable and irreversible emotional trial of the three cerebral courts: shame, ridicule and the bioethical system's tribunal of guilt.

Another interesting case appears in *Wicked Carabel*, a delightful novel by W. Fernández Flórez. Carabel is an honest bank employee who watches how his colleagues profit from their deceitful and 'dirty' practices, while he, incapable of bribing, deceiving, betraying or flattering, is condemned to his miserable wage and to the lowest position in the company. One fine day he decides to join the wicked game of his ambitious workmates but, though he tries once and a thousand times, he always fails in his attempts. He wants to be evil, but he cannot. This argument, though somewhat exaggerated in the letter, does not seem preposterous in the spirit. An individual may have received from his infancy such a strong ethical program that he cannot be 'rotten', however he may try. Individual election is very limited. The individual cannot de-program his neural computer as he wishes or in the time he wishes.

The Ethical Game and Hierarchy

In the ethical world, all men are born equal, but they do not live or die in a state of equality. The life of a man is partly an ethical game where, as in all games, matches are won and lost and a precise hierarchy is created in terms of 'good' and 'bad' persons. We may notice that the politician, the columnist, the priest, the film producer, the person who speaks or writes from some platform, is a preacher who wishes to 'sell' some moral philosophy or fairy-tale moral. The husband preaches to his wife and the wife to her husband. Man is a keen enthusiast of giving free lectures on some specific ethic or moral. Political parties, churches, sects, nations, congregations, all try to convince the rest that their ethical system is the best.

At the end of this life, a person is judged and classified as an ethical hero or as a disqualified player or loser in the ethical game of life. The lay and the religious churches build an altar where the icon, image or statue of some ethical hero is venerated. We do not find a monkey worshipping another monkey that died years or centuries ago, or placing the picture or icon of an ethical supermonkey in the living room, in a temple or in the public square. Marxists did not eliminate the cult of the icons of the Russian Orthodox Church. They merely replaced the icons of St George or of Mary with the gigantic portraits of the ethical heroes of Marxism: Marx, Lenin or the current party leader. Brides and bridegrooms who once deposited a garland before the altar of Mary now did so before Lenin's tomb.

No human being is indifferent to the emotional whisper of the *Homo ethicus*: 'You will be venerated like Marx, like Lenin, or like St George if you behave as an ethical hero' (according to the rules of the ethical game of each creed). In the majority of religions, and in the cults to ethical heroes of this world, a precise hierarchical classification is made for the afterlife. The rational department of the brain may whisper into the individual's ear that the cult offered to him after death is pure illusion and vanity of vanities, at least in this world. However, his bioethical program releases a pleasant feeling every time the mental projection hall shows him a documentary in which he is the hero venerated by future generations after death. Such documentaries form part of the bioethical program of the human being, and would surprise an ape if apes could be surprised at such things.

A person is always taking part in the daily ethical game, as John Smith or as member of his beehive (territorial, ideological, religious, generational, economic, political, sexual). If the neural computer detects the loss of a point or a round, it punishes him with the appropriate emotional fine. If he wins, it pays him the pleasure reserved to the winner, in precise correspondence with the victory obtained. Each time that we condemn someone as the loser in some ethical game ('he's a liar, a scoundrel, an upper-class pig, a male chauvinist, a "commie" . . . '), from whichever moral code, we are affirming our ethical superiority. Cain did not kill Abel for having lost the economic or political game, but for having lost the ethical (and in this case also religious) game. Benito Pérez Galdós, as always, hits the anthropological nail on the head when he presents Fortunata, the lover of a married Madrid aristocrat, as the rival of Jacinta, the wife, on the ethical field. The day that Fortunata discovers that Jacinta has also committed ethical infractions in the sphere of sexual infidelity she exclaims, throwing off the emotional rock borne by the loser: 'At last, the same!'

Wise and cautious Nature has installed the urges to win the ethical game in the neural computer of every last son of Adam, within and without his own beehive. Every human being, pressed by this emotional mechanism, spies on every other continuously, trying to catch him red-handed in some moral lapse. The loser of some serious ethical match can additionally lose many points in the economic/political game. This is why in the deadly fights between tribes or nations (territorial societies), the strategy of disparaging the rival beehive in the ethical arena is resorted to time after time. This is why in the contests between political parties, politicians rummage through each other's 'closets' in search for 'skeletons'. This is why the neighbour obtains such delight in spreading gossip about other neighbours. Nature, as the CIA or any intelligence agency, pays large emotional commissions from the cerebral banks to any citizen who discovers such 'juicy' information. 'You know Little-miss-goody-two-shoes? We'd all swallowed her saintly act, hook, line and sinker. Well, get this: she's having an affair with Senator So-and-so.' 'No! You're joking! That beats everything!' In these types of conversations, we see two human beings thrilled at the discovery of a moral infraction committed by a person with a virtuous reputation. Nature pays a healthy dose of pleasure to the person who discovers that someone – especially someone with whom he plays the economic game of house, district, car, furniture, coats, restaurants, holiday trips – by losing some ethical points on the scoreboard, is inferior to him.

'For every ethical point won, an emotional commission is paid by the cerebral bank of the bioethical department.' This is one of the emotional laws of the bioethical game installed in the neural computer. Why are journalists so keen on being the first to obtain a 'scoop' on a 'juicy' scandal? Why does scandal sell so well? Why is scandal 'juicy'? The answer to these questions is the law we have just stated. The public figure knows that his rivals, his neighbours, journalists, and even his 'friends', will spy on him to 'catch him out', to discover some 'skeleton in his ethical closet'. He knows that on the day they uncover some shocking scandal they will all obtain great pleasure by feeling superior to him in the ethical game. Thanks to this most clever innate programming of the *Homo ethicus or bioethicus*, every human being is a guard with his eyes constantly peeled to detect infractions of the rules of the ethical game of the beehive, hopeful of cashing a good pleasure pay-cheque at the brain's bioethical bank. At the same time, the neural computer warns every human being of the peril undergone if he does not respect the rules of the moral game.

Ethical Arrogance

Two men went up into the temple to pray; the one a Pharisee, and the other a publican. The Pharisee stood and prayed thus with himself, God, I thank thee, that I am not as other men are, extortioners, unjust, adulterers, or even as this publican. I fast twice in the week, I give tithes of all that I possess. And the publican, standing afar off, would not lift up so much as his eyes unto heaven, but smote upon his breast, saying, God be merciful to me a sinner.[8]

This is one of the best-known parables in the whole of the Christian community. When this parable is told, the brain of any human being immediately recognizes the winner and the loser of the ethical match it recounts. Bragging about the possession of an ethical Rolls-Royce, boasting that one is a millionaire of virtue, scorning others as the ethical lower class, is the most immoral act, this evangelical story warns. Once again we come across two opposing programs which, when installed, and according to the firmness with which they become rooted in the brain, push the human being with emotional levers in contrary directions: 'Judge, condemn and you will obtain the delightful pleasure of feeling victorious in the ethical arena' versus 'Do not judge and you will not be judged; do not condemn and you will not be condemned.' It is even possible to present oneself as a despicable sinner to win the ethical game of humility: ethical arrogance disguised as humility. Can the human being win the ethical game without stooping to the ethical arrogance of the Pharisee in the parable?

In a private dinner with Their Majesties the King and Queen of Spain, I had the honour of speaking privately with Queen Sofía. She asked me several questions about my working hypothesis that man is genetically programmed as a competitive animal pressured by emotional mechanisms to win the game on any field. 'Even saints are players,' I said to her, 'They play one of the most difficult games: the game of sanctity. They want to prove that they are superior to all the rest in this arena.' 'But then they are not saints,' answered the Queen with serene majesty. 'How embarrassing!', I thought, stumped by her reply. Here I come across one of the scientific puzzles I have been unable to solve. Can the human being win the ethical game without worrying about this very game? I have not managed to escape from this scientific labyrinth, as with so many others. (We should not, however, commit the fallacy of thinking 'if I cannot resolve a scientific problem, I cannot resolve any scientific problem'.)

Bioethical Programming

The ethical system, as we have already indicated, is installed in the neural computer by a process of multiple recordings in a step-by-step fashion, as is language – English or Spanish. The brain is equipped to unconsciously decipher the ethical rules of play from the information the sensorial agents feed it. It discovers that killing an innocent human being is a reproachable and penalized act, from which it infers the following ethical rule: 'It is forbidden to kill.' The brain discovers the penalty; the penalty allows the brain to detect the infraction; the infraction reveals the rule. *Penalty → infraction → rule.*

According to a Hindu proverb, 'The crab teaches its little crablings, "always walk forwards", and then walks backwards.' The crab sends two different and opposing messages to its young: one is the message of words – 'always walk forwards' – and the other, the message of deeds – 'walk backwards like me'. Consider a father who shouts at one of his children, 'How many times do I have to tell you not to shout at your brother?! Talk, don't scream. If you had any manners, you wouldn't shout like that.' He is sending two opposed messages to his child's brain: that of words ('shouting is wrong, morally reproachable') and that of deeds ('whoever is in charge has the last word and the right to shout'). Both messages are assimilated by the brain. It seems that the mute language of deeds is the most eloquent and effective of all. 'Actions speak louder than words.' This saying points in a direction that seems scientifically accurate. The neural computer of a child acquires a bioethical program to a great extent by observing the way in which his parents follow the rules of the ethical game.

Many sociologists assert that children are becoming aggressive by watching a continuous stream of violent scenes on television and in films. Each time a guitar student hears a piece and each time he practises or plays, the neural computer modifies the biomusical program that is being installed on the art of playing the guitar, for better or for worse. Each time the neural computer observes human behaviour – on television or in the home – it takes good notes and modifies the bioethical program accordingly (as we have seen, only the bionatural programs remain immutable and unalterable, impermeable to the sensorial information that reaches the brain). But the neural computer seems to be genetically programmed to give much greater importance to the behaviour of parents than to that of characters in books or television melodramas. Baby crabs will grow up walking backwards, following the example of their parents.

This is not the only factor, or an absolutely determining one, but it seems to be the most important. A child that is born and grows up in an exemplary family atmosphere where his parents preach with the language of deeds a sermon of bullet-proof honesty, fidelity, sacrifice and love, will acquire within his neural computer a very different bioethical program from that of a child whose parents hate, insult, fight with, rob from, lie to and cheat on each other, and furthermore mistreat and beat him. Each time a human being is tempted to take a path which is ethically out of bounds, his neural computer will show him the behaviour of his parents. If a married man feels the 'temptation' of 'becoming entangled' with his sweet, young and attractive secretary, his neural computer will immediately hand him a report about the behaviour of his father with his mother. If his father was scrupulously faithful to his mother for forty years, his neural computer will project him a documentary in which the father tells him, 'My son: do not backstab your children's mother in such a vile manner. Today you feel proud of me. Do you not wish that your children will feel proud of you tomorrow?' This is not the only emotional mechanism that may prevent the executive in question from initiating a romance with his secretary, but it is an undeniable fact that: (1) the behaviour of the true father with the mother is an emotional mechanism much superior to that of the father of a Hollywood film with his wife; (2) this is an emotional mechanism of prevention which the son of a father who made his wife suffer by sleeping with many young women does not carry in his brain.

Within the department of bioethics 'live' the father and the mother with the example of their own lives. This seems to be one of the most important factors which contribute to the recording of the bioethical rules of play in the brain. Manuel Fraga Iribarne, in *Memoria Breve de una Vida Pública*, describes the bewilderment of an American professor who carried out a study on the influence of the father's behaviour when he discovered that Franco, the most faithful of husbands, was the son of a man who had a mistress. Many other factors intervene in the bioethical programming. No factor is wholly determinant. But it is clear that in the genetic strategy the behaviour of parents, as the Hindu proverb about the crabs suggests, is one of the most profound and lasting factors.

'Brainwashing'

In December of 1983 I was invited by the Smithsonian Institution in Washington D.C. to participate in an international symposium on George Orwell's famous novel *Nineteen Eighty-Four*. All of the participants seemed to agree with this well-known British novelist's central argument: Big Brother, the totalitarian dictator, by means of a daily indoctrination, after forty years eventually manages to completely 'brainwash' the main character, Winston, a worker who represents the average simple man. Through a system of communications media which invades the life of this besieged citizen, or more accurately subject, the dictator has managed to beat into this man's brain the most irrational ethical and mental code imaginable. Winston finally accepts the ethical creed gladly. The last sentence in the book sums everything up: 'He loved Big Brother.'

I begged, with the highest respect towards George Orwell and towards my distinguished colleagues, to differ from the central thesis of this original political parable, otherwise brimming with incisive intuitions, brilliant ideas and profound thought. I am not at all certain of Big Brother's power to 'brainwash'. I made allusion to Franco's case. For forty years Franco attempted to 'brainwash' the Spanish people, preaching an ethical/political creed which held that 'freemasons, communists, liberals, democracy and the devil' were the moral scum that every Spaniard should detest. After Franco's death, at the first general elections, the Spanish people voted against this ethical creed and immediately adopted democracy. At these elections, only a single deputy to the Spanish Parliament was elected who preached the Franquist creed. From the second elections onwards, there has been no representative of this dogma in the Spanish Parliament.

A man, gun in hand, may assault a woman: 'Your sexuality or your life.' The woman may have no choice but to let herself be raped. This armed man, however, cannot say to the young woman, 'Your love or your life; either you fall in love with me or I'll kill you.' A very interesting British film, *The Collector*, deals with this topic. A youth who sees a young woman at the bus stop every day kidnaps her and shuts her up in the basement of a house isolated in the middle of the British countryside. Scream as she may, no one will be able to hear her. This young man wants his captive to fall in love with him: 'Your love or your life.' After several days of seclusion, she has an idea: 'If I surrender my intimacy to him, feigning a smile, I hope he will set me free.' This unfortunate woman decides to put her plan into action. She invites him to dinner one night. He must buy delicious food and choice wines, decorate the table with an elegant tablecloth, silver candlesticks and fresh flowers, and light the living room fireplace with dry firewood. The abductor accepts the plan and follows her every suggestion to the last detail. After dinner, when she initiates the prelude to the erotic symphony as they sit on the sofa, he suddenly pushes her away violently and angrily accuses her, 'You're trying to seduce me so that I will set you free. I don't want your sex. I want your love.' 'You're mad,' she replies, 'Who's going to fall in love with you by force? You can't make someone fall in love with you by kidnapping them at gunpoint.' 'That's not true. You're not really trying. If you made an effort, you would begin to love me.' (I quote the dialogue from memory.) Naturally, he does not manage to make this young woman love him. Each day she hates him more until eventually she tries to kill him, banging him on the head with a metal object. Something similar occurs when any Big Brother, any Franco, any Joseph Stalin, any dictator, tries to impose his code by means of physical coercion, making people swallow an ethical medicine by force. The brain seems to be equipped to emotionally reject a forced love or an ethical code imposed by brute force. It is not possible to 'brainwash', as the kidnapper of *The Collector* or the author of *Nineteen Eighty-Four* imagined.

On the other hand, it is possible that a person may hold a great sway over the minds of others. 'I cannot live without Blue Apple (Chiang Ching)', Mao confessed, once this astute woman had bewitched him. From that moment on, Chiang Ching, having conquered Mao's mind, dedicated herself to the regulation of the Chinese nation, persecuting Beethoven, academics, dogs, sparrows and the Chinese. In the same way, a skilful preacher – political and/or religious – may hold his audiences in a spell, especially young people and particularly young people hungry for faith, for hope, for ideals. We come across countless gurus, leaders of sects of every type, and telepreachers 'Made in America' that 'take over the minds' of their faithful, in other words, that manage to install a bioethical program in their brains, subsequently being able to direct these brains as one may direct a radio-controlled model car.

The Mechanism of 'Conversion' and 'Perversion'

The human being is born in the heart of a society – no less today than in earlier times – where a variety of preachers, from various pulpits, attempt to 'take over his mind'. A never-ending variety of creeds and moral recipes fight it out with each other to reach the brain through lectures, films, radio and television programmes, conferences, and especially through the continuous interaction with parents, brothers, schoolmates, colleagues and partners at the table or in bed. A Marxist/atheist married a young, strict Roman Catholic woman (Navarre, Spain, 1920). This man had acquired the bioethical program of Marxism, which included a fierce hatred of anything that gave off the faintest odour of incense and sacristy, a militant atheism, and a radical anti-clericalism. His wife had limitless respect and admiration for him, and never uttered so much as a word to change his ways. After thirty years of marriage he 'converted' to the Catholic faith. The example of his wife, whom he admired and idolized, had finally won the bioethical battle.

In this example, two opposed systems play a bioethical chess-game within a human brain for many years. However, the day that this man decides to abandon Marxism and atheism, and to adopt a new ethical code, he cannot eliminate the Marxist bioethical program from his neural computer, as one may remove a computer disk and replace it with another. From now on this convert will dedicate himself tenaciously to deepening his new bioethical program, struggling against the previous program still in operation. The new program will gain in strength and the earlier will deteriorate with the passing of the years. Or perhaps gradually the earlier program will again resurge for a few rounds and win the game. In the film *The Great*

Dictator, the brilliant Charles Chaplin portrays a 'Tomanian' (i.e. Nazi) general who has been converted to the anti-Tomanian cause ('perverted', from the Tomanian standpoint) and who attends a secret meeting where a conspiracy against 'Hilken' will be plotted. At the end of the meeting he stands up and exclaims 'Heil Hilken!' with his right arm outstretched.

The neural computer of the convert will react automatically, on various occasions, according to the bioethical program that is being suppressed but which cannot be torn out of the brain altogether. The brain acquires the programs gradually and also stifles them gradually, following its own laws. Fortunata struggles as hard as she can to love her husband – who has been imposed on her – and to stop loving the married man who has enamoured her. But she fails to advance a single millimetre in either case. Sometimes an atheist would like to believe, as Fortunata wishes to love the husband she does not. But the individual does not choose an ethical system, as he does not choose to fall in love or to fall out of love with a person who has already 'taken over his mind'. We are dealing with unconscious processes by which the neural computer creates, enlarges, or diminishes certain programs in the light of information received from the words and especially the deeds of a whole multitude of people whom we come across along the road of life, in most cases by chance. (The scientist can neither affirm nor negate the influence of certain invisible beings – God, the devil, the saints, etc. – in the process of conversion or perversion of human beings.)

Marxists and Christians: the Individual as the Founder of an Ethical Society

When we define human beings as 'Marxists' or as 'Christians', we give no information concerning the contents of a professed doctrine or morality. We simply affirm that certain human beings are followers or adepts of Christ or Marx, to the point of denoting themselves with a name derived directly from theirs: Christians, Marxists. In the human species, the individual is not equipped to function as a human being until his neural computer has acquired the elementary cultural programs of every human society (the linguistic, ethical and other programs). Once the individual has acquired these programs, he can contribute his 'grain of sand' to various different degrees, and create more or less dominant variations on cultural themes.

Christ created a new ethical code which included the forgiveness of enemies, the judging of no one, the treatment of prostitutes and thieves as our ethical equals, the giving of wealth to the poor, the suppression of boasts about religious practices, the sacrifice of life for others, and the sharing of love with all. Christ preached and put this new moral code into practice himself. Although he had a few followers, he was condemned to death by the religious and political authorities of his two contemporary societies: the Jewish and the Roman. His few disciples abandoned him and one betrayed him. Only a single disciple, his mother, and a prostitute assisted him, and they did so in his moment of agony and solitude ('My God, My God, why have you forsaken me?'). His failure was spectacular. Nevertheless, the wary anthropologist never knows where the pioneering work of an individual may lead – in the ethical domain and in others – though his contemporaries may poison him (as happened to Socrates); make him forswear his 'error' (as Galileo was made to do); or crucify him (as with Christ). Paradoxically, the failure and death of Christ became the best advertisement for the new 'Christian' ethical code. After twenty centuries, millions of human beings dispersed throughout five continents call themselves Christian (though we do not know whether Christ would agree with this name).

When Karl Marx died, he was buried in an 'ordinary' grave at London's Highgate Cemetery. Since then, a colossal monument or mausoleum with a gigantic bronze bust has been erected there. Many human beings 'have become Marxists' through seeing Karl Marx not as a scientific theoretician, but rather as a prophet of or liberator from the abuses and ethical corruptions men commit at each other's expense. Those who have imposed Marxism by brute force, repression, torture, executions and prisons have disappointed the fervent believers in this ethic. Once again we can observe how the neural computer rejects an imposed program. Physical or military coercion has its own limits.

Although it is true that the individual's neural processor unconsciously and automatically records the rules of the ethical game of his society (or societies), a Marx, a Socrates or a Christ may emerge who alters these norms of play by creating new codes and founding a new ethical society or *ethicopolis*. Neither Marx nor Christ may exist in the society of bees or of monkeys, nor may bees, therefore, become 'Christians' or 'Marxists'. 'How did Man, a descendant of the ape (if this indeed be the case), become an ethical animal? How or when did man begin to feel guilty, to distinguish between right and wrong, and to classify men as good or evil?'

Ethical Origins

According to the Book of Genesis, Man first became an ethical animal[9] – he came 'to know good and evil' – when he committed his first sin or ethical infraction: eating the forbidden fruit. But how could it be possible to commit an ethical infraction before having learned any ethical code? It is impossible to break a rule without knowing about it. No monkey may commit an ethical infraction, having no genetic passport to enter ethical territory. From a scientific point of view, there is no satisfactory explanation for the origins of morality. Sigmund Freud was taken in by the same sophistic trick. This distinguished thinker fabricated a myth or story – influenced by J. J. Atkinson, according to Evans-Pritchard – which recounts how during Man's semi-primate stage the father had a monopoly over the females.[10] One fine day, in order to end this monopoly and obtain direct access to the females the sons killed their father. At this point they felt the feeling of guilt for the first time. This is how the feeling of guilt and the ethical world from which religion is derived was born.

But why don't the monkeys, which continue to compete for females, kill their father again, become ethical animals, and begin to build temples? Why do some monkeys become ethical and religious animals while others continue to be monkeys that 'monkey around'? Freud fails to explain anything, but cheerfully asserts what he cannot prove. A monkey cannot commit an ethical infraction before knowing the rules and the ethical world. Freud is taken in by a similar sophism to Proudhon's, who must have felt flooded with pleasure when he coined a phrase which has been quoted a thousand times as the finest revolutionary flag: 'La propriété privée est un vol' (Private property is theft).[11] This ingenious French sophist did not realize that he affirmed what he tried to deny. Nothing can be robbed if private property does not exist previously. Theft presupposes the concept of private property.

If the human being descends from the ape, we continue to be ignorant of why, how and when a few monkeys began to feel guilty, smile, blush, laugh, dress, adorn themselves, pray to God, talk – in short, to become human beings. And why, on the other hand, other monkeys continued to be monkeys. Whenever we are unable to resolve a problem of this nature, we must follow the prudent advice of Socrates and, in a spirit of humility and scientific honesty, admit and confess that 'we have no idea'. What we do know, however, is that: (1) Man, unlike apes and all other animals, is genetically equipped with a neural computer which includes a pre-installed feeling – the feeling of guilt – and hardware which contains an empty disk where one or even various ethical programs may be recorded; (2) human societies, unlike the societies of other animals, produce ethical systems – part of the wax and honey of the human beehive; (3) the human brain automatically and unconsciously acquires these ethical codes from the information provided by its sensorial agents; (4) once the cultural/ethical code of a particular society has been installed in the brain, it becomes a biological and biosocial system which functions with a total independence from the subject, following its own laws and activating the appropriate emotional mechanisms; (5) the subject has the freedom to break certain rules of the ethical/bioethical code, but he cannot remove or eject this bioethical 'disk' from his neural computer, nor can he prevent the latter from making him pay the relevant emotional penalties.

12

Emotional Laws of the Religious System

Homo religiosus

We cannot imagine a cow begging God to concede it a good birth, or a wolf thanking God for helping it to capture and kill several lambs, or an elephant praying for the eternal rest of its mother's soul. Even less plausible is the scene of a monkey proclaiming, with flaming passion, its radical atheism.[1] Of all animals, the human being is the only one whose brain is genetically equipped to decipher and record a religious program. The society of bees produces wax and honey; human society produces, among other cultural products, a religious system. Here we discover another hidden genetic frontier between ourselves and apes. The monkey has no genetic passport to penetrate into the religious territory. Nor can any animal trainer take the most intelligent dog, the most astute lion, or the most imaginative dolphin and have a single religious concept or feeling 'get through its skull'. No animal society contains a neural computer capable of assimilating a religious program.

As occurs with the linguistic, culinary and other cultural systems, there exists a great variety of religious systems. If a child grows up in a society where English is in use, his neural computer will acquire this linguistic system. If the child is raised in Spain, his neural computer will acquire the religious program of the Catholic religion, in the majority of cases.

Origins of Religion

Much has been written about the origins of religion. From the conclusion that the 'savage' possesses an inferior mind, many anthropologists or philosophers have searched for the premises – shooting first and aiming afterwards. Thus, for Lévy-Bruhl,[2] religion originates in the mind of the savage, a 'pre-logical' and 'mystical' mind that replaces natural causation, of which it is ignorant, with supernatural causes. According to Edward Tylor,[3] religion also originates in the mind of the savage, who is unable to explain the phenomena of sleep, wakefulness and dreams, and thus invents the concept of the soul, from which he deduces the idea of God. But we might ask: why doesn't the monkey invent these spiritual and religious concepts? Why does our species occupy or preoccupy itself with such metaphysical business as the ultimate causes of life and death, dreams, the origin of the world, or the fate of the individual after death? If the 'savage', awed before the splendour of the Sun, transforms this heavenly body into a god, why doesn't the monkey do the same? We have no valid answers to all of these questions. We do not know how, when or why a truly atheistic ape (in Greek, atheos = 'godless'), unable to decode the concept of god or to feel any religious feeling whatsoever, from morning to night, becomes a religious animal. We have as much scientific information and as many proofs on this question as the famous medieval scholastic debates over the sex of angels and over how many millions of angels may fit on the head of a pin.

Durkheim distinguished between the world of magic and that of religion. According to him, the magician has a clientele, like a doctor, but religion is a social matter. The synagogue, the church, the temple is always a place where the community comes together. Totemism is the most elementary form of religion. Therefore, if we explain the meaning of totemism we will have finally discovered the origin of religion. Each clan worships a totem, generally an animal. But it is not the animal itself that is important. The animal represents the clan. Therefore, in reality, what is worshipped is the clan itself. Society is something superior to the individual. It is there before his birth and continues to exist when he dies. When he worships God, a human being worships his society. The deified animal is the deified society. The above is a hurried summary of several hundred pages of

Durkheim's book *The Elementary Forms of Religious Life*.[4]

Durkheim, one of the great pioneers, who has left us a legacy of many new concepts towards our understanding of what human society is, has understood the crucial role religion plays in the functioning of society better than anyone. However, he explains nothing about the origins of religion. Society, as a superior being, gave man the idea of God, and the deified social totem is society itself, Durkheim affirms. However, why have bees failed to derive the concept of the God of the beehive, or why have they not deified their colossal and omnipotent queen? Why have wolves not deified the alpha wolf, the leader of the pack? Why has society failed to engender the concept of God in other animal species? We find no satisfactory explanation.[5]

The origin of religion has been sought in the cult which the 'savage' begins to offer the dead. But we come to the same dead end. Why does the 'savage', unlike the monkey, bury the dead, 'store' them – in Unamuno's words – or pray for the eternal rest of their souls? 'Well, the "savage" wanted to soothe the pain caused by the death of a loved one, making up the story about the afterlife, God, and the rest of it,' proponents of such a theory, or rather sophism, would argue. But why doesn't the monkey, pained with the death of a son or lover, invent 'the story about God and the afterlife'? None of the evolutionist accounts which try to explain how the monkey became religious and stopped being a mere monkey take us anywhere. We must be satisfied, at least for the moment, with trying to discover how this system functions, how it reaches the brain, and how it becomes a biocultural program regulated by emotional mechanisms.

Hunger for God: *theophilia*

Humans and apes feel urges to eat, to drink, to eat, to copulate. As we have seen, without hunger a human being cannot eat. Only a human individual from his youngest infancy feels hunger for God. Religion, like food, is regulated by emotional mechanisms in the brain. 'But society puts these concepts into the child's head! It's a question of education!', it is said quite naively. Once again we insist that no cultural program, religious or otherwise, which has not been foreseen by the genetic plan and by appropriate hardware, can be introduced into the neural computer. The DNA, the genetic blueprint, does not include a religious program, in the same way it lacks French or English. But the brain of *Homo sapiens*, unlike the brain of a 'lesser' ape, is equipped to record French or the Catholic religion. Although God is not already installed as a program, the neural computer pressures the child with the emotional mechanism of the urges to ingest bodily foods (breast milk) and cultural ones: language and religion, among others. The brain does not accept just any food or program, but only the genetically foreseen ones. The neural computer pays the child with a pleasant sensation for feeding, for learning the mother tongue, and for learning the 'mother religion'. This emotional mechanism of urges for God – or *theophilia*, if we translate the concept into Greek, following the Occidental scientific tradition – allows the child's neural computer to assimilate the religious program.

Fundamentally, in all religions the key of the religious program is a God conceived and felt to be a just and beneficent father, creator of the clouds and the rivers, the fish and the birds, the lights and the shadows, man and woman; a God that directs the great orchestra of the world; a God that saves man from the abysmal precipice of the void into which death pushes him when he is most distracted by stock-market fluctuations, family worries and growing bills; a God who, like Shakespeare – in Madariaga's words – wants to 'tell us something' through the medium of the human tragicomedy in which Hitler and St Francis of Assisi share the stage with Eve and Evita, Bach and Velázquez, Nero and Stalin, characters of every type. The meaning is not in an isolated sound or a loose character, but in the entire orchestra or play in its totality.

In our opinion, the anthropologist has no say in the theological debate over the existence of God. What a biosocial anthropologist can prove and verify is that: (1) every human society has elaborated a religious program with a creative, providential, just and beneficial God who saves man from the existential bankruptcy of the 'sleep of death' – an expression used by Spanish composer Pablo Sorozabal; (2) that the neural computer of a human being from infancy assimilates this program with emotional mechanisms of adaptation and pressure; (3) that according to the degree to which he has received this program, he will receive a great psychological and indirectly somatic energy every time he talks to God, trusts in God, feels His love, His protection and His friendship.

Many human beings begin their day praying to God and placing themselves in His hands. The human being that feels protected by God feels more secure and is better prepared to confront the daily problems, obstacles and misfortunes, and to master his anxieties, fears and worries. If oxygen is energy that allows a human being to think, feel, and live, the presence of God in the believer is energy which charges up the batteries of faith, hope and love. As happens with food, the believer receives daily rations of psychological energy during certain daily 'meals': public and private prayers; religious rites like the prayer in Mecca, in the synagogue or in the church, and so many other rites. 'To the Arabs, Allah is everything', I was told by an executive of Egyptian television (Egypt, 1976), 'Things may be going well or badly. But you feel that Allah is your father and that He knows what he is doing. Allah is a Muslim's greatest strength.' 'When I feel down in the dumps, depressed,' a television producer told me (Hollywood, 1984), 'I walk into a church. I trust all of my problems to God and come out as good as new. The Eucharist is my drug.' The comparison with drugs does not seem absurd. It is an undeniable scientific fact that the human being, as this Muslim in Cairo or this Catholic in Hollywood confessed to me, receives a very beneficial psychological and indirectly somatic energy from the affection felt for his dog, his wife, or God – on different planes. Indeed, the love and trust in God felt by the believer is truly an emotional drug which 'lifts his spirits' and 'cheers him up', helps him to 'get through life'.

'For twenty years I had to live a daily hell. My husband, whom I adored, and my brother, whom I loved with all my heart, hated each other to death and on one occasion even threatened to kill each other, armed with knives. The worst of it was that they were business partners, and there was no way they could be separated. To cap it all, the business flourished. I went to church early every day to receive communion. Believe me: this is where I picked up strength to face that terrible situation. I would never have been able to resist otherwise. For me, mass was the greatest thing' (San Sebastian, 1970). This woman went to the temple every day to recharge her somewhat low emotional batteries. A monkey cannot recharge its emotional batteries when they run down by means of these religious acts (on the other hand, perhaps its emotional batteries do not run down as far as ours). José María Gironella, the Spanish author, told me in a television interview (Arenys de Munt, November 1987) that during the stage of his life in which he was subjected to the excruciating pain of depression, he went three times to the same Mallorcan cliff, to commit suicide. When he was about to throw himself into the sea, Christ, and his wife, were – in his opinion – the ones who in the moment of truth prevented him from falling into the abyss. In this case Christ, and thus religion, functions as a true medicine or therapy against depression and against suicide.

Emotional Mechanisms of Religious 'Reanimation'

'I was surprised by a terrifying thunderstorm in the hills, surrounded by oak trees. Crash! A lightning bolt struck and sliced an oak in two like a hot knife through butter. Blimey, what a fright! My hand reached for my scapulary. I had lost it. I never go anywhere without my scapulary. I've never been so afraid in my whole blessed life' (Eguillor, Spain, 1973). This Spaniard has been programmed with the scapulary of the Virgin of Carmen as a shield which protects him from thunder and lightning. Surprised by the storm in the middle of the hills, and witnessing the lightning strike a nearby oak, his neural computer advises him from this program to grab on to the scapulary for security, like the warrior who uses his shield to cover his chest from the shower of arrows. The scapulary missing, his neural computer unleashes a feeling of fear, of anxiety: 'You've lost your shield when most you needed it.' There exist a great variety of religious symbols (medals, images, etc.) which society offers the individual to protect him from the infinite array of dangers that besiege him from all sides. The cross fulfils this role for Christians, the star of David for Jews, and the half moon for Muslims. Many Muslims carry around their necks, or perhaps in their pockets, a complete microscopic edition of the Koran. We cannot scientifically prove whether the scapulary, the Koran, or a medal hanging around the neck truly protect a person from lightning and in-laws. What we can verify, as a scientific fact, is that these miniscule trinkets – once defined in the brain's programs as protective shields – produce or release feelings of protection, of courage, of self-confidence that permit human beings to confront very dangerous situations.

Rites

It is a fact, as we have seen, that many human beings leave the synagogue, mosque or church transformed, infused with energy, and in high spirits. 'Then why is mass compulsive under the threat of mortal sin? We do not have to force a child to watch his favourite television programme or to go to Disneyland. On the other hand, severe punishments have to be created for those that cheat on their income tax declarations. Something smells rotten here. If mass is a source of such emotional benefits, why must those who do not attend mass be threatened?' Such is the objection brought to me by a militant atheist in my mental village. Rites may indeed become enriching emotional experiences or else turn into events that would 'bore God Himself'.

Sometimes I have imagined the saints at the altar yawning with boredom while the priest drones on with an ungodly series of uninspiring and incoherent phrases. The sincere believer may receive a true spiritual meal at communion, even when the officiant is a frightful bore, the music an insufferable din, and the whole ceremony long, tiresome, and as dry as dust. If the service is well prepared, the preacher eloquent, and the choir angelic, even the most faithless may feel 'transported'. Religious rites have as their social aim the generation of feelings of faith, hope and solidarity, as the kidneys are designed to filter beer. But rites may produce feelings of boredom and urges to sleep in the congregation, in the same way that kidneys may produce stones that are translated into very acute pains.

Certain rites with an annual rhythm can generate very high doses of religious feelings. I remember that during my childhood in Eguillor, a Navarrese village in the north of Spain, we all felt a lump in the throat when we kissed St Michael of Aralar. According to a legend transmitted from grandmothers to grandchildren, Don Teodosio of Goni (a Navarrese village near Eguillor) returned from fighting at the Navas de Tolosa with the King of Navarre, Sancho the Strong. He came across a knight, in reality the devil in disguise, who informed him that during his absence his wife, unlike Penelope, had not remained faithful to him. Don Teodosio, upon hearing such lies, spurred on his horse, entered his house at night, felt two heads in his bed, one male and one female, drew his sword, and bore down on the lovers with it. As he came out of the bedroom his wife appeared with a candle: 'Teodosio! You've returned! I am overjoyed!' 'Whom have I killed?' Don Teodosio had cut off the heads of his parents, who in his absence were sleeping in his bedroom, as the latter was less exposed to the severities of winter. The bishop of Pamplona, as a penitence, commanded him to wander around Mount Aralar in Navarre. The day when the chains that were bound to his legs broke, his penitence would have ended. The day arrived. At that moment, the devil appeared again, this time in the shape of a dragon. Don Teodosio invoked St Michael, who appeared with a sword of fire and slew the hellish beast. From that time on, on the summit of Mount Aralar there has been a romanic church within which can be found the cave from which the dragon emerged and an altar with a statue of St Michael in solid gold and silver.

Once a year, St Michael comes down from his 'Aralar throne' and visits the villages of the North of Navarre. The entire village used to await this visit with incomparable impatience and suspense. The day when 'St Michael arrived', the whole village went to the church in their finest clothes to 'wait for St Michael'. We assembled at the entrance to the church. In the tower, the young boys were ready to ring the bells, two splendid church-bells that could be heard for miles around. Others were in charge of setting off fireworks. The statue of St Michael was transported on a stick, and the lower end of this pole was held in a leather support hanging from straps tied around the shoulders of a strong and privileged youth who walked 'carrying St Michael'. When someone spied 'St Michael' still several miles away, he called out the warcry: 'St Michael! Here he comes!' The sun's rays, reaching the golden statue, made it glimmer and sparkle between the oak and beech trees that were its heralds. Instantly, as if by magic, our hearts began to hammer, the bells clanged joyously, the rockets burst in mad ecstasy, and we all began to sing with unusual fervour: 'Miguel, Miguel, arcangel Miguel' (Michael, Michael, the Archangel Michael). Our neural computers, programmed with the legend heard a thousand times from the mouths of our grandmothers, with an occasional visit to the cave of the Aralar sanctuary, and with the saint's previous visits, activated a high-voltage feeling that truly transported us to a world of bizarre joy. As St Michael came closer – on foot it would take, from the moment he was spotted, over an hour – our excitement progressively grew. Finally, it entered the church. What a thrill it was to see St Michael at such close range! The moment of supreme emotion, the climax of this rite, was when we kissed St Michael, one by one. 'Sancte Michael, ora pro me' (Saint Michael, pray for me) the priest said in Latin, and at that moment we gave St Michael a kiss. This was the moment of the 'lump in the throat'.

I have paused here to narrate in some detail one of the rites that may generate highly intense religious feelings. If someone who had not been programmed with a long previous preparation attended this rite, he would feel nothing. Here we come across the general law of urges, in this case of the urges to see and kiss St Michael. The neural computer generates during the whole year the urges to see and kiss St Michael again, urges which grow on the day we all come out to wait for him. The brain pays an emotional pleasure proportional to the urges generated (the same occurs with the desire to leave jail, to drink, to make love, or to do whatever, as we have seen throughout this anthropological and biosocial excursion through the brain). When we bade St Michael farewell, as he was taken farther and farther away and finally disappeared in the forest that covered the hills, we were flooded with a sensation of melancholy: 'Goodbye, Archangel Michael . . . '. The song was in a minor key, the genetic melody of melancholy (see chapter 8, section on 'The music of language').

The rite of the religious pilgrimage similarly generates highly-charged religious feelings. The pilgrim begins to prepare for the lengthy journey a long time in advance. The longer the preparation, the rougher the path, and the more adverse the circumstances, the greater will be the satisfaction of the pilgrim when he arrives at his destination. Once a year, the 'Javierada' takes place in Navarre. Young people begin their pilgrimage on foot from the four cardinal points to the Castle of St Francis of Xavier. They walk all night without a single stop. When at dawn the pilgrim sees the towers of the castle, a very powerful thrill is experienced, which often leaks out as a tell-tale tear, and which reaches its climax when the sanctuary is entered and a mass is celebrated in the chapel of this Navarrese saint. The pilgrims who travel to Mecca confess that the emotional rush experienced when they arrive and see the Kaaba is 'indescribable', 'the greatest thrill of my life', 'an excitement incomparable with any other', etc. A Muslim is programmed from his childhood with this pilgrimage and with the Kaaba, the 'monumental rock which Adam built, which Nebuchadnezzar attacked, and over which Mohammed spilt so many tears over the human race that he blackened it all'. The neural computer of the Muslim creates a very elaborate and intense program of urges to go and see the Kaaba, from youngest infancy and for years and years. When the individual finally concedes to the neural computer what it has been asking for – to see and kiss the Kaaba – it pays an extremely intense pleasure, proportional to the urges accumulated in the emotional densitometer. Millions of emotional units must be saved in the emotional bank over many years in order to spend them all at once.

In Bali, there is a rite which is celebrated once every century. The entire Balinese people ask God that He protect the community in the coming century and free it from evil spirits. The members of this community celebrate this rite once in their lives 'if they are lucky'. In 1979, the ritual was celebrated, and two of my colleagues at the Department of Social Anthropology at the University of Southern California, Professors I. Abrams and S. Lansing, analysed it in a documentary which received a national award in the United States for its academic and cinematographic quality. The neural computer of a Balinese person receives such an elaborate and constant program from his infancy concerning the celebration of this secular rite, unique in the whole human family, that when he finally participates, he obtains an exquisite and intense pleasure, proportional to the emotional thirst accumulated in the corresponding emotional densitometer.

Opium of the People

One of the phrases coined by Karl Marx in his 'Critique of Hegel's Philosophy of Law', 'religion is the opium of the people', is recorded in the neural computer of millions of human beings. Religion indeed functions as a kind of opium or emotional drug which, by means of symbols and religious rites, 'revives' the lifeless, comforts the sad and lifts the spirits of the disheartened, since every human being in the most important spheres of his life and existence is a humble beggar (Madariaga says that Man stood up to ask God for 'a little eternity, in the name of God's love'). Christ, before Karl

Marx, had already denounced the abuse of religion as a mechanism of exploitation of the poor: 'But woe unto you that are rich!'[6] There are many 'Christians' who view their fortune as a blessing from God, even as a providential sign of being the elected or favourite ones of the great celestial banker who doles out dollars as well as grace: 'Whoever behaves will have Rolls-Royces, Beverly Hills, and Dom Perignon Champagne on Earth and Beverly Hills, Rolls-Royces, and Dom Perignon Champagne in Heaven.' This is a special opium for the rich. Particularly in the United States, I have come into close contact with multi-millionaires who feel favoured by the Almighty every time they are victorious in a hostile takeover devouring a smaller company – today, the larger company swallows the smaller more blatantly than ever – or each time that 'unruly workers', the lower class in Earth as well as in Heaven, are brought under control. This is the opium of the wealthy, whom Christ called, if I have understood correctly, 'whited sepulchres' and 'serpents' (Matthew 23: 27, 33) and whom he violently expelled from the temple: 'My house shall be called the house of prayer; but ye have turned it into a den of thieves' (Luke 19: 46).

Code of Religious Morality

Every religion includes certain rules of the ethical game, though not every ethic includes rules of the religious game. In the code of religious morality, God is the supreme judge, the ultimate court of appeal. Those who have been programmed with this code carry in their brain supplementary or complementary mechanisms of censure: the neural computer warns and threatens the individual with emotional fines in this world and in 'the afterlife'. In the Christian religion, there are two threatening factors in this domain: God may 'catch' the sinner in the act of sinning with a sudden death, something akin to a cunning policeman who hides in a specific spot to 'nab' the driver who jumps a traffic light or stop sign, or who exceeds the prescribed speed limit. Secondly, the sinner caught in a state of 'mortal sin' is headed for a Dantean inferno from which there is no possible remission or amnesty, or even the possibility of eventually carrying out the prison sentence, no matter how many millions of years he suffers. There is no prison so sordid or sinister, or lacking in 'human rights' as the infernal prison. No defence attorney may fight against the squalor and the lack of human rights for the human being in Hell. The tortures of the Holy Inquisition, Auschwitz, Alcatraz and the Gulag pale in comparison with a Hell of interminable horrors.

When I was eleven years old, I heard a Jesuit father who seemed to delight in presenting God as the high Holy Inquisitor, and in using the blackest inks to paint a picture of Hell as the most sordid chamber of horrors imaginable. At that point I was studying at a boarding school in Pamplona, Spain. We slept in a common dormitory, each boy separated from the next by a door which served as a partial screen. My 'next door' neighbour whispered to me, 'Are you scared?' 'Yes, I am,' I answered. That melodramatic and melotragic presentation of eternal Hell had penetrated in our young neural computers with great force. During the years I lived in Los Angeles (1980–7) I recalled the fire-and-brimstone sermons of my childhood listening to the 'Made in USA' telepreachers who intimidate their telecongregation with similar diatribes. The neural computer programmed with the threat condensed in the question 'will my soul be saved?', faced with any ethical infraction, will automatically unleash an emotional unease proportional to the importance of the broken rule and the quality/quantity of the program's recording.

> My God, the Heaven you have promised me,
> Does not move me to love you.
> Nor does the feared Hell move me
> To stop offending you.

This anonymous sonnet, which forms part of the poetic patrimony of the Spanish people (copyright Spain), rejects the practice of loving God for selfish interests rather than disinterestedly: to obtain the reward of the 'promised Heaven' and avoid the 'feared Hell'. To a greater or a lesser degree, according to the recordings of all of these diverse rewards and punishments, the neural computer triggers off emotional mechanisms of threat, reward or punishment which reinforce the rules of the ethical game: the feeling of love for God or the disappointment we give God; the increase or loss of grace;

the hope of entering Heaven or the possibility of being cast into Hell for all eternity. Once more we must be aware of the reality of these programs and of the corresponding emotional mechanisms which contribute to reinforce the ethical code, whether or not the 'afterlife' exists.

Other additional emotional mechanisms also exist or have existed in connection with the various religions. The Holy Inquisition would burn 'heretics' in the public square, a veritable Hell on Earth. Excommunication was a very powerful weapon which left the excommunicated person out of the religious, economic and political game. Today, we do not find penalties of this type in the heart of Christian churches, with a few exceptions. However, a fervent Catholic who divorces his spouse suffers the emotional punishment of finding himself excluded from holy communion. Catholics who have officially received a certificate of 'matrimonial annulment' from the Catholic church have felt 'liberated from a great weight' and that day have greatly enjoyed making love with their now officially 'blessed' spouse. A monkey receives the emotional reward foreseen by its neural computer for carrying out a task useful for its species: copulating with a monkey of the opposite sex. Male humans function with biophysical mechanisms (a penis which changes size and hardness); biochemical mechanisms (alterations in the circulation of sperm, of blood, of the breathing rate); and emotional mechanisms (desires to copulate and deposit semen, and the subsequent satisfaction). These mechanisms are similar to those of the male monkey as it approaches the female. However, the neural computer of a monkey cannot assimilate an additional program of a religious nature which can bother it for not making love according to the canons prescribed by its church: for not having the appropriate licence, in this case the 'annulment'.

One of my students at the University of Southern California, Los Angeles, born and educated within the Mormon church, married a Jew, in full breach of the religious laws of endogamy prescribed by the Mormon ethical code ('every Mormon must marry a Mormon'). Although this young woman lived happily and in love with her Jewish husband, she was punished daily by strong emotional fines which emanated from her neural computer, strongly programmed from her childhood with the Mormon – and for her bioMormon – code.

Theopolis: the Religious Society

We do not find monkeys divided into Muslims, Christians, Hindus, Jews, Sintoists, Buddhists; nor do we observe a wolf burning another wolf at the stake for belonging to a false or heretical religious sect; nor does one elephant try to convert another elephant to the 'true' religion.

The human species, as a society, is divided into competitive teams or societies, with different, opposing and competing sets of denominations, symbols, rites and codes. This is an anthropological fact about the human family. In the same way that there exists no common language (with the exceptions and qualifications already noted), there exists no common religion. Recalling our definition of society (chapter 4), we notice that when we speak of Christians or of Muslims, we refer to human societies. The Muslim or the Christian defines himself as a de-individualized cell (his individuality is irrelevant and unknown) of a community (all share certain common rules of play), which functions as a team versus other teams of this nature.

The Religious Game

What are these teams playing for? One of the games of the religious teams is the game for 'the' truth. Each member of these religious teams believes himself to be in possession of the truth and tries to make the members of other religious teams abandon their team and 'convert' to the true team, the 'true' religion. The members of the 'other' religions are 'pagans' or 'heretics', that is, members of a false religion. An old Latin saying, *cuius regio, eius religio* ('from such a region, such a religion'), gives us an interesting clue about the religious society to which the individual belongs. The individual in the majority of cases is born in a territory where a certain language and a particular religion are in current use, both of which will gradually settle in the software of his neural computer. By the time he is an adult, the individual's brain will have been biologically programmed with the English language and the Anglican religion, or with Arabic and the Muslim religion. He will never be able to eliminate either the biocultural program of English nor of the Anglican religion.

The 'mother' tongue is often spoken about. We could also speak of a 'mother' religion. In a very high proportion throughout the human race, the individual receives from his mother the 'mother' language and the 'mother' religion. Feeding with milk is a biological process, as is nourishment by cultural foods: language and religion. The three are biological, as we have already explained from diverse perspectives. But here we should focus our attention on an important aspect of the biological acquisition of these programs. I have explained the reasons why I disagree with George Orwell's thesis. The brain is programmed to reject certain programs which are imposed by the brute force of some military dictator. On the other hand, the brain very willingly accepts every program, such as religion, which comes from the mother, the person who most cares for the individual, who most knows him, who most understands, feeds, nurtures, defends, pampers, caresses and loves him. Later, when he is an adult, he will be able to 'convert' to another religion, or 'abandon' the mother religion, but in reality he will have to struggle against a bioreligious program that will never completely disappear from his brain.

Theopolis, Geopolis, Ideopolis, and *Econopolis*: Religious, Territorial, Ideological and Economic Societies

What relationship exists between Israel and the Jewish religion, England and the Anglican religion, Saudi Arabia and the Muslim religion, Japan and Sintoism, Mexico and the Virgin of Guadalupe, Russia and the Russian Orthodox Church? This is a fascinating topic to which I dedicated a chapter titled 'The Tribal Religion' in my book *The Rules of the Game: the Tribes.* Although in principle religion has a universal outlook – 'God is the Father of all Men' – the territorial society and the religious society often become the same team. Sometimes the origin of a territorial society is intimately connected with a religious society.

When in the year 711 Tarik invaded what is now Spain in the name of Allah in a *jihad* or 'holy war', the area was divided into many small kingdoms, territorial societies competing in the military game. This invasion led to the formation of a religious–territorial team – the Spanish/Christian team – against the pagans/strangers/invaders. St James became St James 'Matamoros' (the 'Moor-killer'), who captained the Christian–Spanish team. When in 1492 the last Moorish king – Boabdil – surrendered his sword and gave up the last conquered piece of land – the Moorish Gibraltar – the Catholic Kings moved quickly to expel the Moors and Jews so that Spain would be a territorial and religious community.

The Jewish people, expelled from their own territory, and partly living in a diaspora for commercial interests – as occurs to this very day – have maintained their identity as a *geopolis* thanks to the synagogues and to the annual celebration of Passover in the heart of the family, in other words, thanks to having preserved the bioreligious program of a common *theopolis* in their neural archives. Otherwise, having lost the language and the other cultural forms, after many centuries in the Diaspora, Jews would have lost their identity as a territorial and cultural community completely.

During the course of a lecture about the relation between *theopolis* and *geopolis*, I 'innocently' asked my American students at the USC if the United States, as a territorial society, functions in its origins, in its excursions/incursions into other territories ('areas of influence' of the 'superpower'), and in its daily maintenance as a *theopolis* or religious community. 'Obviously you are new here and know little about the history of this country,' one student answered, 'In America there exists a complete separation between Church and State. The president may be an atheist or practise any religion. Furthermore, there is no religious community or *theopolis*, as you call it. In this very class you will find Jews, Mormons, Catholics, Lutherans, Methodists, Adventists and whatever you name.' He seemed quite satisfied with his exposition, and all felt very reassured in their 'tribal' or territorial pride. I invited them to bring out of their pockets a one dollar bill, and to read the inscription printed on all of the banknotes of this territorial currency: 'In God We Trust.' To whom does this 'We' refer?

Although an official separation between religion and nation exists, in a thousand different ways an American has recorded the message 'In God We Trust' in his brain. From the start of the revolution or rebellion of the 'Americans' versus the 'British', this territorial/military game was presented as a 'holy crusade', as a *jihad*. In the final reckoning, God is the 'captain of armies'. 'In God We Trust.' Each president brings out these words *ad nauseam* in his televised sermons and homilies. All sing *God Bless America* (which refers not to the continent, but to the United States) one and a thousand times in temples, in stadiums, in theatres, in cemeteries. Every day in the schools, a religious–territorial ritual is enacted during which the American flag is raised and children stand, place their right hands over their hearts – visual language that does not pass unnoticed by the neural computer – and recite the following pledge/promise/prayer in unison: 'I pledge allegiance to the flag of the United States of America and to the Republic for which it stands, one Nation under God . . . '. God and the flag pass into the neural computer as two mechanisms of the territorial community. This is the God which blesses and protects the United States from the invasion of the 'aliens', 'strangers', or members of other territorial societies. Undoubtedly, we find synagogues and a whole variety of Christian temples, but in all of them we find on the altar, in a visible place and on sacred ground, the flag of stars and stripes. At the start of Congressional sessions, the chaplain prays at length before the whole assembly of statesmen to the God that will bless 'America'.

When Argentina reconquered the Falkland Islands, the Argentinians and the British both publicly and privately invoked God, all convinced that God would support their respective territorial team in this martial–religious match. In the end only the winners organized a religious/military act at Westminster Abbey to thank God for their having emerged victorious. I do not want to press further the relationship between *geopolis* and *theopolis* (for further elaboration, refer to the cited chapter in my book *The Rules of the Game: the Tribes*). The neural computer programmed with 'one Nation under God' and 'In God We Trust' pressures the individual with very powerful emotional mechanisms to play as a participant and/or as a supporter with his *geopolis/theopolis* in the sports, political, economic and martial competitions. A wolf's neural computer pushes it to defend its territory and territorial society with emotional mechanisms, without possessing supplementary or complementary emotional mechanisms related to the God that leads the pack in the fights with other packs.

A human being may be Christian, Chinese, Marxist and/or a millionaire, in other words, he may belong to religious, territorial, ideological and/or economic (class) beehives. Consider an Irish upper-class woman, programmed by an extremely conservative Catholic mother and a militant Marxist/atheist father. With what teams will she play the various games that will emerge? What is more important, her economic society (her class); her religious society (her neural computer has received a strong Catholic program); her territorial society (Irish); or her Marxist ideological society (by influence of her father and some friends she has received a strong Marxist program)? If these teams are at some point opposed, which team will she choose? This question cannot be answered lightly. All of these beehives may be installed in the brain through different channels and pressure the individual with strong emotional levers in opposing directions – which will win the game cannot be foreseen beforehand.

During the life of Christ, his territorial society – the Jewish one – had been invaded and conquered by another foreign and competing territorial society: Rome. Guerrilla movements were organized to regain the 'territorial sovereignty', supported by both territorial and religious emotional mechanisms. Yahve had given them – the Jewish people – that land 'of milk and honey'. The disciples and other Jews followed Christ as a religious/territorial leader who would organize a war to liberate Israel from Rome. Christ distanced himself from this game, clearly separating religion – 'universal love' – from the territorial war. Christ's disciples broke with the Jewish scheme both as a territorial and as a religious society, and began to accept into the midst of this new religious society Jews, Romans, Greeks, Ephesians, in other words, any human being, whatever his territorial society. Twenty centuries later, the Christian society has followed this universal path and today Christians belong to any race, culture or territorial society. Nevertheless, several volumes could be written on how, on so many occasions and in so many martial conflicts between territorial teams, the religious feeling, far from acting as a moderating influence, has functioned as an accelerator of the territorial (or national) feeling.

'Working-men of all countries, unite!', Karl Marx preached with Friedrich Engels from the pulpit of the *Communist Manifesto*. A Marxist worker, whether Chinese, Russian, Jewish or Arab, must militate in the same team – the Marxist one – against the team of anti-Marxists. However, Marxists split into Russian, Chinese, French, Jewish, Arab and even American Marxists (perhaps the most fervent). All sing the *Internationale* and all profess the universal creed of 'Working-men of all countries, unite'. But we have seen the emergence of Chinese Marxism versus the Russian variety, not to speak of Israeli versus Arab Marxism. Marxism has been tribalized and the ideological society has allied with the territorial one. With what team does a British Marxist play if a conflict between territorial societies, such as in the case of the Falklands War, breaks out? With what teams do a Christian Argentinian and a Christian Englishman play in this same martial game? The territorial teams almost always win out. The programming of the territorial society in the neural computer is deep, continuous and extensive (it incorporates almost all of the social systems).

With what team does a person side in a 'civil' war, such as the Spanish Civil War of 1936? Such a struggle is not merely a competition between class societies: the proletariat versus the capitalists. The various societies installed in the neural computers of the players, during all stages of life and with varying intensities, all come into play. A Catholic Basque anti-Marxist may join forces in this civil war with a working-class Basque who is a militant Marxist and atheist, as indeed happened, forming a nationalist team with the aim of obtaining the independence of the Basque Country. In this case neither the class, nor the religious nor the ideological teams coincide. For all of these people, the same territorial feeling predominates: we are Basque first and foremost, and we want independence for our territory.

Other Basques, during the Spanish Civil War, felt primarily Spanish, and in virtue of this predominant feeling allied themselves with Franco's team. Indeed, though Christianity according to Christ has nothing to do with wars between territorial teams, when the moment of truth comes certain bishops, priests and believers will side with one team or with another – the Basque Country, Spain, China, Russia. Part of the game in the Spanish Civil War was the Basque Country and Catalonia versus Spain, and the religious feelings in fact allied themselves with one side or with the other. Part of the game was composed of foreign territorial teams that supported one side or the other, each hoping to obtain a 'piece of the pie'. Part of the game was played by ideological teams which confronted each other, often breaking class alignments. Followers of Franco belonged to very different social classes ('upper', 'middle', and 'lower' classes, according to a classification of no great scientific rigour) by virtue of sharing the same ideological and/or religious creed. Others played in the opposite team, also due to the sharing of the same political creed mentally and emotionally, and despite belonging to different class teams. As occurs with martial games, the winner is whoever wins the match, whether the weapons manage to make the loser 'see the truth' or not. Mr Gun – today, Ms Nuclear Bomb or Mr Missile – has the last word. But guns do not shoot themselves. If Franco had managed to convince the army that democracy and the republic had to be crushed in order to 'save Spain', a *coup d'état* would have resulted. Rather, the army generals – most of them belonging to the same class – allied themselves in different and opposed ideological/religious teams. It is not easy to predict with which team the individual will play in a labyrinth where, unlike monkey society, a great variety of teams exist – religious, ideological, economic, military, territorial, family – which in certain matches unite or oppose, and which may as easily form an alliance as break it. Russia joined forces with the United States in the martial game against Germany, despite a continuing ideological and religious confrontation.

Are the Catholic religion and Marxist society two rival teams? Not always. We have already considered the case of Basque Catholic anti-Marxists who play with Marxist atheists in the common territorial team of a free and independent Euskadi (Basque Country). In fact, today we also find Marxist Catholics and anti-Marxist Catholics, Marxist priests and anti-Marxist priests. The theologians of the 'theology of liberation' feel as Marxist as they do Christian. Today in the United States, Marxist Protestants and Catholics form a team against anti-Marxist Protestants and Catholics.

The key is in the brain. The neural computer of each individual is continually programmed from childhood with the codes of various religious, ideological, economic, military and territorial beehives. Each beehive will pressure the individual, in the case of confrontation, with the appropriate emotional levers in relation to the program installed in the brain.

The Radical *Theopolis*

By the term radical *theopolis*, I understand the religious society which isolates itself completely from the 'world', that is, which disconnects itself completely from the political, economic and military games of the various human beehives – territorial, family and others. Religious societies such as that of contemplative monks – Buddhists, Sufis, Benedictines, Trappists, Cistercians – create a very strict social code and live completely outside of 'the world'. Those individuals who close themselves up in these monasteries, often situated in relatively inaccessible spots, devote their time to meditation and prayer, far away from the 'weariness, the fever, and the fret'. They are unaffected by the struggles of class, of tribes, of the sexes, or of ideologies. (However, a friend of mine who lived in one of these monasteries for some time told me that some monks communicated the results of football games to each other by sign language. The brother porter would obtain the scores from tourists who bought post cards and the news would spread throughout the monastery by means of these signs.) This, more than any other, is a true genetic frontier separating humans from apes.

Other religious societies such as the Jesuits, among others, renounce also playing the economic game (taking the vow of poverty); the political game (taking the vow of obedience); and the family game (taking the vow of chastity). They may, however, participate in and even direct the political, economic and military games between different teams. It would be impossible to understand the history of humanity without a detailed analysis of the influences which the various religions have had, and specifically the 'radical *theopolis*' or religious order. If the Jesuits had not been founded by that Basque-Spanish soldier Ignatius of Loyola, many schools, colleges and universities in the five continents, sources of so many eminent men who have revolutionized the scientific, political and cultural worlds, would never have existed. With its bright and dark spots, the contribution of Jesuits – to cite but one among many of these radical religious societies – to the world of science, politics and culture in the last four centuries has been truly colossal. Until relatively recently, the immense majority of people in our 'Western society' could neither read nor write. It was the monks or members of these religious societies who to a great extent preserved, transmitted and developed the great values of Western culture.

Those who believe that the only way to suppress a headache is to cut off the head make a great show of being horrified before the deplorable spectacle of man pitted against man over religious trivialities, from Cain's murder of Abel out of envy to the Holy Inquisition burning 'heretics' in the public square, and now to the Hindus fighting in India against the Sikhs. It is true that the various languages separate human beings and that these sometimes even kill each other to defend their languages, but this is only one side of the coin. It is neither possible, nor would it be useful, to empty the linguistic ocean of humanity. It is a similar situation in the varied garden of religious plants.

One of the functions of human societies is to produce culture. Thanks to the existence of religious societies which have functioned as competitive teams throughout the centuries, the human family has an extremely varied range of special architectural styles which otherwise would not exist. All tourists, when they visit other lands – geographical and cultural – want to contemplate, view and admire the Egyptian temples; the Romantic, Gothic or modern churches; the mosques; the Buddhist, Hindu and Shintoist temples. Religious societies have created an extremely rich variety of musical forms: Gregorian chant, African drums and chants, Bach's Mass in B Minor, the liturgical choir music of the Russian Orthodox Church. If we removed from museums all of the paintings with religious themes, all the Christs, the Virgins, the saints, occidental art would be left naked. The variety and beauty of many religious symbols and rituals – the pilgrimage to Mecca, the Spanish Holy Week processions, the traditional Jewish weddings – are of incalculable value for the whole human family. Without religion, without diverse and competing religious societies, we would have to suppress religious culture – an extremely rich and varied cornucopia of architecture, sculpture, paintings, literature, music, and folklore – which would impoverish humanity and reduce her almost to a society of monkeys.

No one, I imagine, has criticized the abuses committed in the name of religion as much or with as much virulence as Christ. If I understand Christ's message correctly, the fact that Samaritans and Jews exist – the diversity of religions – should not be condemned, nor should the members of other religions be scorned as bad apples, pagans or heretics who, poor devils, do not belong to the 'true' religion. In the parable of the Good Samaritan, this ecumenical lesson is as clear as water:

A certain man went down from Jerusalem to Jericho, and fell among thieves, who stripped him of his raiment, and wounded him, and departed, leaving him half dead. And by chance there came down a certain priest that way: and when he saw him, he passed by on the other side. And likewise a Levite, when he was at the place, came and looked on him, and passed by on the other side. But a certain Samaritan, as he journeyed, came where he was: and when he saw him, he had compassion on him. And went to him, and bound up his wounds, pouring in oil and wine, and set him on his own beast, and brought him to an inn, and took care of him. And on the morrow when he departed, he took out two pence, and gave them to the host, and said unto him: Take care of him; and whatsoever thou spendest more, when I come again, I will repay thee. Which now of these three, thinkest thou, was neighbour unto him that fell among the thieves? And he [a lawyer who had asked who one's 'neighbour' was] said, He that shewed mercy on him. Then said Jesus unto him, Go, and do thou likewise.[7]

In the eyes of these Jews, the 'bad guy' is the Samaritan, who must be despised for belonging to a false religion. On the other hand, the 'bad guys' in Christ's parable are the two Jews, who are, furthermore, two leaders of this religion – a priest and a Levite – while the 'good guy' is the one who is compassionate with a stranger.

In this century, Mahatma Gandhi has understood this message of Christ better than anyone, and has applied it in his works, in his life, and in his death. According to Gandhi, not only must other religions be 'tolerated' (as an evil which must be put up with), but we must feel proud as members of the human family of the great richness and variety of religions, 'all of them branches of the same tree'. A tree must be a pine tree or an oak, a beech tree or an elm, in other words, a tree of a particular species. An intelligent pine tree – if it could reason – would not only 'tolerate' the fact that not all trees were pines, but would feel proud that the family of trees was so rich and varied. An intelligent pine tree would not wish that all the oaks, palm trees, willows and sequoias would turn into pines. 'How sad! What a loss! How boring,' it would think, 'if we were all pine trees.'

All of us, to a greater or lesser extent, with different qualities and intensities of recording, carry in our mental village certain characters: Christ, Mahatma Gandhi and the priest who despises the Samaritan and who strides contemptuously by a dying man; a Pharisee who thanks God for being good and not a sinner like the ordinary man; and even a Holy Inquisitor who enjoys burning the heretic. All of these characters pressure us with emotional levers from the brain, with different intensities according to the strength they have acquired in their programs. But why does one human being who has received similar programs in his family and in his social sphere become Mahatma Gandhi or Theresa of Calcutta, and not others? It seems to be scientifically necessary to take into account the decisions of the individual himself.

Epilogue

A robot is an ingenious human invention designed to perform certain tasks. Let us suppose that an emotional system could be installed inside a robot. This would imply that the robot could feel a pleasant sensation whenever it obeyed a particular order, and an unpleasant sensation if it failed to do so (proportional to the degree of the infraction). We would thus have created an emotional robot, one which was controlled by emotional mechanisms. We would allow it to infringe certain rules contained in the program codes of its computer, but we would not allow it to avoid feeling pleasant or unpleasant sensations. We thus find ourselves before an impenetrable mystery: what is the nature of that 'I' which feels, that entity which we call José Antonio Jáuregui, the in-dividuum, the not-divided one, the 'je' of Descartes's 'je pense', which I prefer to call the 'I' that feels (*ego sentiens*)? How is that mysterious bridge or connection established between a biological machine, a neural computer, and an individual which it punishes for infringing the law of temperature or the law of the urge to 'make love'? What mysterious process takes place when the neural computer radically wipes out the 'I' that feels from the conscious world, each time it compels him to sleep, or die temporarily, and each time it allows him to feel/think/exist once again, by waking him up, or resurrecting him?

A dog also functions like an emotional robot: if it infringes the law of temperature, it suffers an unpleasant sensation proportional to the seriousness of the infraction, in accordance with the program installed in its neural computer. When its master arrives after a prolonged absence, a dog will feel an extremely pleasant sensation which corresponds to its neural computer's cancellation of the urges to see him. A dog's neural computer also cancels the 'I' that feels during periods of sleep. The difference between human beings and apes lies in their different repertoires of feelings, as well as in the different cultural programs of human societies and societies of apes (the genetic frontiers which I have pointed to throughout the course of this study). However, human beings also have the capacity to discover certain laws, to discover themselves, to create new systems and new societies (Marxist, Buddhist, Freudian or Christian societies), as well as myths, utopias and illusions which mask nauseating, repulsive realities (in other words, those which produce disagreeable feelings).

If the task of the thinker or the scientist consists in separating what we can know from what we can merely believe, what we can prove or demonstrate from what we can only suppose or presuppose, I believe I have demonstrated in this work (the reader may or may not agree) that our brains are equipped with a system, the emotional system, which is governed by its own laws and inescapable biological mechanisms. Thanks to this ingenious system, both the somatic systems (the respiratory system, the digestive system, and so on), as well as the social systems (the culinary system, the ethical system, and so on) are able to function properly. The neural computer, which is unconsciously aware of all the somatic and social codes that need to be respected, informs and pressures the subject so that his organism, as well as the different societies in which he is immersed, may be properly maintained. The neural computer has exclusive control over the whole spectrum of possible feelings or sensations, and activates them according to the needs of each somatic or social system. These systems can only function when they become biological: when the neural computer unconsciously registers the relevant codes. For this reason, we should talk of biosocial (bionatural and biocultural) anthropology. The laws of the emotional system and of the biosocial systems, as well as their corresponding mechanisms, are as precise and rigid as the laws of blood circulation, or of atomic movement. These are the facts which we know and which we can prove/verify.

However, if we follow the Socratic path, we inevitably find ourselves surrounded by a myriad of questions, enigmas and mysteries. What is the nature of the 'I' that feels, that reflects, that believes, that creates, whenever the neural computer allows it to be conscious? We do not know. We cannot know. Were Hitler, Gandhi, Marx and St Francis of Assisi partly free, within the limits imposed by biology, to choose the ethical, aesthetic and political routes which they opted to follow? Who has designed this highly ingenious system programmed within the neural computer? Can the 'I' feel, think or exist without his body and without his neural computer, the latter being the machine that tells him what he has to do at all times, the machine that contains all the registered programs by means of which the 'I' feels or exists, and the machine that allows him to feel or exist every day, and which can reduce him to existential nothingness during sleep or a state of coma?

According to Socrates and other eminent thinkers, these are questions to which we cannot give definite answers. Before drinking the fatal hemlock and declaring in the eloquent language of action that 'primum philosophari deinde vivere', that virtue comes before life, Socrates left us a spiritual testament:

> The state of death is one of two things: either it is virtually nothingness, so that the dead have no consciousness of anything, or it is, as people say, a change and migration of the soul from this to another place. And if it is unconsciousness, like a sleep in which the sleeper does not even dream, death would be a wonderful gain . . . But on the other hand if death is, as it were, from here to some other place, and if what we are told is true, that all the dead are there, what greater blessing could there be . . . I personally should find the life there wonderful when I met Palamedes or Ajax . . . or Odysseus or Sisyphus or countless others, both men and women, whom I might mention. To converse and associate with them and examine them would be immeasurable happiness . . . But now the time has come to go away. I go to die, and you to live; but which of us goes to the better lot is known to none but God.[1]

Socrates knows he is going to die; that much cannot be doubted. He does not know, however, what will happen afterwards; he has the benefit of doubt. Descartes, and before him St Augustine, demonstrated that, even if everything is illusory and nothing in the external world corresponds to our thoughts, at least while we think, we are, to which I would add that as long as we feel, we are. The great frontier between a human being and a robot, or a computer, is not thinking or calculating (a computer can defeat a human being in a game of chess). The great frontier lies in the fact a computer does not enjoy a victory, or suffer a defeat, while a human being both enjoys and suffers. We know that we feel, and we know what it is like to feel. No one doubts the reality of an intensely painful toothache, or of the joy felt when one embraces a loved one after a prolonged absence. We know that we are something as long as we feel, and know what it is like to feel.

What I had not realized before discovering the emotional system is that consciousness, our most intimate possession, is something which is imposed, which is out of our hands, which we cannot control, which is controlled by a biological machine, a programmed computer. The latter plugs us in and out of the world of consciousness every day as if we were electrical appliances.

The *Concise Oxford Dictionary* (1964 edition) defines 'subject' as 'a thinking and feeling entity'. We generally distinguish what is objective from what is subjective. The Spanish writer José Bergamín once said: 'since I am not an object, I am not objective; since I am a subject, I am subjective'. However, the great revelation I have tried to transmit to the reader during the course of this excursion through the world of feelings, is that a subjective entity is, as its etymological meaning indicates, *sub-jectus*, subjected, or governed by a regime of inescapable laws and rigid mechanisms. Our feelings appear to be subjective possessions, but they are in fact objective impositions. Anyone who suffers a throbbing toothache or feels intense urges to commit suicide is indeed a subject, a subjected individual, one who is forced to swallow a bitter medicine. However, anyone who delights in quenching his thirst for water, or fame or money, or in satisfying his urges to be superior to others in a given race, war, election or some other game, is also a subject, a subjected individual who is obliged to savour these pleasant feelings that he can neither cancel, nor increase, nor decrease. A human being can insure his home, his automobile or his lands, but he cannot insure his being, his consciousness or his feelings. He can neither control, nor switch on, nor unplug his consciousness or his capacity to feel, and neither can he control the release of a given feeling, nor the intensity at which it is activated (x degrees of the urge to commit suicide, or y degrees of satisfaction upon having won the Nobel Prize).

Above all, what has not ceased to amaze me throughout this exploration of the brain and its emotional system is the discovery of why we feel what we feel. To feel is to be informed and pressured by our neural computers to co-operate, as conscious pilots, in the maintenance of both our bodies and our society. I now have no doubts about the existence of these laws and mechanisms which govern our conscious world of feelings. Richard Dawkins says that we are 'robot vehicles', and 'the most complicated and perfectly designed pieces of machinery in the known universe'. I have ultimately realized that even consciousness and feelings are part of the machinery, that feelings are in fact the key to understanding the process which makes the robot vehicle function: the brain makes us work for our bodies and our society by employing the emotional whip.

Nevertheless, whenever I dine with Richard Dawkins in Oxford or in Pamplona, exchanging thoughts, feelings, questions, doubts, exquisite meals and friendship, I see the difference between what I know or believe I have discovered, and what I do not know, and know that I do not know: what hides within the body of Richard Dawkins, or within my own? What is the nature of that thinking and feeling entity? According to Parmenides, nothingness cannot generate being, and being cannot generate more being. The neural computer switches on and off that mysterious being which can feel pleasure and pain, but can a machine which is not conscious, and which cannot feel, grant us consciousness and feelings? I believe I have understood the relationship between the computer, the emotional system, and that mysterious thinking and feeling entity, but I do not know what the nature of that entity is.

Perhaps, as Socrates imagined, there is indeed a world in which that mysterious entity can awaken out of nothingness, like the words of a popular Spanish song: 'From the sleep of death I shall awaken to adore you.' Wouldn't my dear colleague and friend Richard Dawkins like to awaken from the sleep of death and be granted the opportunity to meet Charles Darwin? Not long before his own death Madariaga wrote a poem, which he dedicated to his wife (who was also his lover):

> And if after this life has passed,
> Destiny awakens me from nothingness,
> I hope my eyes will open and see you.

Could there be a world in which thinking and feeling entities remained permanently lit, or conscious, without depending on machines or neural computers? Socrates gave us the benefit of the doubt. Pascal, moreover, thought that it was very improbable that a man named Blaise Pascal had emerged from nothingness, and one fine day, in the infinite ocean of time, found himself thinking. Nevertheless, he considered it even less improbable that, once he was there, he would continue to exist.[2]

Quidquid recipitur ad modum recipientis recipitur. This work will have different mental and emotional repercussions on each reader. I sincerely hope, echoing Kant's words, that you have enjoyed taking part in this anthropological excursion as much as I have enjoyed the adventure of writing it.

Notes

Chapter 1 The Emotional System

1   René Descartes, *Meditations on First Philosophy*, sixth meditation. My son Pablo, who studied philosophy at the University of Oxford (Exeter College), has drawn my attention to something that Descartes writes towards the end of this meditation: 'in matters regarding the well-being of the body, all my senses report the truth more frequently than not'. Here Descartes comes close to discovering the informative role which the emotional system plays. However, his dogmatic belief in the superiority of ideas (of reason purified of 'confused ideas', or feelings), blinded him from noticing the precision, swiftness, and clarity of the emotional system. No messages are as direct, clear, and precise (both in terms of quantity and quality) as the emotional messages sent to us by our brains.

2   Sigmund Freud, 'The Unconscious' (*Collected Papers*, iv, first published in *Zeitschrift*, vol. III: reprinted in *Samlung*, 4th series): 'It is surely of the essence of an emotion that we should feel it, i.e. that it should enter consciousness. So for emotions, feelings, and affects to be unconscious would be quite out of the question.' Here Freud was deluded by what appears to be obvious: 'It is surely . . . '. All of us, including Freud, should always keep in mind something that Aristotle noted: 'as the eyes of bats are to the blaze of day, so is the reason in our soul to the things which are by nature most evident of all' (*Metaphysics*, Book II, 1, p. 84).

3   Plato, *Dialogues*, Phaedo, p. 208.

4   Miguel de Unamuno, *The Tragic Sense of Life*, ch. 6.

5   Thomas Aquinas, *Summa Theologiae*, second part of part II, section number 35. In many domains, a human subject is not free: the

neural computer compels him to feel this or that emotion, this or that pleasant or unpleasant sensation, at a particular intensity, and for a particular amount of time. Human beings are not free in the domain of feeling; they are subjected to the despotic government of the emotional system. However, when a human being is caught between two opposed emotional currents (one which pressures him to perform a given act, and one which advises him to refrain from doing so), is the final decision a free individual choice, or is it merely that one emotional force overrides another? This issue, addressed by Spinoza and Leibniz amongst others, is an extremely complex puzzle. We may be able to demonstrate in what domains human beings are not free, but we cannot demonstrate that human beings are not free in any domains whatsoever. At this point we reach the Socratic avenue of 'docta ignorantia': we know that we do not know. Lévi-Strauss, however, appears to deny that the individual is in any way free (see, in particular, the introduction to *The Raw and the Cooked*).

Chapter 2   *The Neural Computer*

1   The term 'metaphysics' was allegedly not coined by Aristotle, but rather by some librarians who classified his works and merely wished to indicate that these were the works that 'come after the Physics'. Irrespective of whether or not this is true, the sensory world has been distinguished from the extrasensory world from Aristotle onwards.

2   Thomas Aquinas, *Summa Theologiae*, part I, section number 16. The whole of Kant's *Critique of Pure Reason* constitutes an attempt to solve this puzzle.

3   Madariaga, *Retrato de un Hombre de Pie* (Portrait of a Man Standing). Although I believe that the reference is found in this work, I have been unable to find it. I shared a close friendship with this eminent thinker and writer during the last ten years of his life. I quote this reference from memory; it may only exist in my brain's files.

4   René Descartes, *Meditations on First Philosophy*, third meditation.

5   Immanuel Kant, *Critique of Pure Reason*, I, part one, ch. 9: 'What may be the nature of objects considered as things in themselves and without reference to the receptivity of our sensibility is quite unknown to us.' Madariaga, *Retrato de un Hombre de Pie* (Portrait of a Man Standing), p. 43: 'The secular antithesis between matter and spirit collapses'; ibid., p. 42: 'Matter is thus dead. May it rest in peace.' As I drove around Milwaukee a few years ago, I heard a Nobel Prize winning scientist, whose name I cannot remember, relate the following story on the radio. A famous physicist who had discovered a new minute particle

of the atom died. When he reached Heaven, he told God with his characteristic impatience: 'My God, I am so happy to finally meet you. I have spent my entire life trying to solve the mystery of matter. Tell me, then: which are the smallest particles that compose matter?' God, with infinite patience, answered: 'That, I am afraid, is a question which not even God can answer.'

We still believe – and this implies that it is a question of faith – that matter is ultimately made up of certain minute particles. However, the more our physical knowledge has advanced, the more the matter of our visual and mental world has evaporated like dew under the morning sunlight. We believe in matter, like we believe in God or in our 'I', knowing that it is something, but without knowing what the true reality of that something is. Physics turns into metaphysics. We mistakenly believe that what we directly see is a tree rather than a photograph of a tree taken with a camera. This, however, can never be the case. What we always see is a photograph of a tree: either a photograph taken with our organic cameras (our eyes), or a photograph taken with a photographic camera. The difference is not that between a tree which is seen directly and a photograph of a tree. The difference is that between two types of photograph: the organic photograph of a tree, which is taken with our ocular cameras, and the photograph taken with a photographic camera. The latter is an organic or ocular photograph of another photograph (one which has been taken with a photographic camera).

6   René Descartes, *Discourse on the Method*, part IV.
7   Some of the greatest figures in the history of Western thought have not understood the nature and function of feelings. Augustine asks himself the following question (which in the context is more an answer than a question): 'However, it may justly be asked, whether our subjection to these affections, even while we follow virtue, is a part of the infirmity of this life?' Augustine concludes that, since feelings are an infirmity of 'fallen' Man, angels do not feel anything at all: 'For the holy angels feel no anger while they punish those whom the eternal law of God consigns to punishment' (Augustine, *City of God*, Book 9, ch. 5). However, Augustine later contradicts himself when he affirms that angels 'enjoy the holy love of which they are inflamed' (Augustine, *City of God*, Book 9, ch. 22). Spinoza, along the same line of thinking, views feelings as imperfect, shameful things, and asserts that God never feels anything: 'God is free from passions, nor is He affected with any affect of joy or sorrow'; 'He neither loves nor hates anyone' (Spinoza, *Ethics*, part V, prop. 17). However, this philosopher also contradicts himself when he says that 'the intellectual love of the mind towards God is the very love with which He loves himself' (Spinoza, *Ethics*, part V, prop. 36).

To describe love as intellectual is, in any case, to confuse two different realities, which is the same mistake Descartes made when he described feelings as 'confused ideas' (a definition we also find in Spinoza, *Ethics*, part IV, prop. 59, def. 48).

It is interesting to observe how human beings, who are ashamed of certain crucial and vital parts of themselves – the genital organs, the urge to win, the pleasure of feeling superior in whatever field, and all feelings in general – have imagined a world of perfection in which God and the angels are free from these 'infirmities'. This feeling of shame is what appears to have guided – or misguided – Augustine, Descartes, Spinoza and other eminent thinkers throughout their mental explorations of the world of feelings. It should also be noted that common sense presents God as someone who loves, hates, becomes angry and feels.

8   Consider the following dialogue (Castaneda, *The Teachings of Don Juan*, part one, 28 December 1963):

> *Carlos Castaneda*:   I really felt I had lost my body, Don Juan [under the influence of a drug].
> *Don Juan* [his mentor, who initiated him into the world of certain 'Indian' drugs]:   You did.
> *C.C.*:   You mean, I really didn't have a body.
> *D.J.*:   What do you think yourself?
> *C.C.*:   Well, I don't know. All I can tell you is what I felt.
> *D.J.*:   That is all there is in reality – what you felt.

This last sentence is true, if we add 'for you at that moment and place' (under the influence of the drug). External bodies, including the body of Carlos Castaneda, exist on their own independently of human feelings. However, Carlos Castaneda's body has a very different emotional reality for him under the influence of drugs, from that which it has when this influence has disappeared. All external bodies – mountains, television sets, beds, and so on – do not change while a human being sleeps 'like a log'. When someone sleeps 'like a log', he becomes a log to himself: like a log, he does not feel anything at all. When someone sleeps 'like a log' (under the influence of the drug which the brain's anaesthetist administers to him), as far as he is concerned, the whole world has disappeared, his own body has evaporated, and his own self has dissolved. For a human being, *to be is to feel* (homo cuius esse sentire est): reality for him is whatever reality he feels. It is the emotional reality which his own neural computer creates for him.

9   See Blaise Pascal, *Pensées*, thought 107: 'I have my foggy and my fine days within me; my prosperity or my misfortune has little to do with

the matter. I sometimes struggle against luck, the glory of mastering it makes me master it gaily; whereas I am sometimes surfeited in the midst of good fortune.'

10   John Locke, *Essay Concerning Human Understanding*, Book IV, ch. 19.

11   See Blaise Pascal, *Pensées*, thoughts 346, 347, and 348. Calvero, the protagonist of *Limelight*, Charlie Chaplin's celebrated film, tries to cheer up a young, beautiful ballerina whom he has just saved from a death by suicide with the following words (I quote from memory): 'The whole of the universe, in spite of all its power, is not conscious, but you are.' Nevertheless, this young girl has tried to commit suicide and liberate herself from that consciousness. The thought that 'you are conscious, while the whole of the universe, in spite of all its power, is not' only has value for this young girl if her neural computer translates it into pleasant feelings.

12   See the section entitled 'Ethical Arrogance', in chapter 11.

Chapter 3   Biosocial Laws

1   Evans-Pritchard, *History of Anthropological Thought*, ch. 6.

2   Ibid.

3   This issue – whether or not there are laws which govern human society, and if so, whether any of them have been discovered or will be discovered in the future – permeates the whole of his *History of Anthropological Thought*. Evans-Pritchard explicitly addresses this problem in the first chapter of *Essays on Social Anthropology*. Edward Leach sides with Evans-Pritchard in this controversial debate and affirms that 'social anthropologists are bad novelists rather than bad scientists' (Leach, *Social Anthropology*, p. 53), and that 'social anthropology is not, and should not aim to be, a 'science' in the sense of natural science. If anything it is a form of art' (Leach, ibid., p. 52). Marvin Harris agrees with Montesquieu, Comte, the evolutionists, Radcliffe-Brown and all of those who have attempted to discover social laws, conceiving of social anthropology as a science as exact or inexact as any other natural science. Marvin Harris believes he has discovered a fundamental social law which he refers to as 'cultural materialism', an academic variation on the Marxist theme of 'historical materialism' ('It is not the conscience of men which determines their social existence, but rather, their social existence determines their conscience,' Marvin Harris, *The Rise of Anthropological Theory: A History of Theories of Culture*, ch. 8, p. 12). Clifford Geertz leads the group of those who think that Harris is wrong. I do not have space in this anthropological excursion to present this (emotional)

debate between Harris and Geertz, between 'materialist' and 'idealist' anthropologists. This study aims to put forward a new view on this old anthropological and philosophical debate: are human society and culture regulated by laws as rigorous as those which govern the universe of atoms and stars? Are human beings governed by social and cultural laws? What are these laws? What power do these laws have over the individual? Who has designed these laws? Can an individual discover, disobey, alter or eliminate these laws?

4 Seneca the Elder, *Controversiae*, ch. 1, p. 44.

5 Pérez Galdós, *Novelas*, vol. 1, p. 1202.

6 David Hume, *Treatise of Human Nature*, Book II, part III, section I.

7 Immanuel Kant, *Critique of Pure Reason*, Introduction, III.

8 In our Western/Christian culture, we find various systems of belief concerning fortune: (1) a system which attributes certain events to pure chance: bumping into a particular person, an accident, the fact that one was born during a given period, in such a place, on a given day, with a given sex, and so on; (2) a system which attributes what seems to be pure chance to two mysterious forces: destiny and luck; (3) a system which attributes what seems to be pure chance to the providence of God; (4) a system which attributes certain actions which seem to have occurred by pure chance to certain malevolent spirits, such as demons and witches. All of these systems, which are opposed to each other, are installed in the brain of a member of Western culture to a particular extent, and lead him to attribute a certain event to chance, luck, destiny, the providence of God or the influence of Satan. Here I shall merely touch on a fascinating issue which requires much more space.

Those who attempt to prove 'scientifically' that pure chance is responsible for establishing all of the laws in the universe – including the law of gravity and the laws of evolution, such as the 'survival of the fittest' – are probably more blind, dogmatic and fanatic than anyone else in 'the land of truth' (Kant, *Critique of Pure Reason*, I, part two, ch. 3). Aristotle suggested that they were drunks: 'When one man said, then, that reason was present – as in animals, so throughout nature – as the cause of order and of all arrangement, he seemed like a sober man in contrast with the random talk of his predecessors' (*Metaphysics*, Book I, 4).

In a lecture delivered in 1969 on Jacques Monod's book *Chance and Necessity*, Salvador de Madariaga related the following anecdote (I quote from memory): 'After spending all day writing about how pure chance is responsible for everything that happens – the honey produced by the beehive, the pears which grow on trees, or the trunk an elephant is born with – a renowned French scientist was served a delicious salad by his wife. As he savoured this exquisite dish, he turned to her and said: 'Darling, let me ask you something. If the tomatoes, the olives, the lettuce, the onion, the salt, the oil, and the vinegar had been combined by pure chance in this beautiful bowl, do you think we could have obtained this salad?' 'Well, it wouldn't have been as good,' she answered employing a bit of common sense (and, as Aristotle would have said, without inebriating herself with the fanatic belief in chance).

9   In the light of our current scientific knowledge, I believe it is more prudent to work separately towards the discovery of biosocial (bionatural and biocultural) laws of human society and of the human brain. To equate human beings and apes – in other words, the biosocial laws which govern the societies and the brains of human beings and apes – does little to illuminate our understanding of ourselves, and may easily lead to utter confusion. Leach is right when he says that human beings and apes cannot be classified in the same biosocial category 'unless you are prepared to argue that Koko the gorilla might become a Christian' (Edmund Leach, *Social Anthropology*, p. 120).

Darwin, however, believed that if not Koko, at least dogs (especially his own) are religious, ethical and even superstitious animals (such a far-fetched belief illustrates how faith, including pseudo-scientific faith, can move mountains). 'A dog looks on his master as on a God' (Darwin, ch. III, *The Descent of Man*). 'I agree with Agassiz that dogs possess something very like a conscience' (Darwin, ch. IV, *The Descent of Man*). 'The tendency in savages to imagine that natural objects and agencies are animated by spiritual or living essences, is perhaps illustrated by a little fact which I once noticed: my dog, a full grown and very sensible animal, was lying on the lawn during a hot and still day, but at a little distance, a slight breeze occasionally moved an open parasol which would have been wholly disregarded by the dog, had anyone stood near it. As it was, every time that the parasol slightly moved, the dog growled fiercely and barked. He must, I think, have reasoned to himself in a rapid and unconscious manner that movement without any apparent cause indicated the presence of some strange living agent . . . ' (Darwin, ch. III, *The Descent of Man*). Leach (*Social Anthropology*, p. 109) says: 'no one has suggested that apes have the imagination to be superstitious!' Darwin, however, does appear to have suggested this. It could be said that at times Darwin the dogmatic believer imprisoned Darwin the socratic, independent thinker.

It is beneficial to be aware of all of the discoveries of non-human sociobiology in order to gain a better understanding of biosocial anthropology. It may be useful to one who is studying the social laws concerning hierarchy amongst chickens to analyse the cultur-al/biocultural laws of hierarchy in the Catholic church (and vice versa). However, no chickens, no Kokos, and not even Darwin's dog – although this animal sounds like he must have been a real genius – are partly governed by their brains through ethical, magical and religious laws, through laws on equality, democracy, humility, celestial retribution in the afterlife, and so many others. The worlds of human beings and apes – the laws which govern the societies and the brains of these two animals – are, unlike what Darwin supposed to be the case, two very different worlds. Certain biosocial laws – of territory, hierarchy and sexual attraction – may be similar or common. However, even in these cases, we must be extremely cautious before reaching any conclusions, because human beings are simultaneously subjected to other opposed laws, unlike Koko and even Darwin's dog. The latter may copulate with any female dogs, including its sister, mother or daughter, without being subjected to other opposed social laws which, once installed in the brain, function with the same emotional mechanisms as all biosocial laws: ethical, religious and legal laws concerning incest, adultery, celibacy, prostitution, and so on.

10   See note 2 of chapter 1.

Chapter 4   Human Society

1   Edmund Leach, *Social Anthropology*, p. 85: 'Perhaps a future gen-eration will come to recognize that the most misguided, though well intentioned, feature of our present age was that, having discovered by the methods of genuine science that man is a single zoological species and thus a unity in his physical nature, we tried, by political coercion and propaganda, to impose on man, as cultural moral being, a comparable sense of unity which contradicts the very essence of our human nature.'

2   Leach, *Social Anthropology*, pp. 82–3. Lévi-Strauss falls into the same Rousseaunian trap (see chapter 1, 'Nature and Culture', of his book *The Elementary Structures of Kinship*). See also chapter 3 of *History of Anthropological Thought*, by Evans-Pritchard, entitled 'Ferguson'. This chapter contains Sir Edward's last lecture (University of London, 1973), which I attended. Evans-Pritchard rediscovers Ferguson, who in his view, 'although much neglected, is one of the major figures in the history of sociological thought' (p. 18). Ferguson, as opposed to Hobbes and Locke, maintained that everything which is cultural is natural (although not everything which is natural is cultural). At one point in his lecture, Evans-Pritchard, like someone who has suddenly

awakened from a dream, asks himself and his audience: 'Did not Aristotle long ago insist that man is by nature a political (social) creature?'

3   Jean-Jacques Rousseau, *Discourse on the Origins of Inequality*, part I.

4   Hobbes, *Leviathan*, chs XIII and XV.

5   'Present-day anthropologists regularly write about "societies" and "cultures" in the plural. The "societies" usage is mostly just a manner of speaking.'

    'In practice "a society" means a political unit of some sort which is territorially defined . . . The boundaries of such units are usually vague. They are determined by operational convenience rather than rational argument.' Leach, *Social Anthropology*, p. 41. See the whole chapter 'Units of Culture and Society' (pp. 41–3).

6   In *Social Anthropology*, Leach has suggested that hierarchical actions speak louder than egalitarian words: 'Egalitarian Rousseau lived out his life as the spoilt plaything of eccentric aristocrats' (p. 80). (It could also be added that this champion of equality, who coined the celebrated slogan of the French Revolution, 'Liberté, égalité, fraternité', abandoned his five children in an orphanage.) 'Marx spent his last thirty years in very comfortable middle-class circumstances in Highgate and was an employer of domestic servants' (p. 80). (Furthermore, the man who condemned the bourgeoisie for taking advantage of their servant girls did the same with one of his own, whom he made pregnant.) Leach is aware of the problem, but he fails to provide a satisfactory solution.

7   Eric Berne, *Games People Play*. After having written this book, one of my colleagues was kind enough to give me a copy of *Homo Ludens*, by J. Huizinga. I had never even heard of the book, which analyses the 'game' from a theoretical standpoint closer to my own than that of Berne. I have become extremely interested in this book, and it would undoubtedly have been a great pleasure to engage in a discussion with its author. Hegel's dialectic between theses and anti-theses; Marx's struggle between classes; Evans-Pritchard's feud; Darwin's struggle for existence; Huizinga's 'Homo Ludens'; and my own 'rules of the game' all represent different perspectives from which to study the great universal law enunciated by Heraclitus: 'the game is the father of all things' (Aristotle, *Nichomachean Ethics*, VIII, i, 6).

8   Marx, *Communist Manifesto*, ch. 2.

Chapter 5   Emotional Control of the Digestive System

1   Mohandas K. Gandhi, *Autobiography*, chs 6 and 7.

2   Marvin Harris, *Cows, Pigs, Wars, and Witches*, chapter entitled 'Love and Hatred of the Pig'.

Chapter 7   Emotional Control of Fatigue and Danger

1   Although those who view evolution as a continuous and uninterrupted progression of beings (from inanimate to animate, from the amoeba to the reptile, from the reptile to the ape, and from the ape to the human being) may hold that pure chance is responsible for this, they also presuppose and admit that what occurs is a constant harmonious progression from imperfect beings to more perfect ones. If pure chance is responsible for all of this, why is the progression uninterrupted, logical and ordered, rather than utterly chaotic? To speak of the harmonious, ordered influence of pure chance is equivalent to speaking of a square circle. One really needs to have blind faith in order to accept all of these Darwinian contradictions and view them as a scientific solution to what is in fact an irresolvable mystery. Darwin merely replaces 'God' with 'nature' and 'divine providence' with 'evolution'.

It is interesting to observe how, in order to 'prove' that evolution is the divine providence of nature, Darwin tries to justify something that in the eyes of human beings seems ethically unacceptable: 'When we reflect on this struggle, we may console ourselves with the full belief that the war of nature is not incessant, that no fear is felt, that death is generally prompt, and that the vigorous, the healthy, and the happy survive and multiply' (Darwin, ch. III, *The Origin of Species*). But, one could say to Darwin, how are the less vigorous men, the sick, the handicapped, the losers of the game to be consoled? How are we to reconcile the supposedly benevolent nature of Darwinian providence with the cruelty of the spiders that trap flies, the eagles that delight in murdering fawns, or the praying mantis that decapitates her lover during their honeymoon? If an ape could reason, he would probably address Darwin as follows: 'Look, my friend, you are being misled by the anthropocentric dogma which is best summed up by the words of Protagoras: "man is the measure of all things". Your anthropocentric myth on the evolution from ape to man leaves one cold.'

2   Charles Darwin marvels at the extraordinary relations which exist among different species of animals, and even between animals and plants: 'plants and animals remote in the scale of nature are bound together by a web of complex relations' (Darwin, ch. III, *The Origin of Species*). He explains how, when the cat population increases, the mouse population diminishes; and when the number of mice which attack beehives diminishes, the number of bumblebees increases. When

the number of bumblebees increases, continues Darwin, as this is the only species which fertilizes certain flowers (*Viola tricolor, Trifolium repens*, and *Trifolium pratense*), these families of flowers are proportionally propagated. Darwin is awestruck by the existence of such relations between cats, flowers, mice, and bumblebees: 'Hence it is quite credible that the presence of a feline animal in large numbers in a district might determine, through the intervention first of mice and then of bees, the frequency of certain flowers in that district!' (Darwin, ch. III, *The Origin of Species*). Darwin himself, then, was aware of this law, which we could refer to as the 'law of the harmony amongst all species' (including plant species and the 'rational' species). Such a law clashes with the supposed existence of the law of the evolutionary progression of animals from 'inferior' to 'superior' ones.

Chapter 8   *Emotional Laws of Laughter and Language*

1   John Locke, *Essay Concerning Human Understanding*, Book III, ch. 2.

Chapter 10   *Emotional Laws of Anger and Vengeance*

1   Proverbs 16: 32.

Chapter 11   *Emotional Laws of the Ethical System*

1   See note 9 of chapter 3.
2   Bronislaw Malinowski, *The Sexual Life of Savages in North-Western Melanesia*, ch. 14.
3   Not long after having written this paragraph, the Berlin Wall was torn down and Russia adopted the ethical/economic/political system of its old American rival. However, with or without Marxism, Russia will always attempt to win the ethical game in the 'Ethical Olympics', where all territorial societies constantly strive to win as many gold medals as possible.
4   See the *Communist Manifesto*, which is partly an ethical homily, rather than a scientific treatise on economics. *Capital* itself is partly an ethical work in which key words such as 'exploitation' (of man by man), 'avarice', or 'bourgeoisie' belong to the world of ethics, of the 'good' and the 'bad', and are alien to the world of economics. In his essay 'The Protestant Ethic and the Spirit of Capitalism', Max Weber takes

an original approach to the relationship which exists between ethical, religious, and economic systems. Unlike Karl Marx and Marvin Harris, Weber understood the meaning of Heraclitus' dictum: 'the ass prefers alfalfa to gold' (Aristotle, *Nichomachean Ethics*, X, V). Gold, capital and money do not signify anything in themselves without the urges to possess them, the emotional mechanisms which pressure human beings to win the game of stocks, sports cars, properties and art collections. 'Materialism' – whether historical (Marx) or cultural (Harris) – is actually spiritual in the sense that the urges to possess material goods are subjective (although, as I am trying to demonstrate in this study, all feelings are partly controlled, activated, and measured by a biological machine: the neural computer).

5 Not long after having written this paragraph, the tragic incidents of Tiananmen Square took place in Peking. In spite of the halt which this event has represented, the Chinese leaders seem to be willing to give up the Marxist ethic in order to generate a more buoyant economy which may allow cars to replace the bicycles still ridden by the majority.

6 Blaise Pascal, *Pensées*, thoughts 277 and 282.

7 Pérez Galdós, ch. 9 of *Fortunata and Jacinta*.

8 Luke 18: 10–14.

9 Genesis 4.

10 Edward Evan Evans-Pritchard, *Theories of Primitive Religion*, II.

11 In 1840, Proudhon published *Qu'est-ce que la Propriété?* (What is Property?). This is the work in which the famous phrase I have cited appears.

Chapter 12 Emotional Laws of the Religious System

1 See note 9 of chapter 3.

2 Lucien Lévy-Bruhl, *The Primitive Soul*.

3 Edward Tylor, *Primitive Culture*.

4 Emile Durkheim, *The Elementary Forms of Religious Life*.

5 See Evans-Pritchard, *Theories of Primitive Religion*. In a truly Socratic spirit, my mentor admirably demonstrates how the so-called 'theories' on the origin of religion are baseless dogmas which cannot be allowed entry into the 'land of truth'. Evans-Pritchard, however, makes a very important distinction between an original approach, which is always valid and fertile, and an erroneous conclusion. Although he rejects, for instance, the solution Lévy-Bruhl provides for his theoretical puzzle concerning the 'primitive mentality', he applauds his original approach, without which Evans-Pritchard confesses he would have never been able to write his book *Witchcraft, Oracles and Magic*

Among the Azande. (Lévy-Bruhl in turn accepted Evans-Pritchard's criticisms, giving us all a lesson in ethical elegance worthy of the highest praise.)

6   Luke 6: 24; Matthew 6: 24; Matthew 19: 23–30; Mark 10: 21; Luke 16: 19–31.
7   Luke 10: 30.

Epilogue

1   See the final paragraphs of Plato's *Apology.*
2   Blaise Pascal, *Pensées*, thoughts 205 and 222.

Bibliography

Augustine, Saint *City of God*. Loeb Classical Library, Harvard University Press, 1958.

—— *Confessions*. Loeb Classical Library, Harvard University Press, 1912.

Ardrey, R. *The Territorial Imperative*. Fontana/Collins, 1966.

Aristotle. *Categories*. Loeb Classical Library, Harvard University Press, 1938.

—— *De Anima*. Loeb Classical Library, Harvard University Press, 1957.

—— *Generation of Animals*. Loeb Classical Library, Harvard University Press, 1953.

—— *Metaphysics*. Loeb Classical Library, Harvard University Press, 1933.

—— *Nichomachean Ethics*. Loeb Classical Library, Harvard University Press, 1934.

—— *Politics*. Loeb Classical Library, Harvard University Press, 1932.

—— *Posterior Analytics and Topics*. Loeb Classical Library, Harvard University Press, 1960.

Bacon, Francis. *Essays*. Oxford University Press, 1985.

—— *Novum Organum*. Open Court, 1994.

Bergson, Henri Louis. *Laughter*. Johns Hopkins University Press, 1980.

Berne, Eric. *Games People Play*. Grove Press Inc., 1967.

Castaneda, Carlos. *The Teachings of Don Juan: a Yaqui Way of Knowledge*. University of California Press, 1968.

Cervantes Saavedra, Miguel de. *Don Quixote*. Oxford University Press, 1992.

Chomsky, Noam. *Knowledge of Language: its Nature, Origins and Use*. New York, Praeger, 1985.

Comte, Auguste. *Introduction to Positive Philosophy*. Hackett, 1988.

Darwin, Charles. *The Descent of Man and Selection in Relation to Sex*. Princeton University Press, 1992.

—— *The Expression of the Emotions in Man and Animals.* University of Chicago Press, 1965.

—— *The Origin of Species.* Harvard University Press, 1975.

Dawkins, Richard. *The Selfish Gene.* Oxford University Press, 1976.

—— *The Blind Watchmaker.* Harlow, Longman, 1986.

Descartes, René. *Discourse on the Method, with Meditations on First Philosophy, and Principles of Philosophy.* Everyman, 1992.

—— *Passions of the Soul.* Hackett, 1988.

Dumont, Louis. *Homo Hierarchicus: Caste System and its Implications.* University of Chicago Press, 1981.

Durkheim, Emile. *The Elementary Forms of the Religious Life.* Allen and Unwin, 1965.

—— *Rules of the Sociological Method.* Macmillan Press, 1982.

Eco, Umberto, *Theory of Semiotics.* Macmillan Press, 1977.

Evans-Pritchard, Edward Evan. *A History of Anthropological Thought.* Basic Books, 1981.

—— *The Nuer: Description of the Modes of Livelihood and Political Institutions of a Nilotic People.* Oxford University Press, 1987.

—— *Theories of Primitive Religion.* Oxford University Press, 1967.

Freud, Sigmund. *Complete Psychological Works.* Hogarth Press, 1951.

—— *Psychopathology of Everyday Life.* Penguin, 1991.

Gandhi, Mohandas K. *An Autobiography.* Beacon Press, 1957.

Geertz, Clifford. *Interpretation of Cultures.* Fontana Press, 1993.

Harris, Marvin. *Cultural Anthropology.* Harper and Row, 1987.

—— *Cows, Pigs, Wars, and Witches.* Vintage, 1974.

—— *The Rise of Anthropological Theory: A History of Theories of Culture.* Routledge and Kegan Paul, 1969.

Hawking, Stephen. *A Brief History of Time.* Bantam Press, 1988.

Hegel, Georg Wilhelm Friedrich. *Lectures on the Philosophy of World History* (trans. H. B. Nisbet). Cambridge University Press, 1975.

—— *Logic* (trans. W. Wallace). Oxford University Press, 1975.

—— *Phenomenology of Spirit* (trans. A. V. Miller). Oxford University Press, 1979.

Hobbes, Thomas. *Human Nature and De Corpore.* Oxford University Press, 1994.

—— *Leviathan.* Cambridge University Press, 1991.

Huizinga, Johan. *Homo Ludens.* Alianza, Madrid, 1987.

Hume, David. *Enquiries Concerning Human Understanding and Enquiry Concerning the Principles of Morals.* Greenwood Press, 1980.

—— *A Treatise of Human Nature.* Oxford University Press, 1978.

James, William. *Principles of Psychology.* Dover Publications, 1957.

Jáuregui, José Antonio. *Las Reglas del Juego: los sexos.* Barcelona, Planeta, 1982.

—— *Las Reglas del Juego: Las Tribus*. Espasa-Calpe, 1977.

—— *Dios Hoy, en la Ciencia, en la Cultura, en la Sociedad y en la Vida del Hombre*. Oviedo, Nobel, 1992.

Kant, Immanuel. *Critique of Practical Reason*. Macmillan, 1993.

—— *Critique of Pure Reason*. Everyman, 1993.

Leach, Edmund. *Social Anthropology*. Oxford University Press, 1982.

Leibniz, Gottfried Wilhelm. *Discourse on Metaphysics*. Manchester University Press, 1988.

—— *Monadology*. Routledge, 1992.

Lévi-Strauss, Claude. *Structural Anthropology* (vol. 1). Penguin, 1993.

—— *Structural Anthropology* (vol. 2). Penguin, 1994.

—— *The Raw and the Cooked: Introduction to a Science of Mythology*. Penguin, 1992.

—— *The Elementary Structures of Kinship*. Tavistock Publications, 1970.

Lévy-Bruhl, Lucien. *How Natives Think*. Lilian A. Clare, 1926.

Locke, John. *An Essay Concerning Human Understanding*. Everyman, 1993.

Lorenz, Konrad. *On Aggression*. Methuen, 1966.

Madariaga, Salvador de. *Retrato de un Hombre de Pie*. Madrid, Espasa-Calpe, 1979.

Machiavelli, Niccolo. *The Prince*. Cambridge University Press, 1988.

Malinowski, Bronislaw. *Argonauts of the Western Pacific*. Routledge, 1992.

—— *The Sexual Life of Savages in North-Western Melanesia*. Routledge, 1929.

Marx, Karl. *Capital*. Penguin, 1990.

—— (and Friedrich Engels). *Communist Manifesto*, Oxford University Press, 1992.

Montaigne, Michel de. *Essays*. Penguin Classics, 1993.

Montesquieu, Charles L. de. *The Spirit of the Laws*. Cambridge University Press, 1989.

Morris, Desmond. *Naked Ape Trilogy: 'Naked Ape', 'Human Zoo', 'Intimate Behaviour'*. Cape, 1994.

Orwell, George. *Nineteen Eighty-Four*. Penguin, 1990.

Pascal, Blaise. *Pensées*. Penguin, 1970.

Penrose, Roger. *The Emperor's New Mind*. Vintage, 1989.

Pérez Galdós, Benito. *Fortunata and Jacinta: Two Stories of Married Women*. Penguin, 1988.

—— *Obras Completas*, Madrid, Aguilar, 1970.

Plato. *Apology*. Loeb Classical Library. Harvard University Press, 1914.

—— *Protagoras*. Loeb Classical Library. Harvard University Press, 1915.

—— *Symposium*. Loeb Classical Library. Harvard University Press, 1925.

—— *Parmenides*. Loeb Classical Library. Harvard University Press, 1926.

—— *Republic*. Loeb Classical Library. Harvard University Press, 1930.

—— *Laws*. Loeb Classical Library. Harvard University Press, 1941.

Popper, Karl (and John Eccles). *The Self and Its Brain*. Springer-Verlag, 1977.

Rose, Steven. *The Making of Memory*. Bantam Press, 1992.

Rousseau, Jean-Jacques. *Discourse on the Origin of Inequality*. Oxford University Press, 1994.

—— *Social Contract*. Oxford University Press, 1972.

Saussure, Ferdinand de. *Course in General Linguistics*. McGraw, 1966.

Schopenhauer, Arthur. *Essays and Aphorisms*. Penguin, 1970.

—— *The World as Will and Representation*. Dover Publications, 1977.

Spinoza, Benedictus de. *Ethics*. Citadel Press, 1986.

Thomas, Aquinas, Saint. *On Being and Essence*. Pontifical Institute of Medieval Studies, Canada. 1968.

—— *Summa Theologiae*. Sheed, 1988.

—— *Treatise on Happiness*. University of Notre Dame Press, 1984.

Tiger, Lionel (and Robin Fox). *The Imperial Animal*. Frogmore, Herts, Paladin, 1974.

Tylor, Edward. *Primitive Culture*. John Murray, 1981.

Unamuno, Miguel de. *The Tragic Sense of Life*. Dover Publications, 1976.

Van-Gennep, A. *The Rites of Passage*. University of Chicago Press, 1960.

Weber, Max. *Protestant Ethic and the Spirit of Capitalism*. Routledge, 1992.

Whorf, Benjamin Lee. *Language, Thought, and Reality*. MIT Press, 1956.

Wilson, Edward O. *Sociobiology: The New Synthesis*. Harvard University Press, 1980.

Young, J. Z. *Programs of the Brain*. Oxford University Press, 1978.

Index